£50-00

AF746833

THE ECONOMIC REGULATION OF AIRPORTS

In memory of Martin Kunz

This book is dedicated to our erstwhile colleague and friend Martin Kunz, who was one of the principals founding GARS. Sadly Martin died shortly before the first meeting. We especially miss his well-founded and provocative advice in airport regulation, which was his main field of research.

The Economic Regulation of Airports

Recent Developments in Australasia, North America and Europe

Edited by
PETER FORSYTH
DAVID W. GILLEN
ANDREAS KNORR
OTTO G. MAYER
HANS-MARTIN NIEMEIER
DAVID STARKIE

Published in Association with the
German Aviation Research Society (GARS)

ASHGATE

© Peter Forsyth, David W. Gillen, Andreas Knorr, Otto G. Mayer, Hans-Martin Niemeier and David Starkie 2004

All rights reserved. No part of this publication may be reproduced, stored in a retrieval system, or transmitted in any form or by any means, electronic, mechanical, photocopying, recording or otherwise without the prior permission of the publisher.

Peter Forsyth, David W. Gillen, Andreas Knorr, Otto G. Mayer, Hans-Martin Niemeier and David Starkie have asserted their right under the Copyright, Designs and Patents Act, 1988, to be identified as the editors of this work.

Published by

Ashgate Publishing Limited
Gower House
Croft Road
Aldershot
Hants GU11 3HR
England

Ashgate Publishing Company
Suite 420
101 Cherry Street
Burlington, VT 05401-4405
USA

Ashgate website: http://www.ashgate.com

British Library Cataloguing in Publication Data

The economic regulation of airports : recent developments in Australasia, North America and Europe. - (Ashgate studies in aviation economics and management)
1.Airports - Law and legislation 2.Airports - Economic aspects
I.Forsyth, Peter
387.7'36

Library of Congress Cataloging-in-Publication Data

The economic regulation of airports : recent developments in Australasia, North America and Europe / edited by Peter Forsyth ... [et al.].
p. cm. -- (Ashgate studies in aviation economics and management)
Published in association with German Aviation Research Society (G.A.R.S.).
Includes bibliographical references.
ISBN 0-7546-3816-2
1. Aeronautics, Commercial--Government policy--Case studies. 2. Aeronautics, Commercial--Deregulation--Case studies. I. Forsyth, P. (Peter) II. Series.

HE9777.7.E28 2004
387.7'36--dc22

2003063923

ISBN 0 7546 3816 2

Printed and bound in Great Britain by TJ International Ltd, Padstow, Cornwall

Contents

Acknowledgements

The book is a compilation of selected papers presented at three workshops organized by the German Aviation Research Society. We would like to thank the HWWA - Institute of Economic Research, the University of Bremen and the University of Applied Sciences Bremen for acting as hosts. We are also grateful to Hamburg Airport, Lufthansa and the Wolfgang-Ritter-Stiftung for providing financial support.

John Hindley of Ashgate Publishers was encouraging with his active participation in founding GARS and establishing a book series. His commitment was critical.

Our thanks also go to Andreas Arndt, Jürgen Müller, Wolfgang Strehl for their support.

Editors and Contributors

Doug Andrew is Lead Infrastructure Specialist of the World Bank. He was Group Director of Economic Regulation at the UK Civil Aviation Authority, a founding commissioner of Eurocontrol's Performance Review Commission and a member of Eurocontrol's Regulatory Committee. Previously, he was deputy secretary in charge of regulation and tax policy in the New Zealand Treasury, and was educated at Princeton and Auckland Universities. In addition to his career in the New Zealand Treasury he had secondments as economic adviser to the New Zealand leader of the opposition (David Lange) and to the World Bank in the Australian Executive Director's Office.

Bernhard Duijm has been a lecturer in Economic Policy at the University of Tübingen since 1996. His current position is Temporary Professor of Economics. He received his PhD in Economics from the University of Tübingen in 1990. Research interests include competition policy in European integration, interdependence of competition policy and international trade policy, and the institutional design of competition and regulation authorities.

Peter Forsyth has been Professor of Economics at Monash University, Australia since 1997. Prior to this he held posts at Australian National University and the University of New England. He holds degrees form the University of Sydney and the University of Oxford. He has specialised in the economics of transport, especially aviation, privatisation and regulation, and the economics of tourism. Most recently, he has been paying particular attention to the privatisation and regulation of airports, and to the use of computable general equilibrium models in evaluating the economic impacts of tourism. He has recently published an edited volume of classic articles on the economics of air transport (Edward Elgar).

David W. Gillen is Professor in the School of Business and Economics, Wilfrid Laurier University, Waterloo, Canada. He also holds the position of Visiting Professor in Civil and Environmental Engineering and Research Economist, Institute of Transportation Studies, University of California-Berkeley. He obtained his PhD in Economics from the University of Toronto in 1975. He has held positions at the University of Alberta, University of British Columbia and Queen's University. He has published over 60 articles and 15 books in the areas of transportation economics, transportation management, industrial organisation and management strategy. His current research covers airline strategies, airport performance measurement and strategy, network economics and competition issues in airlines and airports.

Anne Graham is Senior Lecturer in Air Transport and Tourism at the University of Westminster. She has specialised in the research, consultancy and teaching of airport economics and management for over 15 years.

Cathal Guiomard is an economist and Head of Economic Affairs at the Irish Commission for Aviation Regulation (www.aviationreg.ie). Previously, he worked for the Irish Central Bank, and as a member of the Economics Department of University College Dublin.

Nienke Hendriks is Senior Price Control Review Manager at Ofgem (the Office of Gas and Electricity Markets) and currently works on the Electricity Distribution Price Review. Previously, she worked as economic policy analyst at the UK Civil Aviation Authority. She holds an MSc in Economics and Finance (Warwick Business School).

Oliver Hogan is with the Irish Commission for Aviation Regulation. A graduate of Trinity College Dublin, where he studied economics to Masters Degree level, he was previously employed as an economist with the Office of the Director of Telecommunications Regulation (ODTR), Dublin from 1999-2001.

Thomas Immelmann is Director of Corporate Communications, Marketing and Sales at Hamburg Airport since 1997. Before that he was Director of Strategic Planning & Product Management of the German Airline LTU Lufttransport-Unternehmen GmbH & Co. KG in Düsseldorf, and Vice Director Public Relations and Manager Environmental Affairs for LTU.

Michael Klenk is General Manager, Infrastructure Cost Management for Deutsche Lufthansa AG, Frankfurt. A lawyer, he joined Lufthansa in 1994 as a manager of "collective agreements cockpit staff". From 1999 until 2000 he was a manager of "airport charges" until appointed to his present position.

Andreas Knorr is Professor for International Economics at the Department of Business Studies and Economics, University of Bremen, Germany. His main fields of research are: transport economics, international trade in services, competition policy and environmental economics.

Peter McKenzie-Williams is with the Transport Research Laboratory (TRL) UK. A highly experienced aviation economist, with 24 years' specialist work in the sector, he joined TRL in 1998 as Head of Aviation. His career began at the Civil Aviation Authority where he was ultimately responsible for monitoring the financial health of a number of major British airlines. Since entering consultancy with Travers Morgan in 1989 he has worked for a wide variety of clients including Governments, local government, airports and airlines. He has become recognised as a leading expert in the comparison of airport charging systems and operational and financial performance.

Otto G. Mayer is Head of the Presidential Department of the Hamburg Institute of International Economics (HWWA). He is also managing editor of *Wirtschaftsdienst* and of *Intereconomics*. From 1995-2000 he was a member of the board of the Gesellschaft für Wirtschafts- und Sozialwissenschaften - Verein für Socialpolitik (German Economic Association).

William Morrison is an Associate Professor of Economics in the School of Business and Economics at Wilfrid Laurier University. He graduated with a PhD in Economics from Simon Fraser University in 1993, specialising in Industrial Organisation, Microeconomics and Game Theory. Dr. Morrison's research includes applied theoretical works on transportation markets, dynamic evolutionary games and experimental economics. In transportation economics, Dr. Morrison has contributed to research reports on Canada's airport system and the price elasticity of demand for air travel.

Hans-Martin Niemeier is professor of transportation economics and logistics at the University of Applied Sciences, Bremen. He received his PhD in economics at the University of Hamburg and worked in the aviation section of the State-Ministry of Economic Affairs of Hamburg. His research focuses on airport regulation and management.

Friedrich Schneider is at the Department of Economics, Institute of Economic Policy, Johannes Kepler University of Linz, Austria. His research fields: general economic policy, taxation, shadow economy, environmental economics, privatization and deregulation policies. He is the author of numerous articles and editor and referee for various scientific journals.

David Starkie is a Director of Economics-Plus Ltd and Co-ordinator of Transport Programmes at the Regulatory Policy Institute, Oxford. A former aviation adviser to the UK House of Commons Select Committees he is now general economic adviser to the Irish Commission for Aviation Regulation.

Mike Toms is Director of Planning and Regulatory Affairs at BAA plc. He was previously the corporate strategy director, and has worked in the industry for 22 years, including a spell as Chief Economist of ACI in Geneva. He has degrees from the universities of Durham and Nottingham.

Jaap de Wit is Professor in transport economics at the University of Amsterdam. He was recently appointed as Director of the new research and consultancy institute Amsterdam Aviation Economics. Prior to this he worked for almost two decades in different functions within the Directorate General of Civil Aviation of the Dutch Ministry of Transport. As the chief aviation economist, he was responsible for the preparations of Amsterdam airport's privatisation.

Hartmut Wolf belongs to the transport research group of the Kiel Institute of World Economics. He studied economics at the University of Cologne and received his PhD from the University of Kiel. His main fields of research are industrial, institutional, regulatory and transportation economics. He has published articles and books on air transport deregulation, airport privatisation and regulation and also on the auctioning of airport slots. Recently, he was engaged in researching the effects of mobility taxes and road pricing on the spatial pattern of the German economy. Currently, he works on a project analysing institutional obstacles for overcoming bottlenecks in air transport infrastructure.

Introduction and Overview

Over the past decade, across much of the world, there has been extensive reform of airports. In several cases, airports have been fully or partly privatised, and in other cases, they have been restructured as corporations and required to prepare accounts in a corporatised format. Ownership and incentives have been changed with a view to making airports more commercially oriented. Since some airports possess considerable market power, these changes in ownership and incentives pose the danger that they will use this market power and raise prices to increase profits and achieve excessive returns. In most cases, this danger has been recognised, and the economic power of airports has been restrained by regulation.

The ownership and regulatory problems associated with airports have only recently attracted much attention. For many years, virtually all but the smallest airports were either owned by national or regional governments, or by local communities. There was a presumption that they would not use their market power to increase charges and profits, and the modest profitability of most airports seemed to confirm this presumption. When economists turned their attention to airports they did not focus on the regulatory or incentive problems. From the late 1960s on, problems of congestion, pricing, and allocation of scarce capacity were analysed in some depth (Forsyth, 2000). Another area on which economists focused was on the evaluation of investments in airport capacity; the costs and benefits of new airports or runways and on the economic impacts of airport extensions on local economies. More recently, there has been a recognition of the environmental impacts of airports, such as their impacts on noise and air quality, and there has been interest in devising economic instruments that mitigate these efficiently.

Apart from these aspects, there was little questioning of whether airports were operating in an institutional setting, which gave them the incentive to produce and price efficiently. It was presumed that publicly and locally owned airports would keep prices close to costs, set price structures efficiently, provide the range of services that users were willing to pay for, and keep costs down to a minimum. The analysis of other publicly owned utilities and transport industries, over the past three decades, has shown that these presumptions could be far removed from reality (see chapters 10 and 14). While publicly owned firms did not charge prices well above costs (and indeed, often allowed revenues to fall short of total costs), they did not necessarily produce at minimum cost, and often did not supply what the users were willing to pay for.

The result of this has been extensive reform of the utility and transport sectors in most OECD countries. There has been privatisation or corporatisation of public enterprises, and associated with this there has been the introduction of incentive regulation (see Armstrong et al, 1994; Newbery, 1999). In countries, such as the US, which already operated a regime of regulated private utilities, there was a move from cost plus regulation towards incentive regulation. In a number of cases, but by no means all, markets were opened up, to the extent feasible, to competition. There was an extensive attempt to alter the institutional framework in which utility and transport industries operate, such that they face stronger incentives to perform efficiently, and where they possess some market power, the use of this is constrained in a way that does minimal damage to incentives to perform efficiently. Evidence from most countries that have embarked on programmes of reform suggests that performance overall has improved significantly, though the new environment has introduced its own new problems (such as greater risk of financial failure of regulated firms).

While governments have been active in reform of telecommunications, water, energy, surface transport and airline industries, they have been slow to tackle airports. Nevertheless, there have been substantial changes, mainly in the last decade. However, the move towards private ownership has been slower than in other industries. In many cases, governments have opted for partial privatisation rather than full privatisation. In North America, even though there is a long tradition of privately owned utilities and transport industries, there has been a reluctance to move away from public or local ownership of airports. The move towards full privatisation has been strongest in the UK and, later, Australia and New Zealand - both countries which formerly relied on the UK model of public enterprise, and which followed the UK with extensive privatisation programmes. In continental Europe, there has been a preference for partial privatisation, with the public sector remaining with majority ownership.

These changes in ownership have usually been accompanied by the introduction of explicit regulation. The first example of this occurred in the UK, where the major London airports owned by the British Airports Authority were privatised in the mid 1980s and RPI-X regulation was introduced. In the mid to late 1990s, Australia followed this pattern (since changed), while New Zealand privatised its three main airports (following corporatisation) but did not subject them to an explicit form of regulation. There has been partial privatisation of major airports in several European countries, including Germany, Austria, Greece, Switzerland, Denmark and Italy. In some of these cases, explicit regulation has been introduced (e.g. in Germany). In Ireland, the airport company has been corporatised, although not privatised, and it is subject to economic regulation. In the Netherlands, the government intends to partially privatise Amsterdam airport subject to economic regulation. Canada has chosen not to privatise airports, although the major airports are now under the control of local authorities. In the US, however, there has been little change, and the publicly and locally owned airports are not subject to price regulation, although they are subject to regulation of investment and financing.

Not much of a pattern has emerged in the types of regulation implemented across the different countries. When BAA was privatised in the UK, the government chose to implement RPI-X regulation. In this respect, the approach taken was similar to that adopted in other privatisations in the UK. This regulation was designed to avoid the problems which had become associated with more cost plus forms of regulation, such as rate of return regulation. The objective was to give the firm an incentive to maximise profit but to constrain its use of market power in a way that did not weaken, to any great extent, its incentive to minimise costs. In reality, such regulation encounters practical problems; in particular, regulators find themselves under pressure to set the allowable prices with some reference to the firm's actual costs, and this weakens its incentive to minimise costs. In spite of this, it is generally accepted as a good compromise, which in its variants that include "incentive regulation" and "earnings sharing regulation" in the US, has wide application across the world. (Note that by RPI-X or CPI-X regulation we mean regulation whereby the allowable price or revenue is set for a forthcoming period during which it must fall in real terms by *X* per cent per annum; by price cap we mean regulation whereby the allowable price is set in advance. Not all price caps take the CPI-X form.)

In spite of the popularity of this model (full privatisation combined with RPI-X), the UK is currently the only country which implements it for its airport industry, and then only in relation to its major London airports. (Manchester airport is also subjected to price caps, although it has not been privatised.) When Australia first privatised its airports, it adopted this model, but it has since moved to a much more light-handed form of regulation or price monitoring. New Zealand did not formally regulate its airports, although it did provide for a review of airport pricing behaviour with the threat of more explicit regulation should this behaviour be unacceptable; a recent review recommended that Auckland airport be regulated. In Germany, price-caps are imposed on the partially privatised Hamburg airport, but rate of return regulation is imposed on Dusseldorf, and Frankfurt airport is required to negotiate long-term contracts with airlines. In Austria, the majority public ownership of Vienna airport is partly relied upon to prevent excessive use of market power, although it is also price capped. At Amsterdam airport, rate of return regulation is foreseen in the near future. Formal price regulation does not exist for the North American airports.

What are the objectives of these institutional and regulatory reforms? A simple answer would be to promote economic efficiency. This involves production at minimum cost, provision of services at a quality level which users are willing to pay for, efficient levels of investment, price structures that reflect cost or ration capacity efficiently where it is in short supply, or which enable cost recovery at minimum dead-weight loss. It also involves provision of adequate services to facilitate competition at the airline level, and the development of non-aeronautical services which are complementary to the main business. The institutional and regulatory framework should create incentives for the pursuit of efficiency, although it must be recognised that a balance between objectives will normally have to be sought, and that a first best is rarely attainable.

It is to be recognised that governments have other agendas beyond efficiency. Governments may wish to maintain the dominant hub position of the preferred national carrier (see also the discussion on peak charges later on), or to ensure low cost access to busy airports for commuter and regional carriers. They may be keen to reap the cash proceeds from privatisation and, at the time of privatisation, they may set regulatory parameters such that these are increased. Some governments (especially local governments) wish to use airports to foster regional development. Airlines and airport corporations may be powerful in their own right, and they may influence choice of airport policy. The environmental aspects of airport growth are now very important, and governments will wish to lessen adverse environmental impacts. Some of these objectives are consistent with overall efficiency - for example, efficiency requires that environmental externalities be taken into account. Other objectives are less consistent with efficiency goals.

By way of example, the UK government chose to privatise the nationally owned London airports as a group, and not to sell them separately; it thus missed the potential for competition between the airports. This would probably have yielded a lower sale price. The Australian government abolished formal price regulation just before it privatised Sydney airport; this would have enhanced its sale price. Environmental constraints have long held up the expansion of London and other airports. Even busy North American and Australian airports are required to make special provision for commuter traffic, which is likely to have a low willingness to pay, even though peak capacity is scarce. When new, and different price regulatory systems are introduced and, as, for example, in Hamburg, attempts are made to ensure that none of the stakeholders is affected too negatively. Regulators need to take into account the view that publicly owned corporatised airport authorities, with easy access to revenue flows, may not have strong incentives to minimise costs and avoid over-investment in facilities, as has been argued to be the case with Aer Rianta, the airport owner in Ireland.

Thus, the actual ownership and regulatory environments of airports across the world represent compromises between conflicting objectives - efficiency has been one of the main motivations for change, but only to an extent. The very different approaches to the airport problem adopted across different countries possibly reflect different views on the best ways to pursue efficiency objectives, but it also reflects the different non-efficiency objectives that governments are pursuing in their airport policies. Some governments are keener to maximise revenues on privatisation than others, some are more keen to promote airline competition, some are more willing to become involved in detailed economic regulation than others and some take the view that the the threat of regulation will be sufficient to discipline pricing behaviour.

There are several tasks for the economist in analysing airport regulation. One of these is to observe the ownership and regulatory pattern in a city or country, and seek to explain it in terms of efficiency and other objectives. Another task is to outline which approaches to airport ownership and regulation are most likely to be conducive to efficient operation of airports - have some countries implemented promising models, and are the approaches taken by others as flawed? Finally, there is the task of assessing which ownership and regulatory frameworks can best promote efficiency while recognising the constraints imposed by the non-efficiency objectives imposed by governments - does a particular framework represent a good compromise between objectives and is it possible to meet the non-economic objectives at less cost in terms of efficiency?

Common Themes in Regulatory Diversity

In the light of the diversity of ways in which countries have tackled the airport ownership and regulatory problem, are there some common themes? For practical reasons, in the organisation of this book, we have chosen a geographical structure. The drawback with this approach is that it highlights the diversity rather than draws out unifying themes. In fact, while the packages adopted in different countries do differ considerably, they are mostly responses to common problems, and they use similar regulatory instruments.

In this introduction, we seek to cut across the geographical contributions to distil the common themes. In particular, we look at the issues being faced by governments around the world when designing policies towards airports, and on the reliance they have on specific instruments. A number of policy issues and instruments occur repeatedly in the regionally based contributions to this volume. Some of the key issues and instruments which emerge are:

- The Institutional Framework
- Airport Ownership and Incentives
- Market Power and Competition
- Choice of Regulatory Structure
- The Working of Price Regulation
- Investment Incentives under Regulation
- The Contractual Option
- Light-handed Regulation
- Commercial Development under Regulation
- Excess Demand, Congestion and Regulation

We consider each of these in turn.

The Institutional Framework

Achieving a desirable regulatory outcome is not simply a matter of choosing a regulatory system and then implementing it. Some institutional arrangements are more likely to break down or to perform poorly. There are several aspects which merit consideration. For example, there is the problem of regulatory capture (chapter 15). Industry specific regulators are regarded as more prone to capture than are general regulators (who may also be competition regulators). The close and long term relationship between the firm and its regulator may result in the regulator becoming dependent on the firm and accepting its way of thinking.

The commitment of regulators is another problem - regulators may set up regulatory arrangements, but will they adhere to them (chapters 7, 13, 14)? They may change regulation after having set it in place, under pressure from the government, the media or the firm. As a result the firm is faced with regulatory risk. The short term nature of regulation is also a problem; regulatory parameters may be set for a short term (three to five years), but the firm needs to invest for the long term, and it will be unsure what will happen after the end of the current term.

A related issue is that of the regulator's discretion (chapter 14). Is it desirable for regulators to be locked into contracts with the regulated firms, or should they have the discretion to alter arrangements if circumstances change? Flexibility is desirable because it is never possible to forecast all of the relevant variables in advance when the arrangements are set in place. On the other hand, discretion also gives the regulator the ability to behave opportunistically. For example, a regulator subject to populist pressures may force the firm to push down prices, but at the expense of investment incentives and the long-term efficiency of the firm.

Airport Ownership and Incentives

This volume is primarily about regulation rather than ownership, which is a large topic in its own right. However, it does make good sense to be aware of the ownership options countries have chosen when regulation is discussed.

The question of privatisation is considered by Schneider in chapter 10. Schneider discusses the reason why public ownership of utilities in general, and airports in particular, has come into question around the world. Some countries have fully privatised many of their airports, including the UK (chapter 7), New Zealand (chapter 2) and Australia (chapter 1), but a number of other countries have chosen to partially privatise, leaving the airports in majority public ownership. Thus, Vienna Airport is still majority owned by the government (chapter 10), as are major German airports such as Hamburg (chapter 11), Frankfurt and Düsseldorf (chapter 12). Partial privatisation may be seen as a means of introducing commercial motivations and incentives to minimise costs, while not creating too great an incentive to raise prices - essentially this is an internal form of regulation (chapter 14). Notwithstanding this, Germany prefers explicitly to regulate its partially privatised airports. The Netherlands also decided on a partial instead of a full privatisation of Amsterdam airport, but this was mainly inspired by the idea that majority foreign ownership could be excluded in this way (chapter 6). Interestingly, neither Canada (chapter 3) nor the US (chapter 4) have privatised its airports. Canada has instituted a major shift in ownership, towards more locally oriented owners rather than central government ownership, possibly with the objective of creating incentives for the airports to reflect local objectives. Most of the main US airports are already under some form of local ownership.

Market Power and Competition

Do airports possess market power and, if privatised and made more commercially oriented, will they use this power to raise prices to increase profits? It is generally accepted that airports do possess some market power, given the limited competition that most city and regional airports face. The market power issue is central to whether there needs to be some form of price regulation. It has been most discussed in those contexts where there has been a decision to rely on light- handed forms of regulation, such as in Australia (chapter 1). Even in those jurisdictions which have opted for light-handed regulation, there is a recognition that market power could be used. In Australia, there is monitoring combined with the threat of explicit regulation should airports be seen to be abusing their market power. In New Zealand, the airports were not formally regulated, but they were informed that their pricing would be reviewed. As it has turned out, the review found that one airport had been charging higher prices than could be justified on a cost basis, and the review recommended explicit regulation (chapter 2). It did not find evidence of charges being substantially above costs; probably because the airports were disciplined by the threat of regulation. In the Netherlands, airport competition and airport market power was discussed intensely during the preparations for a new regulatory system based on the specific geographical position of Amsterdam airport (chapter 6).

Significantly, few authors mention the argument that the complementarities between aeronautical and retail services at airports, together with high margins in the latter, incentivise management to seek passenger volumes by ameliorating charges (Starkie, 2001). One exception is the contribution by De Wit (chapter 6) in relation to Amsterdam airport. Nor do authors canvass the countervailing power argument, namely that airlines are powerful corporations, and that they possess strong countervailing power that they can use to force the airports to keep their charges down. For airlines to have countervailing power vis-a-vis an airport, they need to have a viable alternative airport to use - and in most instances, this is not the case. Most major full-service airlines cannot credibly threaten to shift business away from an airport if they wish to continue serving the city in which the airport is located. There are some airlines, specifically the new low cost carriers, which may be able to use secondary airports - this gives them some leverage over the major city airports. However, this only affects a small proportion of traffic, and most of the traffic at a city airport is effectively captive to it. For this reason, most large privatised airports face some sort of imposed pricing restraint.

Choice of Regulatory Structure

The choice of regulatory structure is an issue for all privatised airports, and it may be an issue for part privatised and public airports. The first example of privatisation of state-owned airports was with the formation of BAA plc in the UK and RPI-X was chosen for regulating its three London airports (chapter 7). This was a natural choice, given that RPI-X had been recently developed in the UK as an alternative to rate of return regulation for the privatised public utility monopolies. The objective of RPI-X and price caps is to give the regulated firm a strong incentive to minimise costs, by allowing it to keep any profits it earns, and eliminating its ability to use its market power to increase profits. It is also likely to give the firm an incentive to adopt an efficient price structure. Manchester airport, which is under local government ownership, is also regulated in this way. Australia has tended to follow the British model of privatisation and regulation, and it implemented price caps initially when the major airports, except Sydney, were privatised (chapter 1). Hamburg airport, which is partly privatised but remains under majority public ownership, is also subject to a price cap (chapter 12).

Price caps are not the only available option. Rate of return regulation is also an option, although it has been distinctly out of favour around the world since the 1980s because of its poor incentive properties. Being a cost plus form of regulation, it gives the firm little incentive to minimise costs, and it can create incentives to over-expand its capital base. Nevertheless, it has been adopted as the form of regulation for the partly privatised Düsseldorf airport (chapter 12). In addition, prior to privatisation in 2002, a form of rate of return regulation was imposed on Sydney airport (chapter 1). It is also intended that rate of return regulation will be introduced for Amsterdam airport in the short run (chapter 6).

A notable absence from the regulatory menu for airports is earnings sharing or profit sharing regulation. This is a form of regulation which seeks to strike a balance between incentive regulation, such as price caps, and cost-based regulation, by setting the allowable prices partly, although not entirely, with reference to the firm's actual costs. This mixed approach is common in the US, where regulators have sought to move away from the rate of return regulation that is in place towards incentive regulation (for the telecommunications case, see Sappington, 2000). This approach is less common outside the US and the limited regulatory change to which US airports have been subjected has meant that the issue of which regulation to adopt has not arisen. There is an element of this in the sliding scale arrangements that were adopted for a time at Hamburg airport (chapters 11 and 12) and which are in place at Frankfurt (chapter 9). The pricing rules adopted meant that unit charges fell with increases in output.

The range of different approaches to regulation has been greatest in the case of part privatised airports. This has possibly been because the part public ownership has been relied upon to act as a constraint on the use of market power. Some part privatised airports, such as Hamburg (chapter 12) are price capped, while another, Dusseldorf, is subject to rate of return regulation (chapter 12), and another, Frankfurt, operates with contracts between it and major users (chapter 9). The New Zealand airports were part privatised for most of the 1990s, and during this time they were not explicitly regulated, although there was the threat of regulation (chapter 2).

The Working of Price Regulation

Except in the case of BAA's London airports and Manchester, there is not much of a track record of price regulation of airports, since most of the regulatory systems have been in place only a few years. Nevertheless, some issues have emerged. One of the most complex of these concerns investment, which is discussed separately below. The implications of regulation for the choice of price structure and its relationship with excess demand at busy airports, are also handled separately.

One issue that has arisen is the extent to which regulation has become, de facto, cost based. Even price regulation systems that do not take account of costs explicitly, such as pure price caps, can become cost based. Price caps are normally set for a period, but at the end of this period, new caps are set for the next period. In resetting the cap, regulators often take the firm's costs and profitability into account - indeed they may undertake elaborate assessments of the firm's capital base and set out an allowable rate of return. Thus, over time the price cap tends to approximate cost plus regulation, and its incentive power is reduced (although the firm still can keep the profits it earns during the period of the cap). This trend towards cost plus regulation has occurred in the UK (chapter 8), and it is an issue that has been recognised in the recent review of regulation, when a longer term price cap was proposed (chapter 7). The concern that price regulation would become more cost-based was a factor in the Australian government abolishing price capping of airports and replacing the caps with monitoring.

Another problem concerns the volatility of profits under incentive regulation. Price caps are a rigid form of regulation, which normally do not take account of unexpected shocks, such as a downturn in demand, for example after September 11, 2001. If a shock results in a financial crisis for a firm or industry, the government will come under extreme pressure to change or remove regulation (although to preserve the incentives for efficiency, it is necessary for the government to commit to *not* altering the price cap). The UK had scarcely privatised its Air Traffic Control System than it encountered a financial crisis, and the regulator was forced to alter the price cap. In Australia, the downturn in demand resulting from the September 11 attacks, combined with the collapse of the second largest domestic airline, Ansett, resulted in a sharp fall in revenue for some airports. The government's response was initially to suspend price regulation, and then to abolish it entirely (chapter 1). The revenue crisis also forced the regulator of Hamburg airport to alter the formula (chapter 12). This is an interesting case, because the formula that was implemented initially allowed for changes in demand to be reflected in changes in allowable prices; while this could have given flexibility to the price cap, the fact that the formula was asymmetric caused problems, and the demand responsive aspect of the formula has been removed. It is worth noting that the contract between users and Frankfurt airport also provides for prices to be adjusted downwards as demand grows. The London and Manchester airports were also affected after September 11, though not greatly, so that the price caps were not altered. Overall, in three out of four cases, price caps of aviation infrastructure have been altered in response to revenue shocks - this poses the question of whether price caps can be better designed to cope with demand shocks in the future.

Investment Incentives under Regulation

The problem of reconciling price regulation with incentives for efficient investment is a perennial and difficult one, and no generally acceptable solutions to it have been proposed. Granted that airports are very capital intensive, and under-investment can be costly (for example, when it leads to congestion), how investment is handled is a critical issue. One option is for users and the airport to come to an agreement on how much capacity is to be provided - this option is considered separately below.

If regulation takes a cost plus form, the danger, which has long been recognised, is that there will be excessive investment. Managers may act as output maximisers, and total profit will depend on the size of the capital base. This over-investment is often discussed, and it is noted, in the case of the German airports, by Niemeier in chapter 12.

Incentive regulation, for example price caps, can produce the reverse problem, namely that of under-investment. It is important to distinguish between investments that produce increased *capacity*, such as an additional runway at a slot-constrained airport, and those that increase the *quality* of the services provided, such as a runway extension which makes it feasible for airlines to fly longer non-stop sectors. Additional capacity will enable increased output, and the price-capped airport will gain additional revenue if it constructs a new runway. However, for the allowable prices to give the correct signal to add to capacity, it is necessary that they be set at a level no lower than will cover the incremental cost of that capacity. For an airport that faces the rising costs of expanding capacity (such as London Heathrow), prices which achieve this could be high and lead to very high current profitability. The task of the regulator is a difficult one, since it needs to set prices just high enough to make capacity expansion worthwhile, although it is unlikely to have accurate information about the costs of airport expansion.

The airport's immediate customers, the airlines, are not likely to be of much help. With slot-constrained airports, the profits from inadequate capacity tend to accrue to the airlines. Airlines appear to have *de facto* if not *de jure* property rights with respect to slots at busy airports, and they are able to set fares to these airports at levels which reflect the shortage of capacity – i.e. above cost. The airlines are unlikely to press the regulator to allow the airport to increase the prices they are charged in the short term, so that the airport has an incentive to provide more capacity in the long run, because this would deprive the airlines of their profits from scarce slots.

In the other case, when investment by the airport serves to improve the quality of service, it need not lead to any significant increase in output. Most of the benefits from the investment accrue to the users. To this extent, and unless the airport is able to charge higher prices for better service quality, the airport will have an incentive to under-invest. Hence, quality monitoring or regulation might be needed to accompany price regulation, or provision might be needed to enable the airport to increase prices above those permitted under the cap for investments which are judge to be worthwhile.

This investment problem has been recognised by several countries as they regulate their airports. In the UK, much of the recent CAA review of regulation of London airports focused on creating better incentives for investment (chapters 7 and 12). Longer term price caps were suggested, along with upward adjustments to price caps if greater output was achieved. When Australia applied price caps to its privatised airports, the investment problem was recognised through the adoption of a mechanism that allowed for upward adjustments to the price cap should approved investments be undertaken. While this mechanism did work, and several investments were approved, the airports considered that it imposed very high compliance costs - it did result in very detailed involvement on the part of the regulator. The same danger may result from the Dutch approach, where investments in essential facilities at Amsterdam airport have to be safeguarded after privatisation by separate instruments. One of these is an an operator licence, which can be withdrawn if an adequately equipped airport is not provided.

The Contractual Option

Rather than have direct regulation of an airport, it may be feasible to rely on negotiations between users and the airport in setting prices and investment programmes. This option does not resolve the market power problem, since the airport will have much more discretion over the level of charges than will the users. Significantly, the contractual approach is only used extensively in those cases where there is at least majority public ownership of the airport; for example, in Canada, the US and at Frankfurt.

Airports and their customers can negotiate over the price formula and paths. This has taken place in Frankfurt (chapter 9). In North America, there is a long history of negotiations between airports and airlines over the provision of investment (chapters 3 and 4). Airlines may fund specific investments, or they may agree on prices and may effectively underwrite investments by the airport.

This approach does have its advantages over the regulatory option. Only those investments users are willing to pay for will be given approval, and the airlines have a mechanism for inducing airports to invest where they would like facilities to be improved or expanded. Facilitating agreements between airports and their users was one of the reasons why the Australian government moved towards price monitoring. There are problems with the contractual approach, however (chapter 3). Users are neither homogeneous nor united, and one airline (a carrier that dominates a hub) may support an investment that another (an new entrant) would not be prepared to pay for, but nonetheless will make use of if it is provided. Further, it is difficult to write contracts which cover all contingencies (chapter 13).

Light-handed Regulation

Not all privately owned airports are subject to explicit price regulation. In New Zealand, the private airports are not price regulated. Since 2002, the Australian private airports have been subject to price monitoring, not regulation; and in the UK, airports other than BAA's three London airports and Manchester are not subject to price caps.

In New Zealand, only two of the three "privatised" airports have majority private ownership (chapter 2). Auckland and Wellington airports have had majority private ownership since the late 1990s. While the New Zealand airports have not been regulated, there has been the provision that they can be. A recent review concluded that Auckland airport had charged prices that were excessive, and that it should be subjected to explicit regulation. It also concluded that Wellington airport had not charged excessive prices. The threat of explicit regulation may have been effective in disciplining the use of market power and, significantly, while the review concluded that Auckland airport had made excessive use of its market power, it did not do so to any large extent.

Australia has moved away from explicit price caps to a price monitoring system, although the exact nature of this system has yet to be determined. There is provision for the review of performance and the re-imposition of direct regulation should performance be unsatisfactory (though the criteria for unsatisfactory performance have not been announced). In the UK, while BAA has the freedom to price its Scottish airports as it chooses, it is well aware that its other airports in the UK are regulated, and that there are natural pricing benchmarks in the charges of other airports in the UK.

In some senses, some publicly owned airports are subject to either light-handed regulation, or no regulation. The US airports are subject to some general pricing rules (chapter 4), which might be characterised as light-handed cost plus regulation. The Canadian airports (chapter 3) are not directly regulated. Public, and especially local public, ownership may result in managers not wishing to exploit market power to any great extent, thus public ownership may act as a substitute for regulation.

It is difficult to be conclusive about light-handed regulation of airports. The threat of a sanction, such as imposition of direct regulation, seems important in disciplining pricing behaviour, although it remains to be seen how effective it is. It will also be some time before the performance of light-handed regulation in ensuring efficient investment becomes evident.

Excess Demand, Congestion and Regulation

For many busy airports, the big issue is congestion, or at least, how to ration the excess demand. Other airports face excess demand for part, although not all, of the day. Regulation can impact on how well the excess demand problem is solved.

Consider the case of moderately busy airports first. Does the regulatory system in place set up incentives to moderate the costs of excess demand at the peaks by instituting an efficient price structure? Higher charges at the peak may resolve the excess demand problem. Of the different types of regulation, price caps or incentive regulation are generally more likely to induce efficient pricing structures (chapter 12), though it is an issue which warrants further research. Alternative forms of regulation may not give airports much incentive to set up efficient price structures. For example, rate of return regulation, as implemented at Dusseldorf airport, may give too strong an incentive to the airport to resolve its excess demand problems by building more capacity, rather than by rationing its existing capacity efficiently. Certainly, the response of German airports in the past to excess demand has normally been to invest rather than ration (chapter 12). The same thing is perhaps true of the US airports - the strong cost plus environment (chapter) may be a factor in explaining why they have rarely adopted pricing solutions to congestion or excess demand problems. The preference to invest rather than ration is also related to the role of transfer passenger volumes at hub airports (40-50 per cent at major hubs in Europe). These passengers are the least captive to the hub airport, but they are extra costly since they are mainly accommodated during the peaks. Therefore, the opposite of peak pricing can be observed where various European hub airports apply reduced passenger charges for transfer traffic (chapter 6).

With very busy airports, it may not be a matter of simply instituting higher peak prices, since the airports may be in a situation of excess demand for the whole of the day. When airports are not busy, or only moderately so, weight- or passenger-based charging systems have been regarded as a tolerably efficient means of covering the costs of the airport while creating minimum distortion in demand patterns. Hogan and Starkie in chapter 5 suggest that the marginal damage cost of using the runway could be significant; this cost would need to be taken into account, along with proxies for elasticity, in the design of efficient price structures. However, apart from this, weight-based charges are no longer efficient when excess demand is present: such airports have a problem of rationing demand, not covering costs. BAA has moved away from weight based charging towards a more uniform charging system at its busy London Heathrow airports. This move is consistent with better rationing of excess capacity, and it may have been induced or facilitated by the system of RPI-X regulation (although it has put a heavy emphasis on passenger-related charges, which may not be fully justified by passenger costs).

It is apparent that price structures alone, whatever the form of the regulation in place, are not likely to be sufficient to ration capacity in the busy airports. Very high price levels are likely to be ruled out by price caps. Thus, these airports have needed additional mechanisms, such as administrative rationing systems or the trading of slots in a secondary market to ration demand to capacity. These systems operate at very busy airports such as London Heathrow (albeit informally in the case of the secondary market) in tandem with the price regulatory system. Administrative rationing is also used at many less busy airports, such as Sydney, Hamburg and Canadian airports, whilst a few US airports use a formal trading market.

Future Challenges for Airport Regulation

It will be apparent from the papers in this book that there are many problem areas with airport ownership and regulation which remain imperfectly resolved, and that there remain significant challenges for the future. Indeed, the main contributions of this book may be to identify what the main problems are, and to examine how they have been handled across the world. The papers are suggestive of the way to go, but they do not point to definitive solutions as to how to handle some of the less tractable problems. A number of challenges for the future can be identified.

The Diversity of Approaches

Something which is evident is that there is great diversity in the approaches taken by different jurisdictions to the airport ownership and regulation issue. Different ownership patterns are in place as well as different regulatory systems, different regulatory institutions, and different emphases on local community input. There is not much evidence, so far, of any convergence towards favoured models. It is not as though there is an obvious recommended model of privatisation or regulation. Unlike with other industries, there has not been much full privatisation accompanied by deregulation (e.g. airlines) or by incentive regulation (telecommunications).

It needs to be remembered that most of the changes in airport ownership and regulation (with the exception of the UK) have taken place only within the past decade. There has been little scope to evaluate the different models that countries have adopted. Indeed, those economists who have been turning their attention to evaluating the efficiency performance of airports have not yet revealed a link between ownership and regulation. Establishing whether airports subjected to incentive regulation are performing better than rate of return regulated airports, and exploring the relative performance of private, partially private, local and fully government owned airports might be a priority for the future.

Partial Privatisation

While there has been a definite move towards privatisation recently, often this has taken the form of partial privatisation. Is this just a precursor to full privatisation, as it was in New Zealand, or does it represent the conscious adoption of a hybrid public/private model? This hybrid model appears particularly popular in Europe where governments have been reluctant to privatise fully. As the contributions to this book indicate, by retaining majority public ownership, there may be an intention to moderate the use of market power, while sharpening the incentives to achieve productive efficiency.

Local Ownership and Incentives

Many airports have a local geographic dimension that is missing in most other transport and utility industries. With several airports, there is a strong local component to ownership - this is so for the Canadian and US airports, for German and Austrian airports, for some of the medium-sized British airports, and for some New Zealand and Australian airports.

Local owners should have a strong interest in the performance of the airport, since they will see it as stimulating development, and many of its users will be local residents. Hence they may have strong incentives to ensure productive efficiency, that investment is neither excessive nor inadequate, and to keep charges down. Local ownership may be a substitute for the private/regulated model. Granted that there are problems with regulation, however well designed, in ensuring commitment to keeping costs down and facilitating efficient levels of investment, so local ownership could be an efficient alternative.

This is the theory. In practice, local owners may not be as rigorous in enforcing cost minimisation as they should be, and they may be prone to empire building. Local authorities may be easily convinced that big new investments will "bring development to the region", and thus they will over-invest. Regulatory reviews of the long-standing price-regulated local authority owned Manchester airport suggests that this is the case. Much will depend on the relationship between the local community and the airport management, and whether the former can articulate clear incentives for efficient performance, and whether the latter are constrained to serve their owners well.

Again, it is an empirical matter whether a local component of ownership is a spur to improved performance. The pricing and productivity performance of local airports, and their investment policies, need to be compared to those with other ownership structures.

Resolving Investment Problems

Books on regulation tend to conclude that one of the least satisfactory aspects of regulatory systems concerns their incentives for efficient investment. This book is no exception. No ownership or regulatory approach for airports has yet been shown to handle the investment question very satisfactorily. Admittedly, however, many systems have only been in place for a short period. Price regulation is directed towards limiting the use of market power, and it has difficulty in reconciling this with provision of incentives for long run efficiency. Investment issues can be addressed by the regulator, for example in the assessment of quality enhancing investments at a price capped airport, or in evaluating a large addition to capacity. However, this does rely on the regulator having extensive discretion, and it may require detailed involvement by the regulator in decisions about investment.

There are some attempts to come to grips with this problem. In its initial proposals, the CAA has sought to incorporate better investment incentives within a structure of price regulation for the BAA London airports which it regulates. Contractual arrangements between airports and airlines, taking place within a framework or regulation or monitoring, may be capable of resolving investment problems. Given that airports are capital intensive, and many of their efficiency problems stem from poor investment decisions, this is a problem area which is a research priority.

Regulation and Capacity Rationing

Many regulated airports are subject to excess demand all, or part of, the day. In most cases, prices charged only play a minor role in allocating scarce capacity. Normally, the capacity allocation role is undertaken by a separate administrative system of slot allocation. While such mechanisms achieve their objective of limiting demand to capacity, and thus avoiding serious congestion, they are not the least cost means of doing so. Slot allocation is based on arbitrary criteria, and tends to perpetuate the dominance of the incumbent airlines. Certainly it would appear that price-regulated airports could do more, through the adoption of peak pricing, to allocate capacity efficiently at airports that are not busy for all of the day. A greater, though not necessarily complete reliance, on pricing rather than slot allocation, would be preferable. The incentives facing price capped, or otherwise price regulated, airports to move towards efficient price structures are not clear, and this is an issue worth further investigation. So too is the separation between price regulation and capacity rationing at very busy airports - could better integration of the two tasks improve the outcome?

The Working of Light-handed Regulation

Light-handed regulation has the advantage that it does not require detailed involvement by an imperfectly informed regulator. Some countries have taken the step of removing formal price regulation from privately owned airports, although in each case there is either an explicit or implicit threat of formal regulation should behaviour be unsatisfactory. It is difficult to tell how well this will work, since, with the exception of BAA's Scottish airports, these moves have been made only recently. Much will depend on how serious a threat airports perceive they are facing (though no doubt the New Zealand airports see regulation as a real option now), and what the criteria for unsatisfactory performance are. While giving flexibility to airports and their customers is desirable, such systems may also mean that the regulator is given much discretion when it comes to determining whether an airport has not performed satisfactorily. How light-handed systems work in the airport context will be an interesting issue for the near future.

The Prospects for Airport Competition

Most of the discussion in this book has taken as read that strong competition between airports is not feasible. Indeed, in some cases, the scope for competition has been limited by policy, for example, when BAA's London airports were privatised as one company. With improvements in surface transport, airports may be able to compete with one another, especially in densely settled countries such as the UK. Competition seems to be developing between main and secondary airports for low-cost carriers; these airlines and their passengers are price conscious, and are willing to travel further to save money. Full service airlines are less likely to switch airports unless the price differential is substantial. This competition may not eliminate the market power of the main airports, although it will put limits on it, especially in the role of serving budget conscious passengers. So far, the main airports do not seem to have responded much to competition from secondary airports - they have maintained their prices and let them have the traffic. If the market share of the low-cost carriers continues to grow, the main airports may be forced to respond, and alter their price structures so that they do not lose too much traffic - this will require higher prices for the less footloose traffic. They will need to do this within the context of the price regulation they face. It does, however, raise the bigger question of whether, in more competitive circumstances, there is a continued need for formal price regulation.

References

Armstrong, M., Cowan S. and Vickers, J. (1994) *Regulatory Reform: Economic Analysis and British Experience*, Cambridge, Mass. MIT Press

Forsyth, P. (2000) "Models of Airport Performance", Ch.37 in D. Hensher and K. Button, *Handbook of Transport Modelling*, Pergamon, 597-608.

Newbery, D. (1999) *Privatization, Restructuring and Regulation of Network Utilities*, Cambridge Mass. MIT Press.

Sappington, D. (2000), "Price Regulation and Incentives", in: M. Cave, S. Majumdar, and I. Vogelsang (Eds.), *Handbook of Telecommunications Economics*, http://bear.cba.ufl.edu/sappington/papers.

Starkie, D. (2001) "A New Deal for Airports?" in C. Robinson, *Regulating Utilities*, Cheltenham, Edward Elgar.

Part A
Australasia

Chapter 1

Replacing Regulation: Airport Price Monitoring in Australia

Peter Forsyth

Introduction

Australia provides an interesting case study of airport regulation. In the mid to late 1990s, most of the major airports in Australia were privatised, and subjected to price-cap regulation. Yet, within five years this regulatory system had been rejected, and replaced by price monitoring.

One objective of this paper is to explore why this occurred. Price regulation had given rise to several problems, and further problems were expected to emerge. Critically, airports had been unprofitable under regulation, and the events of September 2001 imposed a financial crisis on them. The government's initial response was to remove or modify regulation, on a temporary basis. It later decided to remove regulation altogether, and replace it with price monitoring. This reflected a concern with the financial implications of regulation, and the longer term implications for incentives to pursue efficiency.

A second objective is to explore how price monitoring might work. The details of the monitoring regime to be imposed are sketchy. The system does embody a sanction for unsatisfactory performance - a return to direct regulation. Critical to the working of any monitoring system are the triggers for the imposition of the sanction; these are yet to be determined. There is some chance that they will be cost based, depending on the actual relationship of costs to revenue. If so, they will embody poor incentives for productive efficiency. It is not necessary for this to be so however - the triggers for sanctions could be designed so as to be consistent with incentives for productive efficiency.

Another aspect of monitoring is the scope for flexibility. This could be important in the light of history, whereby regulation proved too rigid to allow for the adverse external effects which impacted on the airports. Ex post assessment of performance can allow for the impact of external factors on the airports more readily than regulatory rules set in advance can. This aspect of monitoring is analysed. The flexibility advantage could be a real one, although it comes at the cost of greater discretion on the part of the monitoring body.

The chapter has a brief review of developments in price regulation of airports in Australia. The problems that arose with regulation, and led to its replacement, are considered next. Some of these problems could have been mitigated by better design of regulation. The new price monitoring arrangements, and the options as to how they might work, are analysed. This move to price monitoring does present opportunities for introducing more flexibility. The paper concludes with some lessons from the Australian experience.

Airport Policy: A Brief History

Until 1996, nearly all of the airports serving passenger traffic were either owned by the federal government, or by local authorities. All of the large, international airports, with the exception of that at Cairns, were owned by the federal government, and were operated by a public enterprise, the Federal Airports Corporation (FAC). These airports were not directly price regulated, though they were subject to a form of price monitoring, called "prices surveillance", by the Prices Surveillance Authority (PSA), which was later merged into the main competition regulator, the Australian Competition and Consumer Commission (ACCC) in 1995. The PSA produced one report into airport charges in 1993 (PSA, 1993).

From the mid 1990s, all the airports owned by the FAC were privatised, beginning with the second and third biggest, Melbourne and Brisbane, and Perth, in 1997. Most of the other airports followed a year later, however the largest airport, Sydney, was held back from privatisation, partly because of the problems it posed for future development. The airports were sold in trade sales, and major investors in them included BAA (Melbourne) and Schiphol Airport (Brisbane).

Formal price regulation, to be implemented by the ACCC, was introduced at the time of privatisation (for more details, see Forsyth, 2002). Five year price caps of the CPI-X form were set individually for each of the airports. The "X" factor was set with reference to expected traffic growth; for example, the "X" for Brisbane was set higher than that for Melbourne because of higher expected traffic growth. There was provision for an inquiry into regulation at the end of the five year period. Price-caps of this form had been used to regulate a number of industries in Australia, and some of the problems that could emerge had been anticipated. For example, the risk of reductions in quality was noted, and quality of service monitoring was put in place. The problems with inadequate investment under price-caps were also recognised, and a mechanism was put in place such that the airport could obtain an upward adjustment to the price-cap if it undertook investment that was approved by the regulator (ACCC, 2000).

Sydney airport remained in public ownership, although it was slated for privatisation in 2001. Prior to this, the airport sought a price increase of over 100%. Using its prices surveillance powers, the ACCC undertook a review of this increase - it initially suggested that an increase of 76% would be in order. However, the government did not accept all of the ACCC's analysis, and it instructed it to allow items (including a dual till) which would have the effect of making the allowable price increase about 100% (ACCC, 2001). This was implemented in 2001.

The privatisation of Sydney did not take place until June 2002; this was because the events of September 2001 (the September 11 terrorism incident and the collapse, a few days later, of Ansett, the second largest domestic airline) caused a sharp drop in traffic and considerable uncertainty. Curiously, the government offered the airport for sale before it had determined what regulatory environment it was to operate under, even though this was likely to change from the price surveillance which had been implemented up to that time. It had just received a report on price regulation, but had not announced its policy, when it took bids for Sydney, although it had announced its policy changes when the short list of bidders was announced.

The government entrusted the five year review of airport price regulation to the Productivity Commission (PC), its main microeconomic advisor. The PC commenced a review in late 2000, and produced a draft report in August 2001. This report canvassed the option of relying solely on price monitoring rather than regulation, but it also raised the possibility of continuing price regulation (of the price-cap form) on the major airports, with price monitoring or no regulation for the smaller airports. The airports strongly supported the first of these options; they had been critical of price regulation, partly because most had been unprofitable, and because they saw regulation as too intrusive. The airports also possibly saw the regulator as behaving opportunistically, taking advantage of every opportunity to keep charges down regardless of the merits of the situation.

The September 2001 crisis had a major impact on the airports - some lost nearly a half of their traffic in a week. The airports, which had not been profitable, asked the government to remove or modify price regulation. In October, the government suspended price regulation of most of the airports, although it maintained prices surveillance of Sydney airport, and it maintained regulation of Melbourne, Brisbane and Perth airports. It adjusted their price-caps upwards by about 6-7% however (Forsyth, 2003). With their new-found pricing freedom, the airports increased their aeronautical charges, in some cases by over 100%.

The PC delivered its final report to the government in January, 2002 and the government released it publicly in May (Productivity Commission, 2002a). The report advocated the removal of direct price regulation and the imposition price monitoring for the major airports, to be reviewed in five years time. Price regulation could be re-introduced if the airports had abused their pricing freedom. The government accepted the Commission's recommendations and, from July 2002, all price regulation was removed. The larger airports, including Sydney, are now subject to price monitoring, and the smaller airports are not subject to any controls. The competition regulator, the ACCC, is currently devising a system of price monitoring.

The Experience with Price Regulation

Price regulation of Australian airports was replaced after only a short period of operation. This came about partly as a response to problems that had developed, and partly as a response to problems that were anticipated to develop. As the September 2001 events and the government's response to them shows, price-caps became very difficult for governments to adhere to - they caused too much profit volatility, and threatened the viability of the regulated firms. Apart from this, other problems with price regulation had become evident during the reviews of pricing - most of these are the normal problems associated with incentive regulation.

The problems that develop are symptomatic of the form of regulation. If cost-plus regulation (such as rate of return regulation) is implemented, several problems can be anticipated. Most seriously, the incentive to minimise costs and produce efficiently is weakened, since the firm can simply pass on cost increases. In addition, the firm will have an incentive to overcapitalise, since it can make more profits with a large capital base than with a small one (the Averch and Johnson effect). To the extent that quality is a problem, it is likely that the firm will "gold plate" and supply a level of quality in excess of that required by its customers. Cost-plus regulation does not run the risk of bankrupting the firm, since prices can be adjusted upwards if the firm is incurring a loss.

Incentive regulation has been implemented in many countries since the 1980s in response to these problems. The essence of incentive regulation is that the price that the firm is allowed to charge does not depend on its costs. This is achieved via a price-cap, one form of which is CPI-X regulation. If it achieves low costs, it is allowed to retain the profits; on the other hand, if revenues fall short of costs, the firm must bear the loss. Thus, one problem which does emerge with incentive regulation is that of profit volatility - profits may be very high (which is awkward for a regulator or a government), or negative (this is even more difficult for the government because the supply of an essential service is threatened). Other problems associated with incentive regulation can be a degradation of quality of service, and inadequate investment. On the other hand, incentive regulation does promote efficient production, since the firm has a strong incentive to keep costs down.

Systems of regulation, as actually implemented, rarely fit perfectly into one or other of these types. In particular, when price-caps are revised, as they are periodically, regulators usually take the firm's actual costs into account, and set prices such that they cover expected costs over the regulatory period. There is some concern that "incentive regulation" may degenerate into cost-plus regulation over time, as regulators pay close attention to the firm's costs when setting prices. In Australia, price-cap regulation is often implemented with cost-based resets at the end of regulatory periods - nevertheless, regulation as it is implemented does have some of the properties of incentive regulation. Effectively, in Australia, most of the airports were subject to price-caps, which were due to be revised if such regulation was to continue - this revision might have been partly cost based. Sydney airport had been effectively subject to cost-plus regulation.

The problems that have emerged at Australia's regulated airports are all those which could be expected from the type of regulation. Three types of problems have been of greatest concern; investment problems, problems with incentives to minimise costs, and profit volatility problems. There are other problems that can arise with regulation, for example, quality problems. These had been anticipated, and dealt with adequately. For example, the quality problem was addressed through the implementation of a quality monitoring system. Attention will be concentrated on these three main problem areas.

Investment Adequacy

When price-caps were introduced for the privatised airports, it was recognised that ensuring adequate investment could be a difficulty. As a result, a specific investment incentive was built in. This took the form of the "necessary new investment" provisions (ACCC, 2000). When airports undertook investments to increase capacity to cater for increased demand, or to improve the quality of the service (for example, improving landside access or extending a runway) they could apply to the ACCC to obtain a price increase to cover the cost of the investment. The ACCC might or might not approve the price increase; in several cases it did approve increases, but it did not do so in all cases. It was guided by the responses of the airlines to the proposed investments - if they were in favour, it would be likely to approve them.

The curious feature of these arrangements was that they enabled price increases when investments were required to enable additional traffic to be handled. Normally, additional demand would lead to additional revenue, which would cover the cost of the expansion in capacity. Assuming that this did not entail increasing per unit costs, an airport should have an incentive to invest in capacity to cater for additional demand. A price rise should not have been needed - unless the airports were likely to respond to an increase in demand without increasing capacity, and congestion developed. On the other hand, when the benefits of the investment accrue to the users, as they would with a runway extension, the airport would need some incentive to invest - a price rise would achieve this.

In fact, these arrangements served to correct another problem that was becoming evident - the initial price caps had been set too low to enable the airports to invest in extra capacity and cover their costs. Price rises for capacity expansion were used to compensate for price-caps that were too low.

The airports were critical of the way these investment provisions were implemented by the ACCC. In particular, these provisions resulted in very detailed intervention by the regulator, which was required to make an assessment even for quite minor investments - this led to high compliance costs. These provisions may have been simplified if price regulation had been continued.

These sorts of problems did not emerge with the more cost-based regulation of Sydney airport. If anything, the reverse problem of excess investment may have been present. The airport undertook a major investment programme in the late 1990s in preparation for the Sydney Olympic Games, and it was subsequently allowed to increase its prices very sharply. Whether all the investments it undertook were economic remains to be seen.

Getting investment right is particularly difficult in the case of regulated airports - perhaps more so than in the case of other regulated industries. This is because there is no well behaved long run cost function for airports. There are many indivisibilities, and the cost of additions to capacity vary widely from case to case. For a given airport, increasing capacity by 20% may be quite inexpensive, but increasing capacity by 30% may be extremely expensive, since a new runway on a constrained site may be needed. It is not possible to set prices which simultaneously cover current costs (approximately) and which will also be just sufficient in the longer term to cover the costs of investment.

This inevitably involves the regulator in having a detailed role in the assessment of investment. Some expansions of capacity can only be funded if the airport is granted a price increase, and the regulator will need to evaluate the airport's case. In doing so it will be at an information disadvantage, and it will need to rely heavily on the airport for information (and the airport need not have an incentive to provide accurate information).

This was a problem which the Productivity Commission paid particular attention to in its report (it has been particularly concerned about investment adequacy in other regulatory contexts – see Productivity Commission, 2001). Whether regulation takes the form of incentive regulation or cost plus regulation, the regulator will need to be closely associated with the evaluation of investment. Certainly, light-handed regulation is not feasible. However, this may not be the main problem. Given the information asymmetries, there is a high chance that the regulator will get it wrong, refusing price increases when investment is needed, and granting price increases when they are not necessary.

With the price-caps as they were applied to the Australian airports, significant problems of inadequate or excess investment had not had time to develop. The main difficulty which had developed with the price-caps so far was that of the intrusiveness of the regulation. It probably would have been possible to have revised the arrangements so that the airports were given more discretion over their investment programmes, and to have lessened the close involvement by the regulator in assessing major investments. However, this would not have solved the information asymmetry problem; for major investments, the regulator would need to be involved, and it would have been making decisions based on limited information.

Incentives for Productive Efficiency

The primary rationale for incentive regulation is that it gives the regulated firm an incentive to keep costs at a minimum, although achieving productive efficiency. Most of the Australian airports were subject to incentive regulation in the form of CPI-X regulation. Interestingly, none of the parties to the reviews which took place sought to test whether it had achieved this aim. The ACCC was in favour of continuing price-caps; however, it did not present any evidence on how well they were working in terms of productive efficiency. None of the parties wishing to replace price-caps, for example with monitoring, examined the impacts which regulation had had on productive efficiency.

The way the price-caps worked in the case of the Australian airports should have been fairly conducive to productive efficiency. For nearly five years (until they were adjusted in response to the September 2001 crisis), price-caps were set independently of the airports' actual costs. During this period, the airports had been experiencing poor profitability - partly because of excessively optimistic demand projections, the price-caps that had been set were probably too low for long term viability. In such circumstances, the airports should have been very keen to ensure costs were at a minimum. They may have expected cost-based resets of the price-caps at the end of the five year periods (Australian regulators, especially the ACCC, tend towards cost-based resets of price-caps). If this were so, they would have expected that efficiency gains would be taken away from them at the time of the resetting of the price-cap. Even so, they would have had a considerable incentive to minimise costs for the time of the current price period. While, over time, they may have done so, the price-caps as implemented had not yet degenerated into cost-plus regulation.

As mentioned earlier, not all airports were subject to price-caps: Sydney airport was subject to a cost-plus form of prices surveillance or monitoring. The pressure on Sydney airport to minimise costs was less than that on other airports. Since the doubling of aeronautical charges in 2001, Sydney airport has the highest charges of major airports in Australia. One might have expected that scale economies would have enabled it to have lower per unit costs than smaller airports.

It is difficult to assess how productively efficient the Australian airports are, granted the lack of analysis. Such benchmarking studies as exist suggest that they are not poor performers (see Transport Research Laboratory, 2000, Productivity Commission, 2002a, Ch 2). Low productive efficiency has not been perceived as a significant problem, and the rejection of direct regulation was not the result of an efficiency problem. The Productivity Commission was sceptical of all price regulation, possibly because it considered that even strong incentive regulation would be diluted over time and end up as a variant of cost-plus regulation. To this extent its recommendations would have been conditioned by the expectation of future productivity problems rather than the experience of past problems.

Profit Volatility and Firm Failure

As implemented, price-caps for airports in Australia have constituted a form of incentive regulation. Under incentive regulation, prices are set without reference to the firm's own costs. This gives the firm a strong incentive to minimise costs, since it can keep the profits it earns. However it also imposes considerable risks on the firm.

The price of strong incentive effects is high risk. Some of the variables which affect cost and profitability are under the control of the firm. However many are not. When external events impact on cost or demand, it is not possible for the firm to vary the price; it must absorb the costs in changes to profit. Sometimes the firm may do unexpectedly well and it may be able to earn, and keep, high profits. On the other hand, external factors may be adverse, and the firm may earn a less than anticipated profit, or incur a loss. Within the normal price-cap, there is no mechanism for external events to be taken into account and for the price cap to be revised. To a degree this is recognised in actual regulatory structures; in Britain and Australia, cost-based resets of the price cap act to lessen the volatility of returns (see Mayer and Vickers, 1996), and in the US, earnings sharing formalises this by making the allowable price such that profits are shared between the firm and its customers (Sappington and Weisman, 1996). Even when this is done, the firm may still be subject to considerable risks; for example, cost based resets of the price-cap for the Australian airports would not have avoided the revenue crises that occurred in 2001.

If profits are volatile and unpredictable, there is a risk for the firm, and this risk can be costly. However, the firm does not bear all this risk - typically, the government will be very risk averse towards the returns of the firms it is regulating. If profits are high, there will be a political problem for the government - a monopoly it is supposed to be regulating in the public interest is seen as exploiting its market. Even where the regulated airport earns high profits because it has been able to achieve high efficiency, it is unlikely to be seen as this. The government is likely to have even more difficulties if the firm incurs losses, especially if there is a risk to its survival. Governments are responsible for continued supply, and losses incurred by regulated firms pose a threat to this supply. Even when there is no genuine likelihood of the firm failing, the regulated firm will claim that it may fail, to obtain favourable treatment from the government or regulator. Governments cannot take the risk, knowing that they will be held responsible for interruptions in supply. With airports, sunk costs are a major proportion of total costs, and even if the firm that owns the airport fails, the airport itself is likely to remain viable under a new owner. Long term closure is unlikely, but if the owner of an airport collapses, it may take some time for ownership to be transferred and all property rights to be determined. The interregnum could be very damaging, and would amount to a political crisis for the government.

The attitudes of governments towards profit volatility and firm failure are also reflected in the actions of regulators. Regulators are risk averse. A regulator will be blamed if the firm it is regulating earns high profits - it will not be seen to be doing its job. The regulator will be in even greater difficulty if the firm it is regulating fails, and supply is interrupted. It is not surprising that regulators tend towards cost-plus regulation. Often, when regulation is first set up, it incorporates strong incentive properties, but over time, regulators pay more attention to the firm's actual costs when resetting allowable prices. The initial regulatory system is usually recommended by treasury departments, who have a strong interest in promoting efficiency, but will not have responsibility for day-to-day implementation of regulation. Regulators will be more pragmatic and risk adverse. The price-cap regulation introduced for most airports in Australia was designed by treasury and transport departments; the much more cost-based regulation for Sydney airport was designed by the regulator, the ACCC.

It must be questioned whether governments can commit credibly to incentive regulation. In Australia (Melbourne urban transport, airports), the US (California electricity) and the UK (electricity, Railtrack) governments have implemented price-caps as part of a regulatory package designed to improve incentives for productive efficiency. In all of these cases they have been forced, because of excessively high profits or losses, to modify the price-cap, initiate bailouts or simply remove the regulation. In some cases they may not have needed to act to enable the regulated firm to survive, but (in most cases) they were unwilling to risk its failure.

The revenue crisis of September 2001 was the proximate cause of the removal of regulation of Australian airports. This crisis had been precipitated by the

September events, but it had been conditioned by the longer term unprofitability (revenues being above running costs but below total costs) of the airports under price-caps. This problem may have been exacerbated by airport owners paying too much for the airports when they were privatised - if so this winners curse is afflicting the seller as well as the buyer, and the government may not have been easily able to avoid it. The government responded to the crisis by adjusting the price-cap (in the case of the three largest private airports) or by removing regulation altogether, and implementing monitoring of some airports. Once the government had done this, it would have been difficult for it to have reinstated tight price regulation had it desired to do so.

Could these Problems have been Avoided?

The government's response to the problems that were being encountered with price regulation was to remove it entirely, and replace it with a system of price monitoring, which has yet to be designed. An alternative course of action would have been to improve price regulation. The Productivity Commission discussed both options, and while it did not investigate either of them in great detail, it recommended the monitoring option (Productivity Commission, 2002a).

As noted, one of the main problems with regulation as implemented was that of profit volatility. Incentive regulation inevitably imposes some profit risks on the firm because it sets prices that the firm is unable to alter even when it is incurring a loss. Some of the risk associated with profit is subject to the firm's control - giving it the incentive to minimise costs - but some of the risks are associated with factors outside the firm's control. If it is possible to design regulation such that factors outside the firm's control can lead to adjustment of the price-cap, it would be possible to reduce the volatility of profits without diminishing the incentives to produce efficiently. There are some ways in which this could be done.

Demand Contingent Price-caps or Fixed Revenue Caps

A demand contingent price-cap is one in which the regulated firm is permitted to alter prices if demand changes; for example, if demand is unexpectedly low, it can increase its prices. A system that partly incorporated this mechanism was in operation at Hamburg airport (see Kunz and Niemeier, 2000). However, problems emerged due to the asymmetric nature of the cap, and the mechanism has recently been removed. Alternatively, it may be subject to a cap on total revenue. It is possible to adjust price-caps for other factors that are beyond the firm's control but which may impact on revenue and profitability. In each of these options, if demand falls, revenue, and hence profits, need not fall as sharply, and the volatility of profits is reduced. There are some costs: allocative efficiency is not enhanced, since prices are increased when capacity is most readily available, and the airport will have a reduced incentive to add to traffic (the scope of an airport to increase traffic is often quite limited however). The airport also may not have a strong incentive to invest to cope with demand variability. In spite of these qualifications, if price volatility is a real problem, it can be reduced by mechanisms such as these.

Use of Input Prices in Price-caps

One source of profit volatility lies in variations in the prices the regulated firm pays for its inputs. Firms are typically permitted to adjust prices in line with a general price index, such as the CPI. This is an inappropriate price index for regulatory purposes, because input prices, and hence the firm's costs, may not have any strong relationship to general prices. Replacement of the CPI by an input price index (which does not include prices over which the firm has some control) would lessen profit volatility while preserving incentives.

Ex Post Adjustments for External Factors

The regulatory contract, between the regulator and the regulated firms, is necessarily incomplete, since it is not possible to forecast, and make provision for, all the factors that may impact on the firms' profits. However, if external factors impact, positively and negatively, on the firm's profit, it would be possible for the regulator to adjust the price-cap to take account of them. The regulator would need to be convinced that the factors were genuinely outside the control of the firm before it permitted a variation of the price cap. Incentive properties would be preserved but profit volatility would be reduced. Essentially this is what happened when the Australian government allowed the three largest private airports to increase their prices in October 2001. While some might see this as a weakening of incentive regulation, it could be interpreted as a practical response which preserved the integrity of the incentive regulation. The downside of this option is that it would give the regulator considerable discretion, which it would be under pressure to exercise when inappropriate. The price monitoring option, which has been adopted in Australia, can be seen as a variant of this option, since it involves a review of pricing behaviour after the end of the period (see below).

Yardstick or Benchmark Regulation

Yardstick regulation operates by setting the allowable prices for the firm with reference to the costs of yardstick firms. It may add to profit volatility. However, if all the yardstick firms are similar to the regulated firm (e.g. they are other airports operating in the same country), and are subject to similar shocks from external factors, reliance on yardstick firms' costs can decrease the volatility of returns.

Thus, there are several ways in which the problem of profit volatility might be mitigated by better design of regulation. These methods would not eliminate volatility entirely; some of this is under the control of the firm, and it is desirable that some volatility remains there to preserve incentives. Furthermore, the regulatory contract is inevitably an incomplete contract - it is not possible to specify everything that may impact on the firm's profitability and make allowance for it. It may be possible to allow for more factors ex post than ex ante. These options also only address the profit volatility problem - they do not address the problem of setting prices that are consistent with, and encourage, the efficient level of investment. Incentive regulation probably requires the regulator to have considerable involvement in investment assessment as a prelude to making adjustments in price-caps to accommodate capacity expansion plans.

The Australian move away from price regulation can be seen as a response to the problems the former regulatory system was encountering, or expected to encounter. The problem of profit volatility and the risk of firm failure were important factors in the decision. In the light of the Productivity Commission report, the government was also concerned about the difficulties of ensuring efficient levels of investment under regulation. It was also unconvinced of the general efficiency case for regulation. While regulation may improve allocative efficiency by keeping prices closer to costs (this must be qualified by the recognition that, at airports, marginal costs may be well below or above average cost, to which prices are set close to), it may come at a greater cost in terms of productive efficiency. All regulation has a cost element to it which diminishes incentives for productive efficiency and, over time, the likely move towards cost-based regulation means this problem becomes greater. Less rigid regulation or monitoring might promote efficiency while lessening the risk of firm failure.

Living Without Regulation: The Price Monitoring Alternative

As from the middle of 2002, none of the privatised airports, now including the largest, Sydney, will be subjected to direct price regulation. Instead they will be subjected to a system of price monitoring. In addition, Australia has in place a system of access regulation, whereby a right of access under regulated terms can be obtained for essential facilities owned by a natural monopoly - in principle, airport facilities might be subject to this form of regulation, although it is not clear what this might entail.

The government's response to the Productivity Commission Report, released in May 2002, was to accept most of its recommendations. Price regulation of the airports would be replaced by price monitoring for a period of five years. After this period, there is to be a review of performance under monitoring. If an airport's performance has not been satisfactory, it may be re-regulated. What constitutes satisfactory performance has yet to be determined. The Productivity Commission suggested some broad criteria, but did not go beyond them. The body in charge of monitoring will be the ACCC, and it is currently determining which variables it will require the airports to report on. Ideally, the criteria for satisfactory performance should be set out at the beginning of the probationary period, so that firms can know what is expected of them.

The ACCC has had considerable experience of "prices surveillance" of firms with market power. This has essentially meant that it has reported to the government as to what level of prices it considers is appropriate - in the main, it has assessed the reasonableness of prices with reference to costs. Sydney airport was subject to prices surveillance by the ACCC while in government ownership, and the other airports were also subject to this while they were in government ownership. The sanction for unsatisfactory performance has been decidedly vague, although government-owned firms like the airports were not willing to charge prices in excess of those that the government had signalled its approval. Privately owned firms with market power were also subjected to prices surveillance. In the main they have held to the ACCC's recommendations, but recently tugboat companies increases their charges above the level the ACCC approved – and they do not seem to have been penalised for doing so (Productivity Commission, 2002b).

The system of prices monitoring suggested by the Productivity Commission is more explicit than prices surveillance because it does contain a sanction- that of re-imposition of price regulation. Nevertheless there has been little analysis of how price monitoring might work. If monitoring is to amount to more than a regime for collecting data which are not explicitly acted upon, then it will need to consist of two aspects: first, a set of criteria for satisfactory performance, and second, a sanction for unsatisfactory performance. These two will be sufficient to alter the behaviour of the firm. Price monitoring can amount to a system of flexible regulation, and some of its properties can be desirable.

Sanctions for Poor Performance

Consider, first of all, the sanctions proposed for the airports. Will they be sufficient to deter unsatisfactory behaviour (whatever this is)? If the sanction is imposed, the airport will be price regulated, and probably profits will be modest - the regulator will aim to set prices which cover all costs and no more. Without this regulation, the airport will have more pricing flexibility, and will be able to earn higher profits in the long run, at least after the decision has been taken not to implement regulation.

One option for the airport is to "make hay while the sun shines", and charge profit maximising prices in the period before the review. While this may result, almost certainly, in re-imposition of regulation, the gains in the short term may outweigh the reductions in profit in the long run. If so, the threat of re-imposition of regulation would not act as a constraint on pricing behaviour. If the long run profits under continued monitoring were greater than those under short run profit maximisation, the airport would moderate its pricing in the short run - the sanction would work, to an extent.

The sanction may be seen as discrete, either being imposed or not. However, its impact need not be discrete. The airport will realise that the probability of the sanction being imposed will vary according to its behaviour. The more it raises its price above what it considers the safe level, the greater will be the probability of the sanction being activated. The airport will have to choose a price level for the short term which maximises expected profits over the long term, and the risk of price regulation will motivate it to keep its prices below the short run profit maximisation level. Thus, the threat of imposition of regulation will be a real sanction, although how strong a sanction it will prove to be has yet to be seen. The effectiveness will depend on how precise is the relationship between exceeding the bounds of satisfactory performance and activation of the sanction. If the sanction is automatically activated even for very small deviations from satisfactory performance, it will be a moderately strong sanction. If considerable leeway is given between actual and defined satisfactory performance before the sanction is activated, the sanction will be less effective.

Criteria for Satisfactory Performance

The effect of monitoring will also depend on how the guidelines for satisfactory performance are set. There are two aspects to this - how tightly the guidelines are set and on what variables they are made dependent.

The guidelines might be set out in terms of the relationship of price to cost, or revenues to costs. If the guidelines are set very tightly, in the sense that unsatisfactory performance is defined as revenues that exceed costs by any margin at all, the monitoring system may appear tight, but it will give strong incentives to the airports to price high in the short term and maximise profits, since there is little advantage in the short or long run in keeping behaviour satisfactory.

On the other hand, if allowable prices are above costs, there may be an advantage in keeping prices within allowable bounds in the short term so as to be able to earn higher profits in the long run. If the relationship of prices to costs is the measure of satisfactory behaviour, the minimum ratio that will be sustainable in the long run without provoking sanctions for unsatisfactory behaviour (short run profit maximisation) will be that which delivers the airport this level of profit (in present value terms) over the long run.

The content of the criteria for satisfactory performance is of critical importance. This determines how price monitoring will work. If a cost-based criterion is imposed, price monitoring will have the same incentive properties as cost-plus regulation. Alternatively, if the criterion for satisfactory performance is that prices do not exceed some level set without reference to the firm's own cost, then price monitoring will function as a form of incentive regulation.

The indications are that the criterion for unsatisfactory performance by an airport will be that of earning high profits, or having revenues in excess of costs. The ACCC has normally adopted the criterion of the relationship of revenues to costs when it has undertaken prices surveillance; for example, in its prices surveillance of Sydney airport. It has recently issued preliminary guidelines for data collection from price monitored airports - these suggest it will adopt a cost-based approach to monitoring (although the data collected could be used for incentive monitoring) (ACCC, 2002). When the New Zealand Commerce Commission reviewed pricing at the three major airports, it used a rate of return criterion to determine whether they should be price regulated; while it recognised the relevance of productive efficiency, it gave it little attention (New Zealand Commerce Commission, 2002). It determined that Auckland airport's rate of return had been higher than its cost of capital and recommended price regulation on this basis. Thus, it seems quite likely that the ACCC will adopt a cost-plus approach to price monitoring. If so, the incentive properties will be poor; an airport which increases its profits by achieving efficiencies will be penalised by the imposition of price regulation. The incentive properties of such a system would be worse than those of a mixed system, such as price-caps periodically reset by reference to the firm's own costs, the approach favoured by Australian regulators.

However, there is no need for a system of price monitoring to be cost based. The criterion for satisfactory performance can be one of prices which are no higher than those set with reference to external benchmarks, not the firm's own costs. For example, having prices higher than the average of costs for a group of comparable airports could be the trigger for the implementation of sanctions. Significantly, when the Productivity Commission recommended price monitoring, it suggested that the relationship of prices to the *efficient* level of costs be the trigger (Productivity Commission, 2002a, p. 353). An airport could keep higher profits that were the result of greater efficiency without triggering the sanction. If need be, adjustments can be made in the allowable prices to take into account external factors which may influence costs, such as unexpected changes in demand (in the same way as a demand contingent price-cap might work). If it were considered that a performance criterion which was solely related to external information, such as benchmark airports' costs, imposed too great a risk on the airport, it would be possible to also take into account the airport's own costs. The price monitoring system would then be comparable to earning sharing or sliding scale regulation - this is often considered to embody the best balance of risks and incentives (for some discussion, see Sappington and Weisman, 1996, and Mayer and Vickers, 1996, who are less keen on it). Indeed, it is possible to develop a price monitoring counterpart of any regulatory system - rate of return regulation, CPI-X regulation or any mixed system. Ideally, the monitoring system should embody criteria for sanctions which are the counterpart of the regulatory option that would be chosen were price regulation to be implemented.

The Properties of Monitoring

Perhaps the essential difference between a price monitoring system and price regulation lies in terms of the former's flexibility of operation. The monitored airport is allowed to price as it chooses for a period, after which its behaviour is reviewed - if behaviour is deemed unsatisfactory, a sanction is imposed. Regulatory systems are more rigid - the airport must set prices no greater than those set by the regulator in advance. As noted before, the regulatory contract is inherently incomplete, and cannot take into account all factors which may impact on profit. Even when circumstances change, perhaps dramatically, the airport is not permitted to change is prices.

The advantage of price monitoring is that it is possible for the effects of external events which impact on the firm's costs to be taken into account. When the firm's behaviour is reviewed, it is not penalised for increasing prices in response to adverse events beyond its control. It may be penalised for not passing on to customers the benefits of unexpected good fortune however. Even with more flexible forms of regulation, e.g. with demand contingent price-caps, it is not possible to allow for all contingencies in advance; there will always be some unexpected factors that impact on the firm's costs which ex ante regulation cannot allow for. Under a monitoring system with ex post review, it is possible to allow for these. Thus, if a firm increases its prices to compensate for an unexpected external event, it will not be penalised.

The downside of monitoring is that it increases the discretion of the regulator/reviewer, especially if it attempts to move away from de facto cost-plus regulation. Monitoring might work with the monitoring body collecting data on costs, prices and profits, and the review comparing these and imposing the sanction if revenues over the period exceed costs (in the manner in which the New Zealand Commerce Commission operated). If a simple costs to revenue or rate of return criterion is adopted, monitoring is straightforward and easy. On the other hand, if the review body seeks to implement price-caps, set with reference to benchmarks, with flexibility, it will need to exercise discretion. It will need to determine which factors affecting costs were external to the firm and which were not.

Some of these factors will be easy to allow for - for example, external demand shocks. Others may pose more difficulties. If it wished, the monitor/reviewer could impose pricing criteria without flexibility, and impose the sanction on the firm regardless of why it priced above the trigger level. If it operated in this way, the monitoring system would have no advantage over rigid price regulation. Ex post flexibility has the advantage that the volatility of profits and the risk of firm failure can be reduced, even when compared to a fairly flexible structure of ex ante price regulation. The price of this flexibility is increased discretion on the part of the monitor/reviewer. This flexibility/discretion trade-off has a precedent in the airport regulation system which has just been replaced. Airports were permitted to increase prices to cover the cost of necessary new investment. This gave them more flexibility; however, they needed to convince the regulator that the investments met the criteria - this gave the regulator additional discretion.

Price monitoring, per se, does not make a large difference to the way in which investment and quality issues are handled. Its primary effect will be on the frequency of regulatory intervention. If an essentially cost-plus approach to monitoring is taken, the impact on investment will be much the same as with formal cost-plus regulation. The firm will have no incentive to invest wisely, since it can pass on the costs of excess investment to its customers. At the time of the review of performance, the review authority will assess whether revenues are in excess of total costs, including the costs of capital. The sanction will not be imposed if revenues are not above costs, even if costs are higher than they need to be.

Alternatively, if an incentive approach to monitoring is adopted, the issue of how prices should change in response to investment arises. When the airport invests to increase quality, or to cater for additional traffic, its per-unit costs may increase, and a price rise may be warranted. Under price regulation, as in the system recently replaced, the regulator will need to assess the investment proposal, and determine what price adjustment if any is to be permitted. Under monitoring, the assessment takes place after the event: the review body examines the investments undertaken during the period, and assesses what impact they could be expected to make on unit costs; if the airport has increased prices beyond the level warranted, given its investment, the sanction will be imposed. Individual investments are not assessed, but the investment programme will need to be. The review body can use similar criteria to those which a regulator might use - for example, investments which have met with the approval of the airlines could be approved for price adjustment purposes. The review body still has considerable discretion, but exercises it only once, not continuously as under regulation. Again, regulatory discretion is the price of flexibility.

Price monitoring is more "light handed" than direct regulation in that it involves less day-to-day involvement by the regulator in the decisions of the regulated airport. It may, however result in greater use of litigation (this seems to have been the case in New Zealand). If an airport is setting excessive prices, the airlines may take little comfort in the likelihood that the airport will be penalised at the time of the review, which may be several years away. If they do have any legal options to restrain the airport's behaviour they will use them. Guidelines for behaviour, which are clearly set out and embody flexibility, may lessen the likelihood of litigation.

Formal imposition of sanctions if behaviour is not satisfactory is not the only way in which price monitoring might work. Monitoring sometimes has an effect through "shaming" firms that are behaving badly. Sometimes the purpose of monitoring systems is to highlight poor performance, and thereby encourage government or community disapproval. This disapproval may then work to moderate the poor behaviour. While this may appear to be a form of light-handed regulation, it is unlikely to promote good incentives. Inevitably it will degenerate into weak cost-plus regulation. This is because, in the public arena, high profits enjoyed by a monopoly will be interpreted as poor behaviour; it will be assumed, always, that high profits are the result of exercise of market power. The possibility that they could be the consequence of efficient production is too subtle to be appreciated. When the price-capped electricity firms in the UK earned high profits, the government and regulator were forced by public opinion to alter the price cap to reduce them. Public opinion is a poor means of regulating firm behaviour.

How price monitoring works depends on the criteria set for satisfactory behaviour, and on the severity of the sanctions imposed for unsatisfactory behaviour. If there are strong sanctions, monitoring will work rather like regulation. If the criteria for poor performance are essentially cost-plus criteria, then the system will work like cost-plus regulation. If the criteria pay explicit attention to factors beyond the firm's own control, then monitoring will work like incentive regulation but with an added degree of flexibility, to allow for external events which impact on the firm's performance.

Alternatively, if the sanctions are weak, the firm is given more pricing flexibility. It will have a smaller incentive to keep prices down to the level of its own costs, or the efficient level of costs. On average, prices will tend to be higher than warranted on allocative efficiency grounds (at least for airports which are not subject to excess demand or where the excess demand is rationed by non-price means). There may be an offsetting advantage, in that weak sanctions reduce the link between costs and prices - this link is strongest with cost-plus regulation, but is still present with price-caps as implemented, with some reference to the firm's costs. If this happens, the firm will have a stronger incentive to pursue productive efficiency. Monitoring with weak sanctions can be seen as moving towards a deregulated situation, under which the incentives for productive efficiency are strongest, but the scope for the exercise of market power is also greatest.

Access Regulation as a Substitute for Price Regulation

Australia has a system of access regulation for natural monopoly essential facilities (see Productivity Commission, 2001). A competitor to an integrated firm with natural monopoly facilities can apply for access to these facilities, and if successful can negotiate conditions with the owner. If these negotiations are not successful, there is provision for the ACCC to arbitrate. Thus, a mobile phone company can obtain access on regulated terms to the local loop facilities of the vertically integrated telecommunications carrier. This system applies to airports, and its provisions have been used. In 1999, a car hire firm obtained access to the kerbside owned by an airport, which it needed for its operations.

The issue is whether this right of access regulation could be used by an airport's customers as a substitute for price regulation. Suppose that an airline was unhappy with the prices charged by an airport because these charges were well above the airport's costs. The airline could seek access to the airport's natural monopoly facilities - its runway, taxiways, aprons and, perhaps, terminal. With these it could effectively package its own airport services (and if need be it could sell to other airlines). If negotiations with the airport over charges for these facilities failed, it could ask the ACCC to arbitrate. The ACCC is likely to set cost-based charges. The all inclusive cost of obtaining the airport services package by access would be less than the price the airport charges for the package itself. If this were to happen, access regulation could be used by customers to undermine the high prices charged by the non-regulated airport.

In principle this is possible, although it is not clear how practical an option it is. For a start, would all the facilities necessary for operation be declared for access? Furthermore, the access arrangements in Australia are very slow to implement, with much scope for the incumbent to delay proceedings. Nevertheless, the access route could provide a limit on the extreme use of market power by airports.

There is also the question of whether airlines would wish to go down this route. If an airline pays a high price at an airport, its competitors will be paying the same high price. If airport charges are increased, the airline will normally be able to pass the increase on to travellers (except when excess demand for the airport is rationed by non-price means). Thus, an airline or group of airlines is unlikely to have a strong incentive to incur the costs of mounting an access claim, which may not be successful. There may be some situations where an access attempt could be worthwhile, however. If an airline had a large share of the airport's total traffic, a successful access action might enable it to achieve lower costs than its rivals, and it could profit from this. In spite of these difficulties, there has been an application for runway and taxiway facilities to be declared for access. The new entrant airline, Virgin Blue, has made an application for declaration of airside facilities at Sydney airport. This is being considered by the National Competition Council (2002).

Conclusions

In Australia, regulation of airports has been replaced by monitoring - this has been a response to the problems of regulation, both in ensuring efficiency and, more immediately, in ensuring the viability of the regulated firms. As implemented, price regulation was threatening the financial viability of the airports. This problem is not unique; it has occurred in several industries and several countries. Significantly, regulation had not yet degenerated into cost-plus regulation, and there was no evidence of productive inefficiency. The government chose to replace rather than redesign regulation - it would have been possible to have redesigned regulation to impact less on profitability while still preserving the desirable incentive properties. Governments find continued commitment to incentive regulation difficult.

Another factor behind the decision to replace regulation was the view of the government's advisor, the Productivity Commission, that regulation was not conducive to efficiency. The allocative efficiency gains from keeping prices close to costs were likely to be outweighed by productive efficiency losses from regulation.

The government opted for price monitoring, although the parameters of this are vague. The effectiveness of price monitoring in keeping prices close to costs depends on the strength of the sanction imposed for poor performance. The sanction proposed, that of re-imposition of price regulation, will have some effect, although it is not sufficient to force prices to be equal to or close to costs.

The criteria for triggering sanctions are crucial. These can parallel the content of regulatory systems. Criteria can be cost based, triggering the sanction if the airport earns profits, regardless of whether these are the result of the use of market power or achievement of productive efficiency. Alternatively, they can be based on the relationship of prices to the efficient level of costs. This would be consistent with incentives to achieve productive efficiency. Within a monitoring system it would be feasible to allow for the impact of external factors, thereby reducing the volatility of profit and the risk of firm failure.

Price monitoring can work like price regulation, though, depending on how it is implemented, it can allow more pricing freedom for the airport. Monitoring has an advantage in that it can allow more flexibility, since it is always possible to allow for unexpected external factors which impacted on the airport's performance at the review stage. This flexibility is not costless, as it involves more discretion on the part of the monitoring body. However, in the light of the recent history of the Australian airports under regulation, this flexibility would be valuable.

The prospects for airport price monitoring in Australia are problematic. The approach to monitoring, and the objectives that it might achieve, have been ill thought out. The criteria for poor performance are vague, but there is a real chance that high profits, per se, will be taken as the criterion of poor performance. This would be consistent with the ACCC's history as a price monitor, and its suggested guidelines for data collection. In short, there is a distinct risk that monitoring may become a form of light-handed cost-plus regulation.

This outcome is not inevitable. Price monitoring could be consistent with incentives for efficiency, and it could operate in a more flexible manner than the price regulation did. It can combine strong incentives for efficiency with flexibility to allow for external factors that impact on the airports' performance, thereby lowering the risks of profit volatility and firm failure. To achieve this, it is necessary that clear criteria for poor performance, which are consistent with incentives for efficiency, be established. Relying on vague criteria will increase the likelihood that monitoring will degenerate into a form of cost-plus regulation.

Acknowledgements

I am grateful to the Discussant, Hartmut Wolf, and participants in the seminar, for helpful comments.

References

Australian Competition and Consumer Commission (2000) *New Investment Cost Pass-Through. Position Paper*. Melbourne

Australian Competition and Consumer Commission (2001) *Sydney Airports Corporation Ltd: Aeronautical Pricing Proposal Decision*, May

Australian Competition and Consumer Commission (2002) *Airports Reporting Guideline, Draft*, August

Forsyth, P. (2002) "Privatisation and Regulation of Australian and New Zealand Airports", *Journal of Air Transport Management*, 8, 19-28

Forsyth, P. (2003) "Regulation under Stress: Developments in Australian Airport Policy", *Journal of Air Transport Management*

Kunz, M. and Niemeier, H.- M. (2000) "Regulating Airports: Some Lessons from the UK and Germany", Air Transport Research Group, Conference, Amsterdam, July

Mayer C. and Vickers, J. (1996) "Profit Sharing Regulation: An Economic Appraisal", *Fiscal Studies*, 17 1 February, 1-18

National Competition Council (2002) *Application by Virgin Blue for Declaration of Airside Services at Sydney Airport*: Issues Paper, November

New Zealand Commerce Commission (2002) *Final Report. Part IV Inquiry into Airfield Services at Auckland, Wellington and Christchurch International Airports*, August

Prices Surveillance Authority (1993) *Inquiry into the Aeronautical and Non-Aeronautical Charges of the Federal Airports Corporation*, Melbourne, August

Productivity Commission (2001) *Review of the National Access Regime; Report No 17*, AusInfo, Canberra

Productivity Commission (2002a) *Price Regulation of Airport Services; Report No 19*, AusInfo, Canberra

Productivity Commission (2002b) *Economic Regulation of Harbour Towage and Related Services. Position Paper*, Canberra, June

Sappington, D. and Weisman, D. (1996) *Designing Incentive Regulation for the Telecommunications Industry*, Cambridge, Mass. MIT Press

Transport Research Laboratory (2000) *Airport Performance Indicators 2000*, TRL, Crowthorne, August

Chapter 2

A Shift Towards Regulation? The Case of New Zealand

Peter McKenzie-Williams

Summary operating and financial data for the airports mentioned in this paper are to be found at Annex 1, together with sample levels of aeronautical charges.

Background

The process of moving New Zealand's three principal airports at Auckland, Christchurch and Wellington from the public to the private sector began in the late 1980s, when the airports were corporatised and given more demanding targets in terms of producing greater returns for their shareholders. Since then, the ownership structure of the three airports has evolved in different ways. In July 1998, the Crown disposed of its holdings in Auckland airport and a public float and listing on the New Zealand Stock Exchange took place. A total of around 42 per cent of the issued shares remained in the hands of Auckland City Council and two other nearby City Councils. Shortly afterwards, the Crown disposed of its 66 per cent holding in Wellington airport by means of a trade sale to NZ Airports, a consortium lead by Wellington-based Infrastructure & Utilities NZ Limited (Infratil NZ). The remaining 34 per cent of shares remained in the hands of Wellington City Council. In contrast, Christchurch airport remains entirely in public ownership, with 75 per cent of shares held by Christchurch City Council and the remainder by the New Zealand government.

At the time that the partial privatisations at Auckland and Wellington took place, no system of price regulation was put into place, but the government announced that the question of whether or not price regulation should be introduced would be the subject of a public Inquiry by the Commerce Commission. The process for such Iiquiries in New Zealand consists of a period of consultation, during which interim submissions may be made to the Commission, culminating in a Conference, following which the Commission issues a report.

It was originally intended that the Conference would take place in 1999, but it was subsequently decided to defer this until 2001, so as to be able to take advantage of new disclosure of information legislation.

The Transport Research Laboratory (TRL) was retained by Air New Zealand to assist in the preparation of its case for the Inquiry. Air New Zealand was particularly concerned about the levels of aeronautical charges at Auckland, its principal base, which it regarded as being excessive. TRL was asked in particular to apply its long-standing methodology used in producing aeronautical charge comparisons in its publication *Review of Airport Charges* (Transport Research Laboratory (1)) together with its wider airport benchmarking work used in its publication *Airport Performance Indicators* (Transport Research Laboratory (2)) to establish an accurate assessment of the comparative position of Auckland.

This work began early in 1999 and continued until mid-2001, by which time Air New Zealand was facing severe financial problems which culminated in the New Zealand government taking control of the company. As a result of this situation, Air New Zealand played only a minor part in the Inquiry, which took place in the first half of September 2001, with its case being made by the New Zealand Board of Airline Representatives.

In July 2001, the Minister of Commerce withdrew the original request made to the Commerce Commission and issued a new request under the Commerce Amendment Act 2001, requiring the Commission to address three key issues:

1. to assess whether competition is limited or likely to be reduced in markets in which airfield activities are supplied;
2. to assess whether control is necessary or desirable in the interests of acquirers of airfield activities. To address this question the Commission examined the pricing behaviour of the airport companies, and compared this to what it considered to be appropriate pricing principles;
3. to make a recommendation on whether market conditions were such that the Minister should recommend control.

This chapter begins by outlining the work carried out by TRL in assisting Air New Zealand. This included:

1. a discussion of general issues relating to airport charging;
2. a discussion of different systems of airport price regulation;
3. a case study on Manchester airport;
4. factors specific to Auckland, Christchurch and Wellington.

This chapter is intended primarily to describe the work that TRL provided to Air New Zealand for input to the Inquiry, and it summarises the content of the Evidence produced for the Inquiry in the period up to September 2001. Additional information in relation to more recent developments has been added as appropriate. In particular, the paper outlines the findings of the Commission, as expressed in its Final Report of August 2002 (New Zealand Commerce Commission, 2002). It concludes by considering whether the relative differences in levels of profitability of airports and airlines constitute a prima facie case for airport price regulation.

General Issues Relating to Airport Charging

This part of the work dealt with four key areas, namely:

1. the pricing principles defined by ICAO;
2. the views of the two leading industry stakeholders;
3. patterns and trends in the setting of charges;
4. observed difficulties in adhering to pricing principles.

Advice from ICAO

As the international body providing overall guidance on most matters relating to civil aviation, the International Civil Aviation Organisation (ICAO) has periodically issued statements in which it has defined guidelines for the setting of airport charges. Its views on the ways in which aeronautical charges should be set by airports are expressed in its publication *Statements by the Council to Contracting States on Charges for Airports and Air Navigation Services*, known as Document 9082 (ICAO, 1997).

This provides a number of broad points of principle, such as that users should ultimately bear their full and fair share of the cost of providing the airport, and that charges should be simple and suitable for general application at international airports. It states that "Any charging system should, so far as possible, be simple and suitable for general application at international airports"; and that "Charges should not be imposed in such a way as to discourage the use of facilities and services necessary for safety".

While Document 9082 is comprehensive in its coverage, in a number of ways it does little more than present a series of generalisations about the subject, which do not constitute particularly clear guidance.

The recommendation above that charges should be "simple and suitable" is not accompanied by a definition of what ICAO regards as either simple or suitable in this context. A reference to the possibility of varying the landing charge scale at a certain level or levels of weight "if considered necessary" is not accompanied by examples of situations which could render such variations necessary.

There is a noticeable lack of reference to, or definition of, what could be regarded as acceptable levels of costs for the operation of an airport. Overall, the document reveals the fact that it was first drafted a good number of years ago, with only perfunctory attention having been given to updating it: for example, there are no references to pricing arrangements at airports that have been partially or wholly privatised.

The Airports Council International View

In industry debates on the issue, the Airports Council International (ACI) often takes the stance that airport charges constitute only a small percentage of airlines' total costs – it has quoted the figures of 4.5 per cent and 4.3 per cent respectively for 1995 and 1996.

While this may be true at a global level, it is also true to say that for short-haul airlines, airport charges can represent considerably larger proportions of total operating costs on a route: for the British short-haul airlines British European and KLM UK, they represented 7.3 per cent and 5.9 per cent respectively in 2001.

The ACI produces its own guidance to airport operators on the setting of airport charges (Airport World 1). It believes that charges should be related to all the costs of operating an airport, including a "reasonable" rate of return and other financial costs, but, like ICAO, it makes no attempt to define a reasonable rate of return.

It suggests that airport operators may offset aeronautical revenues with proceeds from non-aeronautical activities, but that they are under no obligation to do so.

This appears to ignore the fact that many airport operators, whether in the public or private sectors, would normally be expected to have a duty to their shareholders to maximise the return on their assets, while also assuring growth in the business and a good level of service to airline users and passengers.

A somewhat uncompromising line emerges in the ACI's views on consultations between airport operators and airlines on proposed charge increases.

Its view is that consultation implies discussion of proposed charges, which should be notified a minimum of two months before the increase is due to take effect. It is not a negotiation; if there is a failure to reach an agreement, airport operators are free to impose the charges at the level they deem necessary. The ACI's position comes across as being somewhat confrontational, although it could be said that the IATA view (see below) forces it to take this position.

The International Air Transport Association (IATA) View

The views of IATA, the international airline operators' association, are based on a clear belief that airports are natural monopolies, and that their pricing policies often reflect this (Airport World 2).

It believes that there is a clear need for the economic regulation of such monopolies, and that particular attention needs to be paid to productivity improvements and cost control. It supports the principle of single till pricing by airports, under which all airport revenues are used to offset operating costs. It also takes the view that airlines, on the whole, need far more airport infrastructure than they are provided with, and it supports moves towards airport privatisation since this is seen as a means of hastening both greater cost consciousness on the part of airports and airport infrastructure investment.

IATA believes that airlines should be involved in the commercialisation evaluation process accompanying airport privatisations, and it has produced a list of conditions to which airport pricing should comply:

1. Charges should be determined on the basis of transparent, fair and reasonable costs (but again no attempt is made to define the term "reasonable");
2. Charges should be in conformity with international agreements and obligations of the State, and in line with ICAO's policies on user charges;

3. Charges should be subject to a regulatory process, ideally through an independent regulatory body;
4. Charges should be fairly allocated between different categories of users, without discrimination or cross-subsidisation;
5. There should be gradualism in any significant change in an airport's charging structure;
6. If facilities are to be sold, the proceeds should be used to eliminate any existing debt for the airport;
7. Revenue, cost, balance sheet, capital expenditure and traffic data must be available and must be transparent.

It could be said that there is a reasonable degree of common ground in the views of ACI and IATA. Both advocate adherence to the principles laid down by ICAO, although it might be argued that this reflects a vagueness in Document 9082 which enables both parties to use it to support their own positions.

Both parties agree that there should be a clear relationship between charges and costs, and the principle point of divergence seems to be IATA's use of the term "reasonable" in relation to costs.

Since IATA does not offer its own definition of reasonableness in this context, the situation seems to be one in which confrontation may be difficult to avoid; this is further complicated by IATA's calls for more infrastructure which, of course, implies additional costs. Overall, we are left with a situation in which intervention by an independent arbitrator or regulator becomes almost inevitable.

Recent Patterns and Trends in the Setting of Charges

There are a number of patterns and trends in the way that airport charges are set. These are:

1. Annual or periodic increases not subject to a defined regulatory structure.
2. Annual changes subject to a defined regulatory structure.
3. Price freezes.
4. Discount schemes.
5. The introduction of environmental charges.
6. The separate identification of terminal navigation charges.

Although the regulation of airport charges is generally associated that airports which have been privatised, formal price regulation has existed for many years at the public sector US airports. In most, but not all, cases of airport privatisation, price regulation has been introduced at the same time as the privatisation took place.

There are a number of identifiable trends in airport pricing over the past ten years which are not necessarily associated with privatisation. These include the introduction of price freezes or discount schemes; the introduction of environmental charges; and the separate identification of terminal navigation (air traffic control) charges.

Observed Difficulties in Adhering to Pricing Principles

ICAO calls for the production of full accounts by airports, to ensure transparency. There are many cases where this is either not done, or only done on an irregular or untimely basis.

ICAO calls for charges to be "simple and suitable". In many cases, charging structures are complex, particularly in relation to the calculation of noise charges. The principle of using weight-based charges is intended to be simple, but in practice it is not, since a fixed charge per tonne will tend to discriminate against operators of either large or small aircraft. The matter is complicated further by different airports using four different definitions of aircraft weight.

Systems of Airport Price Regulation

Types of Price Regulation

There are three types of price regulation which may be imposed on monopolies or semi-monopolies, namely direct tariff regulation, dividend regulation and price cap regulation. Direct tariff regulation is in use in the US, while most privatised airports, including those in the UK and Australia, operate under some form of price cap regulation. TRL's advice to Air New Zealand focused on price cap regulation, since this is the most commonly used form of price regulation for airports.

The UK Experience of Airport Regulation

Price cap regulation was introduced in the UK with the privatisation of BAA in 1987. It is also used at Manchester, UK. It is applied by means of a CPI – x formula, by which charge increases are limited to x per cent less than the inflation rate, or Consumer Price Index. Charges are reviewed every five years and set for the following five years.

The system has resulted in charges being steadily reduced at Heathrow and Gatwick, where they now represent good value. Average aeronautical revenue per passenger has dropped at the London airports by around 15 per cent in real terms since privatisation in 1988. However, it has recently become the subject of a certain amount of criticism. There are three main criticisms.

The first is that the system is reducing the cost of using Heathrow and Gatwick, which are both heavily congested, whereas the working of a normal market price mechanism would increase charges in order to reduce demand.

The second criticism points to the high cost of the process, which amounted to around GBP6.3 million (US$9.4 million) the last time that BAA underwent its review.

The third suggests that while a CPI – x system may be an appropriate means to protect the interests of users of public utilities, it may be less appropriate in the regulation of airport charges. This is because it could be argued that airline users of airports are in a stronger position to influence airport price increases than individual users of public utilities.

Overall, it appears reasonable that the UK system was put into place at the time of BAA's privatisation, so as to allay the fears of airlines and consumer groups that there was a risk of monopolistic pricing. There may now be a case to suggest that the process has served its purpose, and that BAA has demonstrated a willingness to work closely with its airline customers to provide a good quality service at reasonable cost. It may therefore be the case that a less formal system might serve the industry better, although this would not necessarily be the case had BAA not passed through what amounts to a probationary period in a satisfactory manner.

Airport Price Regulation Elsewhere in the World

There are a number of other formal systems of airport price regulation in place elsewhere in the world. Most of these apply to privatised or semi-privatised airports. The most significant formula-based system, apart from that in the UK, was put in place in Australia when the first tranche of airports privatisations took place there in 1997. The situation there is described in detail by Peter Forsyth (Chapter 1) paper, and will not be repeated here.

The system in the US reflects a fundamentally different philosophy of the role of airports. Charges are generally not allowed to generate revenues in excess of the difference between commercial revenues and operating costs. This reflects a general (though diminishing) belief that airports are public services that should not be run as businesses.

The Future for the Economic Regulation of Transport Services

There is a range of regulatory frameworks in the field of transport operations. The international airline industry has seen a gradual trend towards deregulation, although this is still some way off in a number of markets. This relaxation largely reflects the fact that the competitive nature of the industry makes price and entry (as opposed to safety) regulation superfluous. A similar situation applies in many national bus industries. In contrast, the privatised UK rail operators are tightly regulated, both in respect of price and quality of service.

In the case of the main UK airports which are subject to price regulation, the regulatory authority, the Civil Aviation Authority, began a review of the present system of regulation during 2000, in preparation for the setting of charge limits for the next regulatory quinquennium which begins in April 2003 (CAA). The CAA indicated a preference for the abandonment of the single till principle in favour of a price cap based solely on aeronautical revenues, coupled with some level of reliance on benchmarking as a tool in the regulatory process.

However, the shift to a dual till system was opposed both by the airlines and by the UK's Competition Commission, and the CAA agreed late in 2002 that the single till process would remain in place for the next quinquennium. In practice, the effect on BAA's income is likely to be determined by the level of the price cap rather than by whether regulation is by single - or dual till. At the time of completing this chapter it appears that the cap will be set at a level which will allow BAA adequate revenue streams to finance the construction of Heathrow Terminal 5, and other major infrastructure investment programmes.

Case study – Manchester airport

The experience of regulation at Manchester points to some clear tangible benefits to airline users and, by implication, passengers purchasing airline tickets. Chief among these has been the effect on airport charges which have been held vitually static in absolute terms over the past twelve years, and which have fallen significantly when adjusted for inflation. The regulatory system has also provided the means for actions perceived to be against the public interest to be addressed. So far, this has been carried out by offering an incentive to the airport, in the form of a proffered relaxation in the pricing formula, to comply with the regulator's requirements relating to the provision of choice in ground handling services (MMC).

There are, however, some questions that could be raised as to the results and effectiveness of the regulatory regime at Manchester. Chief among these is the extent to which costs do not appear to have been contained. This may be due to the airport's public sector shareholders not regarding cost reduction as a major priority, particularly if it came as a result of cuts in staff costs.

The answer may lie in the fact that Manchester has enjoyed a period of strong sustained traffic growth in recent years which has generally exceeded expectation. As its pricing formula is set in relation to airport charge revenues per passenger, profits can be maintained without particular attention being paid to costs as long as growth exceeds the levels anticipated at the time of the last regulatory review.

Broadly speaking, the more competitive an industry, the more likely a company is to be acutely cost conscious. Companies in industries that are not particularly competitive (and it is generally reasonable to include airports in this category) may not therefore be under pressure to reduce costs as long as profits which are regarded as satisfactory are being produced. This situation could therefore apply to regulated airports, unless the regulator was minded to impose an unusually draconian pricing formula.

Another question relates to the use of the regulatory regime to eliminate actions deemed to be against the public interest. Whilst the system in place at Manchester appears to have produced useful results, it is not clear that these could not have been achieved by a conventional consumer protection/competition commission. What is important is to have a structure that allows complaints to be referred to the competition body at the time that they are perceived to be a problem. The system at Manchester appears to have been less than ideal in this respect, as the complaints have only been addressed in detail at the five-yearly regulatory reviews.

Overall, the experience at Manchester largely matches that which relates to the London airports. The regulatory system has produced some worthwhile results, and its introduction was necessary given the general level of Manchester's charges at the beginning of the period of regulation. For the future though, a less cumbersome approach, but one able to deal quickly with complaints of actions thought to be against the public interest, might be more appropriate.

The relevance of the Manchester case to the situation in New Zealand lay largely in the fact that, as discussed below, charges at the New Zealand airports are relatively high in a regional context, as Manchester's were at the start of its period under regulation. Furthermore, the New Zealand airports' charges would be very high by international standards had the New Zealand dollar not depreciated to the extent that it has in recent years. If a regulatory structure is ultimately considered in respect of Auckland it would need to provide a reasonable assurance that it would protect users against excessive pricing, while allowing the airport the ability to generate sufficient funds to allow it to provide additional capacity to meet future growth in demand. These aims appear to have been achieved satisfactorily at both Manchester and the BAA London airports. There is no reason to suppose that a similar structure applied to Auckland would not produce similar results.

The New Zealand Environment up to 2001

An important element of the work which TRL was asked to carry out by Air New Zealand was to apply the methodology of *Review of Airport Charges* to the three New Zealand airports. This methodology involves the calculation of the aeronautical charges that would be incurred if a sample of eight different aircraft types arrived at and departed from a sample of airports. The charges are calculated in local currency and then converted to a single unit of currency, the Special Drawing Right (SDR), which is widely recognised in the aviation industry due to its use as a basis for accident compensation payments under the Geneva Convention. Once converted, the airports being sampled are ranked from highest to lowest.

The methodology was applied to the charges at the three New Zealand airports. The results for 2000 charges, as submitted to the Inquiry, are shown at Annex 2, where they appear alongside the results for other international airports included in TRL's sample. These demonstrate that charges at the three New Zealand airports were moderate in world terms, but were the highest in the south-east Asia/Pacific Rim region.

Other points specific to the three airports which were raised in TRL's evidence are summarised below.

Auckland

There would seem to be little doubt that Auckland priced its aeronautical charges fairly aggressively during the period in the 1980s following its corporatisation. It is also probable that this period of emerging commercial awareness saw a trend towards cost containment which may not previously have been particularly apparent.

While there was a period of relative price stability (at least with respect to larger aircraft) for around nine years up to 2001, this period has also seen significant traffic growth, up from 5.4 million passengers in 1993 to 8.4 million in 2000/01. While the pegging of prices over an extended period would normally have the effect of gradually reducing them in real terms, the past six years have seen only a modest level of domestic inflation in New Zealand. Over this period, during which passenger throughput has increased by about 56 per cent, it would be normal to expect that economies of scale would have led to a reduction in unit costs. The profitability level now being achieved therefore reflects the fact that, while unit charges are virtually unchanged, unit costs are likely to have fallen, while the significant increase in throughput means that the gap between income and expenses in absolute terms will have widened significantly.

It does not seem unreasonable to say that Auckland's current financial strength owes much to a level of aeronautical charges which was established some time ago. In a commercial situation where neither competitive nor regulatory pressures were placed on any business in these circumstances, it would not be surprising to see price levels maintained: price maintenance in these circumstances allows the enterprise to enjoy sustained profits growth, while appearing relatively benign through the absence of price increases.

If Auckland was in a more competitive situation – as is the case in the European, South-east Asian and US airport markets – then its ability to maintain prices at their current levels might have been less. Regulation is, of course, often used as a means of moderating prices in markets with a relative lack of competition, although it has not so far been used in this way with the New Zealand airports.

Christchurch

Of the three New Zealand airports, Christchurch is the least reliant on its aeronautical charge revenues to cover its costs. However, its charges are still higher than those of Auckland and are certainly high by regional standards, as is demonstrated by a comparison with Perth's charges: this showed the charges for a turnround of a Boeing 747-400 to be around 85 per cent higher than at the Australian airport. Because it has low costs (as, at Auckland, airline operation of the domestic terminal is a factor) it achieves a high level of profitability, albeit lower in percentage terms than Auckland's. The same absence of regulatory and competitive pressures to reduce charges, as discussed in the case of Auckland, is likely to be a factor in the level of Christchurch's charges.

Although Christchurch is alone among the New Zealand airports in remaining wholly in public sector hands, there is no clear evidence to suggest that its pricing policies are affected by its ownership. Its aeronautical charge structure is unusual in that it is based around a fixed price for a landing by any given aircraft type, including terminal use by passengers regardless of passenger numbers, but varying between international and domestic operations. This structure, and the levels of the fixed charges, have been in place since before Auckland and Wellington were partially privatised and differed significantly from those airports' charging structures at that time.

Wellington

Of the three airports, Wellington (on the basis of our three years' analyses) is the most reliant on aeronautical revenues, and it is the airport with the highest charges. At the same time it is the least profitable, although in comparative terms its profitability is in the top one-third of a sample of world airports. Since it also has a very low level of costs, the more modest level of profitability cannot be due to a lack of cost control. The main reason for the lack of profitability appears to be poor commercial revenues, caused by the relatively undeveloped nature of the retail facilities, coupled with small numbers of passengers per aircraft. In theory at least, the terminal expansion and its associated increase in retail activity will go some way to remedying this situation, leading to an improvement in profitability, in which case Wellington's overall position will become more similar to that at Auckland than at present.

Background to the Commerce Commission Inquiry

Before briefly discussing the findings of the Commission's Final Report, it may be useful to touch on the terms of reference and *modus operandi* under which it worked. The Inquiry took place under the terms of Part IV of the Commerce Act 1986, which seeks to promote competition in markets for the long-term benefit of consumers within New Zealand. Where markets fail to deliver competitive outcomes and fail to operate efficiently, the Act contains provisions for the control of prices, revenues and quality standards of good and services.

The Minister of Commerce had asked the Commission to report on whether it considered that any of the airfield activities supplied by the three major airports should be controlled. The Commission was also asked to report on whether there was evidence that the requirements of the Act were met for the airfield activities supplied by any or all of the airport companies in respect of whether:

- the airfield activities are, or will be, supplied or acquired in a market in which competition is limited or is likely to be lessened;
- it is necessary or desirable to impose control in the interests of the persons acquiring (directly or indirectly) the airfield activities.

The airfield activities are among a number of activities undertaken by the airport companies. Airfield activities are defined by the Airport Authorities Act 1996 as the activities undertaken (including the facilities and services provided) to enable the take-off and landing of aircraft. They therefore included the provision of all airfield facilities, including the provision of runways, taxiways, parking aprons for aircraft, lighting, facilities for air traffic and parking apron control, and the maintenance of all of these. The Inquiry was therefore not required to consider the conduct of any of the airports' commercial activities. Similarly, the Commission decided that it was not required to consider any airfield activities as defined by the Airport Authorities Act provided by parties other than the airports themselves. Thus, for example, ground handling services provided by airlines were not considered.

The Commission took the view that the outcomes achieved by competitive markets, where there is workable or effective competition, are a general benchmark against which to compare the outcomes of other types of market. The Commission developed pricing principles which provide a framework within which it could evaluate whether efficient outcomes and normal returns were being achieved. In brief, the principles the Commission regarded as appropriate were that:

- prices should be as close as possible to their allocatively efficient level over the medium term and
- prices should allow for a normal return to be earned by suppliers over the medium term, calculated on an appropriately determined asset base and rate of return, and cover efficient operating costs, and no more; and
- prices should be dynamically efficient over the medium term; this requires that over- or under-investment is avoided, and that appropriate price signals be sent for investment.

The Commission's Final Report

The Commission produced its final report in August 2002. This recommended that price control should be introduced in the case of Auckland, where it considered that there was limited market competition and that it would be necessary or desirable for airfield services to be controlled in the interests of acquirers. However, it noted that "other less intrusive, and lower cost, forms of control than price cap regulation, which was used as a means of estimating the costs of control, are likely to be available". In the cases of Christchurch and Wellington it was not thought that price control was necessary.

The Commission considered that there would be both direct and indirect costs associated with price control. The direct costs would consist of the compliance costs to regulated entities in terms of staff and management time, coupled with the administrative costs of the regulatory body. The indirect costs would be the "distortion to behaviour caused by poor or uncertain regulatory decision making". The Commission estimated that the direct costs of price control for a single airport would be NZ$1.1 – 2.2 million in a review year and NZ$0.5 – $1.1 million in other years.

In May 2003, the Commerce Minister announced her decision on the recommendations put forward by the Commerce Commission. Her announcement indicated that no controls would be imposed at any of the three airports. She indicated that she had "… taken into account a wider range of matters than those the Commerce Commission was asked to consider. I have given particular regard to the negative net public benefits of control and the relatively small net benefits to the airlines, and indirectly airline passengers".

The Minister also referred to benefits to airlines amounting to NZ$1.7 million per annum, amounting to a 3.1 per cent reduction in total charges payable by the airlines to the airports. It was estimated that if this reduction was passed on in full to passengers it would result in approximately a 35 cent reduction on the average price for a one-way trip. The Minister considered that this level of reduction was insufficient to merit the imposition of control.

The Minister also took into account the fact that, in February 2003, Wellington airport announced a 27.6 per cent increase in airfield activity charges.

A possible admission that the Inquiry process may have been to some extent flawed or compromised emerged in the Minister's statement that "This Inquiry has highlighted aspects of the Commerce Act which may need amending, including the constraints on the Commission in determining what forms of control it may impose when undertaking a control Inquiry under Part 4 of the Act. I have asked officials to report to me on this".

Financial performance results at Auckland

The financial analysis which TRL provided to Air New Zealand was based on results for the three years to F/Y 1999/2000. Data are now available for a further two financial years. Given the Commission's view that price control should be introduced in the case of Auckland, it is instructive to look at the financial performance of that airport to see the levels of earnings (in particular) which led the Commission to its conclusion. (The recent performance of Christchurch and Wellington is not considered as the Commission did not regard price control at these airports as being necessary.) Table 2.1 below shows operating profit and Earnings before Interest, Tax, Depreciation and Amortisation (EBITDA) (both expressed as a percentage of turnover) and Return on Net Assets (operating profit as a percentage of net assets) for the five financial years 1997/98 – 2001/02.

Table 2.1 Financial performance at Auckland airport, 1997/98 – 2001/02

Y/e June	*Operating Profit (per cent)*	*EBITDA (per cent)*	*Return on Net Assets (per cent)*
1998	49.5	71.5	13.8
1999	52.1	72.6	9.5
2000	56.1	75.0	11.1
2001	56.5	74.1	11.5
2002	61.0	78.1	13.7

The Return on Net Assets results are not exceptional, although they have placed Auckland in the top one-third of places in this measure in *Airport Performance Indicators* for the past three years. However, the results for Operating Profit and EBITDA are unquestionably high by world standards in the airport industry. Auckland has for several years been at, or close to, the top of the rankings in these measures in TRL's publication *Airport Performance Indicators*. Auckland's exceptional performance is illustrated by the following results (Table 2.2) extracted from the most recent edition of the publication, relating to data for calendar year 2000 or F/Y 2001.

Table 2.2 Levels of financial performance at airports worldwide

	Operating Profit (%)	*EBITDA (%)*
Highest	Auckland 56.5%	Auckland 74.1%
Lowest	Miami 1.5%	Miami 21.9%
Average of 45	25.7%	47.1%
Australasia		
Singapore	41.8%	66.7%
Sydney	29.4%	54.8%
Europe		
London Heathrow	40.7%	54.6%
Frankfurt	33.8%	53.7%
Amsterdam	25.0%	44.0%
Aéroports de Paris	18.5%	41.2%

It is also interesting to note the unit revenue and cost figures for Auckland shown at Annex 1. Of the airports discussed in this paper, Auckland is the only one at which total revenues per passenger exceed total operating costs per passenger by a factor of more than two.

To give these figures further context, it is interesting to consider corresponding data for the airline sector in the same accounting period, extracted from TRL's publication *Airport Performance Indicators (Table 2.3).*

Table 2.3 Levels of financial performance at airlines worldwide

	Operating Profit (%)	*Return on Net Assets (%)*
Highest	Ryanair 22.7%	easyJet 25.7%
Lowest	Malaysian Airlines (14.8%)	Alitalia (22.9%)
Average of 35	4.6%	6.3%
Australasia		
Singapore Airlines	10.3%	6.6%
Qantas	9.4%	11.4%
Air New Zealand	3.0%	5.4%
Europe		
Air France	7.3%	9.3%
Lufthansa	6.6%	17.5%
KLM	1.5%	1.5%
British Airways	0.9%	0.8%

Comment

A comparison of the performance of Auckland with that of its airport peers gives a very clear indication of the relatively high levels of profitability it achieves. A simple analysis would suggest that this has been brought about by a relatively high level of aeronautical charges being in place at the start of a period of sustained traffic growth.

A comparison of the performance of Auckland and Air New Zealand provides a stark contrast in profitability levels. Corresponding comparisons between the other airport/airline national pairs shows that the New Zealand case is not an isolated one. A qualification on this situation is that in the US it is usually the airlines which are more profitable, due to the nationwide policy of restraining airport incomes. The situation shown in the tables above is typical in the rest of the world, however.

While many factors combined to culminate in the financial collapse of Air New Zealand in the latter part of 2001, it would not be unreasonable to reach the conclusion that high and unregulated levels of charges at Auckland over an extended period played a part in this outcome. This is because Auckland is Air New Zealand's principal operating base. For competing airlines, such as Qantas, the impact of Auckland's charge levels is much less, since operations at Auckland generate a much smaller proportion of those airlines' total costs.

Conclusions

While the scale of the 600-page Commerce Commission Final Report suggests an exhaustive approach to a theoretical economic analysis of airport costs and their proper relationship with charges, its outcome was one in which the relationship between airport and airline profitability did not change at all as a result of the Inquiry. Indeed, the significant price increases allowed at Wellington will presumably have an adverse effect on airlines operating there over time. This outcome may have as much to do with a national psyche which shrinks from "heavy-handed" regulation as with an objective of ensuring that airport pricing is not excessive.

This apparent preference for light-handed regulation has been manifest from the time that Auckland and Wellington were both partially privatised. In virtually every other case in the world where airports have been wholly or partially privatised, a new regulatory structure has been put in place from the outset. In most of these cases the form of the regulatory structure was known to the bidders, who were able to factor the implications of regulation into their bids. In some cases bidders were even expected to make offers with only an incomplete understanding of the likely form or severity of regulation that would be put into place. The New Zealand approach is in marked contrast to these cases.

Two factors stand out from the Inquiry experience. The first is that the process appears to have been flawed from the outset in that the form of control is a matter to be decided under the terms of Part V of the Commerce Act, and the Commission was not formally required to operate under that part of the Act. This outcome seems to point to an omission in the terms of reference given to the Commission, in that under those terms the process was incapable of resulting in the implementation of any recommendations. The Minister's comments seem to add credence to this view.

Coupled with this unsatisfactory outcome is the very extended period that elapsed since the Commission was first given its instructions in March 1998. After a period of over five years nothing was achieved other than the possibility of some form of procedural change for Inquiries of this sort. Even had the Minister accepted the Commission's recommendation in respect of Auckland the timescale would have been, to my mind, unacceptably long. In contrast the UK quinquennial reviews, covering much larger airports with far larger financial outcomes at stake, are normally completed within a three-year timescale.

While accepting that the long term stability of supply of aviation services to the travelling public may not be a primary objective in airport price regulation, it would surely by a desirable outcome. To passengers (and employees) who were inconvenienced by the withdrawal of services at the time of Air New Zealand's financial crisis, the theoretical economist's position that this was merely a case of wealth transfer would have carried little weight. New Zealand's relative isolation and lack of alternative means of travel only serve to underline the need for a financially healthy national airline.

This paper demonstrates that, in both a regional and global context, Auckland airport generates exceptional profits, both in terms of operating profits and profit after interest and tax, and in terms of the difference between total revenue per passenger and total costs per passenger. This situation was recognised in the Commerce Commission's recommendation that price control is needed.

The use of straightforward benchmarking as employed in this paper provides a simple to understand insight into the airport/airline relationship. Since airport price regulation is primarily intended to ensure that airlines are not the subject of monopolistic or excessive pricing, it seems relevant to be aware of that relationship.

References

Airport World (1). *Airport World* (published by Airports Council International). Volume 3, Issue 6, December 1998 – January 1999: Airport Charges: the ACI view.

Airport World (2). *Airport World* (published by Airports Council International). Volume 3, Issue 6, December 1998 – January 1999: Airport Charges: the IATA view.

CAA. Numerous reports and consultation papers published since August 2000. See "Quinquennial Reviews of Designated Airports" at www.caa.co.uk/erg.

ICAO. Statements by the Council to Contracting States on Charges for Airports and Air Navigation Services. 5th edition, 1997.

MMC. Monopolies and Mergers Commission: Manchester Airport plc – A report on the economic regulation of Manchester Airport plc. July 1997.

New Zealand Commerce Commission. Final Report on Part IV Inquiry into Airfield Activities at Auckland, Wellington and Christchurch International Airports, August 2002. www.comcom.govt.nz.

Transport Research Laboratory (1). *Review of Airport Charges.* Published annually since 1999. Previously published by Symonds Travers Morgan between 1990 and 1998.

Transport Research Laboratory (2). *Airport Performance Indicators.* Published annually since 1999. Previously published by Symonds Travers Morgan in 1998.

ANNEX 1
Summary operating and financial data for airports discussed in this paper

Table 2.4 Operating and financial data for airports discussed in this paper

	Passengers (000s)	*Air Transport Movements*	*Total Revenues (US$000s)*	*Operating Profit (% of revenues)*	*Post tax profit (% of revenues)*
Auckland	8,424	147,868	80,428	56.5%	30.9%
Christchurch	4,300	79,907	24,764	39.2%	26.5%
Wellington	3,704	99,744	17,131	46.6%	9.2%
Sydney	26,437	290,492	222,149	29.4%	1.0%
Perth	5,237	57,607	41,227	38.0%	-41.3%
Heathrow	64,311	459,474	1,259,169	40.7%	21.5%
Gatwick	32,131	251,91	493,331	36.4%	26.5%
Manchester	18,604	179,495	342,225	20.5%	12.4%

Table 2.5 Operating and financial data for airports discussed in this paper

	Total Costs per Passenger (US$)	*Total Revenues per Passenger (US$)*
Auckland	4.15	9.55
Christchurch	3.50	5.76
Wellington	2.47	4.63
Sydney	5.93	8.40
Perth	4.88	7.87
Heathrow	11.61	19.58
Gatwick	9.77	15.35
Manchester	14.63	18.40

Source: Airport websites (Christchurch and Wellington), *Airport Performance Indicators 2002* (others). Data relate to calendar year 2000 or financial year 2000/01.

Table 2.6 Aeronautical charges at airports discussed in this paper

US Dollars	*Aeronautical charges applicable to an arrival and departure by a Boeing 747-400*
Auckland	4,793.9
Christchurch	4,520.8
Wellington	6,148.2
Sydney	4,060.1
Perth	2,494.1
Heathrow	4,428.8
Gatwick	3,559.7
Manchester	8,212.8

Notes for table 2.6

1. Includes landing charges, all passenger-related charges, aircraft parking and terminal navigation charges if applicable, for international services.
2. Assumes passenger loads of 279 (Boeing 747-400).
3. Charges calculated on the basis of those applicable at the time of TRL's work for Air New Zealand in September 2000.
4. Assumes parking periods of 4 hours for Boeing 747-400.
5. Charges at Sydney rose substantially after TRL's work for Air New Zealand was completed. Charges for the Boeing 747-400 in mid-2002 amounted to US$6,867.

ANNEX 2
Table 2.7 Airport Charges Index (based on 2000 charges)

	Airport	SDRs	Index
1	Tokyo	48646	100
2	New Jersey-EWR	33587	69
3	New York-JFK	33004	68
4	Vienna	24819	51
5	Moscow	22594	46
6	Mexico City	22374	46
7	Budapest	20747	43
8	Frankfurt	20142	41
9	Paris-CDG	20011	41
10	Lisbon	19386	40
11	Amsterdam	19263	40
12	Vancouver	18620	38
13	Munich	18172	37
14	Jeddah	17942	37
15	Athens	17435	36
16	Berlin	17034	35
17	Chicago	17031	35
18	Stockholm	16518	34
19	Copenhagen	16063	33
20	Oslo	15809	32
21	**Wellington**	**15714**	**32**
22	London-LHR	15082	31
23	Helsinki	14325	29
24	**Auckland**	**14316**	**29**
25	**Christchurch**	**14220**	**29**
26	Madrid	13459	28

Table 2.7 (Continued)

27	Washington	13374	27
28	**Hong Kong**	**12945**	**27**
29	Dublin	12919	27
30	**Singapore**	**12408**	**26**
31	**Sydney**	**12025**	**25**
32	London-LGW	11238	23
33	Johannesburg	11135	23
34	Miami	11069	23
35	**Honolulu**	**10088**	**21**
36	Dallas/Fort Worth	9865	20
37	Orlando	9782	20
38	**San Francisco**	**6425**	**13**
39	**Los Angeles**	**5358**	**11**
40	Dubai	3271	7

Bold: Airports in the Asia Pacific region.

Part B
North America

Chapter 3

Airport Pricing, Financing and Policy: Report to National Transportation Act Review Committee

David W. Gillen and William Morrison

Introduction

We examine the economic debate on government regulation of airports with a focus on the role of airports in fostering airline competition. In the Canadian context this latter concern is important given the latest evolution of the domestic airline market to a single dominant carrier - Air Canada. The Federal government in Canada is currently reforming the legislation underpinning all forms of transportation, including aviation. This process is taking place at a time when many airports have only recently devolved from direct Federal control and operation to become autonomous entities. These events have led to no small amount of interest in how governance structures for the airport system in Canada should be developed. We begin by reviewing the debate on regulation of airports. In the third section, we consider the role of airports in fostering airline competition and in the fourth section we review the evolution of airport policy in Canada and discuss the merits of regulation in the Canadian system, taking airline competition into account.

Should Airports be Regulated?

An airport is a multi-product firm. It has two obvious sides to its business: the airside market (passenger airlines and cargo companies as direct customers and fixed base operators as tenants) and the non-airside market (enplaning and deplaning passengers as direct customers and retail businesses as tenants). Each side gives rise to a multiple of outputs with peak and off-peak periods in both markets.

On the airside, the number of passengers an airport can attract determines the airport's market power (ability to set airside prices). In this regard, smaller (regional) airports often compete with road and rail transportation. For example, the demand for flights to and from Charlottetown in Prince Edward Island was significantly reduced with the completion of a road bridge connecting the island with mainland New Brunswick. In the case of larger airports, the number of flights an airport can attract depends on both the airport's attractiveness as a point of departure/arrival and on its usefulness as a hub for connecting passengers. In the former case, an airport's bargaining power with airlines derives from its geographic proximity to "non-connecting" passengers and the degree to which it competes with other airports for those passengers. In the limiting case, airlines are faced with the choice of using the airport or ignoring that segment of the passenger market. However even in this case, the airport is constrained in its pricing to the extent that non-hub airports prefer to be servicing several rival airlines than one airline with deep pockets. The self-interested desire to have competing sources of airside business thus provides a natural ceiling on airside prices, particularly in Canada, where the domestic carriers in competition with Air Canada are discount or charter airlines with low margins.

Larger airports clearly have location-based market power, both with the services they sell to passengers directly and with the leasing contracts they write with airside and groundside tenants. We can expect rent-seeking behaviour from airports in this aspect of the business, where the bargaining power lies squarely with the airport authority in its lease negotiations. However, this seems less of a competition issue because it simply involves a reallocation of the surplus generated by the location.

Airport Regulation: Options and Experience from Other Countries

In the debate on how to regulate airports, three features are important: the complementarity between airside and non-airside activity, the degree to which airports are congested (capacity constrained) and the level of competition in the industry (or at the airport if it is a hub). With regard to the complementarity issue Starkie (2002) argues that the effect of increased airside movements on passenger volumes and non-airside revenues has a strong effect on airport pricing incentives. Capacity constraints influence the consequences for different price structures and, just as important, the ability of the airport to cover its capital expenses.

The perception that airports are monopolies has figured into the regulation of charges that airports levy. This includes charges for airside activities such a landing and passenger terminal fees but also fees for non-aviation activities.[1] The form that this regulation has taken varies from country to country. In the US, for example, it is required by the Federal Aviation Act that airside fees cover only the costs associated with providing aeronautical services.[2]

In other parts of the world, price (or economic) regulation can include traditional rate of return regulation, price-cap regulation and cost-based price regulation. Other forms of regulation include trigger or "grim strategy" regulation where a light-handed form of regulation is used until the subject firm sets prices or

---

[1] Airside fees would include landing, terminal, security and emergency/policing fees. Commercial fees are those negotiated for concession and lease agreements.

[2] Clearly there will be debate as to what costs should be included and how one allocates common costs between airside and non-airside activities.

earns profits or reduces quality beyond some point and triggers a long-term commitment to interventionist regulation.

The US is the largest aviation market in the world and has the least progressive airport governance and regulation evolution. The power of the carriers, the long-term contracts written between the carriers and the airports, and the traditional funding of airport capital projects by the FAA (through the Airport & Airway Improvement Fund), all these factors contribute to the lack of evolution observed in other parts of the world. The US is essentially a cost-of-service form of regulation although one could argue that those airports that still adhere to the principles of residual financing are under a single till form of price-cap regulation.[3] The airports are required to set aeronautical fees so as to collect revenues that reflect the costs of providing the service. Thus, individual prices are indirectly regulated in the sense that revenues cannot exceed costs.

The US form of regulation provides for neither static nor dynamic efficiency. It also ensures the airlines appropriate the majority of rents at capacity constrained airports. Static efficiency is not achieved since fees reflect accounting rather than economic costs. Any excess demands will be rationed through some quantity method, such as flow control whereby flights within a given time or distance from the constrained airport are not allowed to depart until a slot is available for them. The selection of the time or distance is clearly arbitrary. Dynamic efficiency is frustrated since there are no price signals that reveal the value of added capacity. The excess demand reflects a failure to price scarce resources appropriately and the rent due to slots accrues to the carriers that hold the slots. The rents show up in the form of hub premiums.

In other parts of the world, rate of return or price-cap regulation is the norm. The best examples are the UK, which regulates the BAA; Australia, which regulates its privatized airports, and Germany where Hamburg Airport has a price cap regulation.[4] The major debate concerns whether a single or dual till form of regulation should be used. Rate of return regulation (ROR) is a traditional form of utility regulation and involves allowing a rate of return on an allowed rate base. The firm or airport can set prices at whatever levels or using whatever structure they wish provided the revenues less costs do not result in a return on capital that exceeds the specified allowed return. Here, the key questions are firstly what constitutes a "fair" return on capital invested and, secondly, what capital invested should be included in the "allowed rate base"?[5] This form of regulation is very time intensive and generally involves lengthily regulatory hearings. As Tretheway (2001) points out, ROR regulation tends to be complex, unresponsive and expensive to administer.

---

[3] The single till in discussed in detail below but it is a form of regulation in which a price cap is set and all revenues collected at the airport enter into the calculation - airside and non-airside. Residual financing means at the end of the fiscal year, if revenues are less than costs the airlines are responsible for covering the difference.

[4] Hamburg Airport has been partially privatized recently.

[5] Liquidity ratio, risk and conditions in the economy are considered in setting the allowed rate of return.

Price cap regulation on the other hand was introduced precisely to overcome the problems associated with rate of return regulation and to lower the overall costs of regulation when it is deemed necessary and provide the incentives for firms to act in a way to improve economic welfare. The price cap, expressed as CPI-X involves setting a cap on prices, generally at the rate of inflation, and then deducting an amount (*X*) that is to induce the firm to improve its efficiency and is chosen to reflect the "expected" efficiency gains of the firm. Prices (or revenue) can be increased up to the level of the allowed cap and when inflation rises or costs rise.

A key issue in price cap regulation is what is included in the group of prices to be "capped". Note that it is only the average price that must be at CPI-X, not every price. This feature allows the firm to adjust relative prices in keeping with cost and demand conditions. The most notable feature of price cap regulation is the much lower cost of enforcement and the incentives it provides for innovation and efficiency. Despite these positive features there is considerable debate about the appropriateness of price-cap regulation of airports.

Further, there is also debate about the relative superiority of single till versus dual till price-cap regulation. A single till refers to the use of all airport revenues in the determination of the price cap. This means that both aeronautical and non-aeronautical revenues are included. Alternatively, the dual till system only considers aeronautical revenues in setting airside prices for an airport.

Single versus Dual Till

The essence of the debate of single versus dual till is the impact it has on efficiency. There are some comments on distributional issues but these are raised for the most part by the carriers who would face higher aeronautical charges under a dual (or multi) till system. The Australian system (except for Sydney airport) is regulated using a dual till system, as is the German (Hamburg) airport, while the UK system and South Africa use a single till system.[6]

To evaluate the relative merits of dual versus single till we need to consider two issues. First, do airports have (and exercise) market power in non-aviation sectors and second what represents a "fair" distribution of the rents? Some argue that airports can operate in a competitive environment. In Europe, Schiphol, Frankfurt, Heathrow and Charles de Gaulle all compete for long-haul connecting traffic. In Germany, airports are close enough together that they can be considered in competition to some degree, and in the Maritimes in Canada, airports can be viewed as substitutes. To the extent airports are in the same market, they have limited market power. However, many, if not most, airports have varying degrees of monopoly power in aeronautical services. Whether they have similar market power in other activities is open to debate. To the extent that these are joint activities with the airside market (e.g. check-in desks) these prices might rightly fall into the basket for regulation. Alternatively, if these are not joint activities that

[6] Interestingly, ACI and IATA, lobby groups for the airline industry, have recently persuaded ICAO to undertake a study on the single till principle. The single till clearly favors airlines while the dual till may favor everyone else.

can be offered in varying proportions (including not at all), it is not clear they should be included in the basket.

The major arguments for not including activities such as food, rental and parking concessions under a single till are they result in perverse incentives when airports are capacity constrained and may create costs when airports have lots of capacity. When airports are capacity constrained and a single till is in place, as more revenue is made on the non-aeronautical side, it must be that aeronautical charges must be lowered to remain under the price cap. Thus, in the presence of congestion, prices end up being lowered when efficiency dictates that they should be raised. If profit-maximizing airports are not capacity constrained, they have every incentive to stimulate demand (and revenue) via lower prices on the aeronautical side. Thus in the non-constrained case, single till price-cap regulation is not necessary.

Aside from efficiency considerations, distributional concerns remain as to which parties will capture the rents arising from geographic location and scarcity of supply.[7] Location rents are essential to allocate limited space efficiently (Starkie, 2001). Currently, at capacity constrained airports, airlines holding property rights to peak-demand slots capture all the rents that could be shared with, or allocated to, the airport. Under a single till price-cap, where the tendency is for aeronautical charges to fall, airlines will actually obtain some of the airport's location rents as well.

At an airport without capacity constraints, the incentive is for the airport to lower charges on the airside, due to demand complementarities with non-airside business. Even here the airlines obtain the rents since they do not pass the lower airside fees on to passengers in the form of lower prices, unless the market is highly competitive.

However, this is efficient because the marginal cost associated with excess capacity is likely to be below average cost and consequently the efficient outcome is to promote the use of airside capital. Therefore, non-airside rents are used to promote more efficient use of airside capacity. The airlines might argue that they are responsible for generating the non-airside rents and therefore are as deserving of them as the airport. But it is the airport that undertakes the investments and contracts and therefore takes the risk.

Note that an interesting question now arises concerning infrastructure investments by airports. Would a competitive (profit-maximizing) airport not internalize the demand complementarity when considering the investment decision for more airside capacity? It seems reasonable that the airport would compare the incremental cost of expansion with the incremental revenue from airside and non-airside activities. But if the airport is not allowed to have (in effect internalize) the non-airside revenue it could result in less investment in airside capacity or to an investment at a later date than would otherwise be the case.

The question of dual till price-cap regulation is somewhat more complex. The attractiveness of a dual till approach depends on the level of congestion at the airport and the level of airline competition. Under a dual till, airside charges would rise since they would no longer be cross-subsidized by non-airside revenue. If

[7] Note that these are not monopoly rents arising from market power per se.

airport fees rise, airfares would not necessarily change. The fee increase would be a form of rent tax and, consequently, the more competitive the air service is (higher elasticity of demand), the greater the portion of the increase absorbed by the carriers. Similarly, to the extent that local market demand or hub airport demand elasticities are somewhat lower, a portion of the tax incidence would fall on the passengers.

The impact on economic efficiency when the airport is not congested depends on the extent of cost economies. There is mixed evidence of the degree of scale economies at airports. Our view is that there are no scale economies for airside but significant density economies for terminals. There is also a good deal of lumpiness in airside capital. Because runways and taxiways are added in discrete units, there will be, after an expansion, some degree of excess capacity. This being the case, marginal cost is less than average cost. With a dual till, if fees rise, an airport could experience a reduction in traffic when there is already excess capacity. If this scenario were true, would a profit-maximizing airport not cross-subsidize from non-airside to airside? If there are demand-side complementarities, the airport would set fees on the airside such that the marginal revenue from an additional operation, which would include both airside and non-airside revenue, is equal to marginal cost. In other words they would fully internalize the externality.

While the comparison of single and dual till forms of price-cap regulation clearly favors dual till, there is a strong argument to be made for no price-cap regulation. This is because the implementation of a single regulatory regime will have divergent efficiency and distributional effects across the system given the heterogeneous characteristics (congestion, location-based market power, degree of airline competition) of airports.

In addition, there are two cost-side effects of regulation. First, the determination of allowed capital investment in the rate base distorts incentives for capital, as airports will strategically engage in over-investment. Second, once the regulatory rule is in place, airports have an incentive to minimize costs if the target allowable revenue level is reached. Thus, we would expect over-investment in some infrastructure (gold plating) in order to influence the price-cap and then reductions in operation costs (lowering of service quality) in order to maximize realized profits. In the case of larger "national" airports in the Canadian system, the airport authorities are formally treated as "not-for-profit" entities under the corporation act, so that any profits must be reinvested. The resulting incentive structure therefore exacerbates the gold plating problem.

Finally, what is not often considered in the debate on airport regulation is that airports can directly contribute to the degree of airline competition through pricing and capital investment decisions. Therefore, policy makers should not only consider the welfare effects of airport regulation in relation to airports and their customers, but also the associated welfare effects on airline competition that result from airport pricing and investment decisions under the various regulatory regimes.

Airports and Airline Competition

Airport-related opportunities for airlines to engage in exclusionary practices arise from the pricing and control of airport infrastructure. Specifically, airlines will have an opportunity to engage in exclusionary practices if they dominate passenger throughput at airports. Three central components of passenger throughput are take-off/landing slots, enplaning/deplaning gates, and ticketing desks. Each of these elements might not yield significant or conclusive evidence of a dominant position when viewed independently, but the notion of throughput (the flow of passengers through an airport) points to the inter-relatedness of these elements and the possibility of *cumulative* market power. A dominant incumbent airline with sufficient control of slots, gates and ticketing counters at an airport can present potential entrants with significant barriers to entry, particularly with respect to the business travel market, where price considerations are offset by service quality attributes (availability of travel times, punctuality, convenience for example).

Take-off and Landing Slots

The number and size of runways and aprons determine the take-off and landing slot capacity of an airport. Airlines that control a large percentage of slots hold a dominant position over rivals to the extent that other airlines are prevented from offering routes and schedules during peak demand hours. It is typically during peak demand times (corresponding to the high-value, price-inelastic demand for business travel) that airports are likely to be slot-constrained. By controlling peak-demand slots, particularly at hub airports, an incumbent airline can effectively exclude rivals from this segment of the market.

In 1998, at Toronto's Lester B. Pearson International Airport (LBPIA), the only slot-constrained airport in Canada, Air Canada controlled approximately 74 per cent of the available slots, with 15 per cent controlled by US-based airlines; 7 per cent controlled by Canadian Charter Airlines and the remainder by foreign-owned airlines.[8]

If an airport can alleviate slot capacity constraints, then the potential for exclusionary practices is lessened and the obvious way this might be accomplished is through infrastructure investments in additional runway and air-traffic control facilities. Recently, LBPIA has embarked on a capital expansion program to add two new runways along with new dual taxiways bordering the terminal apron area, a satellite de-icing facility, and an infield access tunnel.[9]

---

[8] DAFFE Competition Policy Roundtable, "Competition Policy and International Airport Services", #16, p. 4, OECD, 1998. Note that following its take-over of Canadian Airlines International in 2000, Air Canada complied with a request from the Competition Bureau to surrender 42 slots at LBPIA. The surrendered slots were spread more or less evenly over the peak periods (7:00am - 9:00am and 3:00pm - 8:00pm) and there have been two rounds of slot allocations thus far. All the slots have been allocated to domestic carriers.

[9] Montreal and Vancouver are the next airports expected to become slot-constrained in the future.

However, there are two factors to consider when evaluating the effectiveness of this sort of investment in airside capacity. First, air traffic movements may increase in the future as a result of an increased demand for business and discretionary travel. Secondly, air traffic movements may increase as a result of strategic adjustments by dominant incumbent airlines. In the case of Canada and Toronto in particular, the sole dominant carrier (Air Canada) might increase its flight frequencies on business routes even if passenger volumes remain roughly constant. The use of smaller aircraft (if merited by passenger volumes) with more frequent service would be a way of maintaining its current dominant market share in the business travel market, while extending its control over an expanded number of slots.

Passenger Gates

A more significant and widespread aspect of airside infrastructure in Canada that affords incumbents the opportunity for exclusionary practices, is the number, type, ownership and control of enplaning/deplaning gates. Even when an airport is unconstrained in its take-off and landing slots, congestion can and frequently does occur due to excess demand for gates relative to the number and/or size of aircraft enplaning or deplaning passengers in the same general time period.

If an incumbent airline owns and operates gates, it can exclude rivals by making sure that its own flights are serviced first and at the most preferred terminal location (to facilitate connections for example). If these gates are equipped with loading bridges, an airline owner can set high prices to discourage use by rivals by raising their relative costs, while at the same time generating revenue for itself.

Counter Space and Baggage Facilities

In the same way that a dominant airline can create barriers through control of slots or gates, it can also create barriers to entry or discourage expansion by competitors through controlling a majority of counter spaces in terminal buildings. By utilizing a majority of the counter spaces, the dominant airline can force longer waiting times on passengers traveling with competitors and increase their potential for delays.

In this environment it could be difficult to show anti-competitive practices, since the airline can argue that its use of counter spaces is part of a strategy to compete on service quality as well as price. Unless the dominant airline matches the prices of low-cost "no-frills" competitors, it can argue that it is charging higher prices in return for increased service. If the price differential between its own fares and those of discount price competitors do not match the cost differential defined by the level of service quality, the airline could argue its product is an "experience good".[10] The argument could then be made that "competitive" pricing is necessary to attract consumers to experience the service quality difference. The issue is further complicated by the uncertainty of proper yield management principles and the degree to which aircraft capacity over and above business fare seats can be used to match, or almost match, competing fares of competitors.

The Cumulative Effects of Control of Passenger Throughput

There is a danger that if a dominant carrier is scrutinized with respect to anti-competitive practices in relation to only one form of infrastructure, that the tests for exclusionary behavior might not produce a correct result. For example, an airline might be judged to operate above avoidable costs on routes connected to its peak demand slots at an airport. However, the airline's real dominance may lie more with its control of gates and counter spaces. If an airline owns and operates a gate that it retains for its own use in conjunction with particular slots, then the avoidable costs of operation should include all relevant opportunity costs including the revenues it might earn from renting its gate to the highest valued user. The point is that the cumulative effects arising from control of slots, gates, counter spaces and baggage facilities make it impossible for rival airlines to offer comparable service (frequency, reliability or passenger time costs).

The Domination of Hubs and Spokes

Like all firms, airlines create value for their customers, and airlines use their hubs in creating this value (consumer surplus). Despite hubs being expensive mechanisms to do this, it allows the firm to exploit economies of density and economies of scope on the demand side with high frequency and large numbers of destinations. The premium (business) traveler will pay a premium for this service. The "fortress or dominated" hub is the means by which airlines survive to be able to price discriminate.

Empirical research in the US to date supports several broad conclusions about hubs:

- On average, fare revenue per passenger is higher on average for trips to and from major hub airports where one or two carriers operate a large fraction of flights (75% or so) than for trips to and from other airports. Hub premiums have existed since the early 1980s, if not before, at some major airports.
- The difference between average fares at individual concentrated hubs and those at less concentrated airports varies widely, ranging from –15% to nearly 70% depending on the airport considered. A few concentrated hub airports have shown large fare premiums for more than a decade.

---

[10] An "experience good" is a good for which consumers cannot easily estimate the utility associated with the good without actually consuming it.

- Higher average fares for travel to and from concentrated hub airports are realized mainly by the carriers operating major hubs there, and do not appear to spill over to other carriers serving those same airports. This suggests that travelers pay higher fares only for travel on flights offered by carriers that dominate service at concentrated hub airports. Fares charged by other carriers serving those hubs are similar to those for travel to and from less concentrated airports.
- Adjusting for differences between concentrated hubs and other airports in flight characteristics that would be expected to make carriers' costs for serving them differ – principally flight distance and average passenger volumes on routes – reduces differences in average revenue per passenger.
- Adjusting the measure further for differences in the fraction of travelers using frequent-flyer award tickets reduces the apparent premium, but still does not eliminate it.
- Travelers' willingness to pay higher fares for the more frequent departures and non-stop connections to more destinations that characterize large hub airports appears to explain some of the fare premium for travel to and from these airports, but it is not clear exactly how much.
- Adjusting for differences in variables other than route distance and passenger volumes that might cause carriers' costs for serving concentrated hub airports to be higher – such as the mix of business and leisure travel – reduces estimated hub premiums to modest levels. However these variables may be correlated with demand characteristics that allow hubbing carriers to identify price-insensitive travelers and to charge them higher fares.

Adjusting for differences in the presence of low-cost carriers – Southwest Airlines in particular – between routes to and from concentrated hub airports and markets between other airports eliminates apparent hub premiums at all but a few concentrated hub airports. These premiums can be due to barriers to entry, lack of competition from low fare carriers and/or due to higher quality service.

Thus, the weight of the collective evidence points toward the existence of hub premiums, although they may be relatively modest. This is also consistent with the fact that the carriers that appear to charge premiums also report operating margins - fare and other revenues in excess of operating expenses - significantly above industry norms. Finally, the fact that substantial entry has been extremely slow to occur at several of the airports where hub fare premiums appear to have existed for long periods provides some evidence that they are a consequence of barriers to entry at airports.

Airport Policy in Canada: Past, Present and Future

Canadian aviation policy has evolved from one in which government played a dominant role as owner, operator and investor in airports, airlines and air traffic control systems, to one in which it is essentially a regulator of safety. From the 1960s through to the mid-1980s, airports were the responsibility of the Canadian Air Transportation Administration (CATA), a division of Transport Canada. Investments in runways, terminals and other buildings were funded out of a capital fund provided by Treasury Board. Revenues were raised through landing fees, terminal charges and a ticket tax and were placed in Consolidated Revenue Fund[11] However, airports were not required to break even; nor was the system to be self-financing. Only at Toronto (Pearson), and in some years Vancouver, did revenues cover operating and maintenance costs. In all other cases, costs exceeded revenues.

As long as the Treasury Board was willing and able to provide subsidies from general revenues, there were incentives for CATA to overbuild capacity. Despite capacity and infrastructure problems at Toronto and Vancouver, Transport Canada had to consider the entire system and demands from other airports even though the latter were not under the same capacity constraints. There were uniform standards, uniform codes of construction, training and conduct. Revenues were pooled to fund the entire national system rather than any single airport or subgroup of airports.

While large increases in Federal government spending occurred in the 1960s, the mid-1970s witnessed an economic slowdown that created much greater competition between government ministries and departments for Treasury Board funds. As a result, greater fiscal prudence was forced upon CATA and Airports came to be seen as an important source of revenues. Financial self-sufficiency for the system became the target and this led to an increase in fees and charges and the introduction of the Canadian Air Transportation Tax (CATT).[12]

Despite an increase in revenues, CATA could not match the demand for airport services. The introduction of larger passenger aircraft along with increased operations and passenger traffic both placed increased pressure on major airports and the system generally. CATA responded by implementing three strategies. First, incremental investments were made to increase capacity. These included high-speed taxiways and added parallel taxiways, for example. Second, operational procedures such as "flow control" were introduced to allocate scarce capacity at peak periods.[13] Third, steps were taken to operate airports on a more "commercial" basis not only in order to generate added revenue, but also to improve efficiency.

---

[11] Revenues went to the consolidated revenue fund and expenditures were paid out of it but the two were not linked.

[12] Fees and charges were set in Ottawa so all airports charged the same amount regardless of the level of demand, or supply of services and capacity.

[13] Flow control is the arbitrary decision criteria to hold aircraft destined for the congested airport on the ground at origin airports that were within a given distance or flying time. This strategy was, and is, not limited to Transport Canada but is used in the US and elsewhere.

While appropriate, the third strategy was not successful because there were no incentives in place to achieve more revenue or to improve cost efficiency. The personnel in CATA were operationally oriented and functionally driven with a supply-side focus: demand pressures were to be relieved by expanding supply rather than using the price system to manage demand or to obtain some sense of the value of added capacity.

The 1980s witnessed a general shift away from active government participation in the economy, particularly in the Canadian airline industry, which was subject to deregulation and privatization. In 1986, the Airport Authorities Group (AAG) replaced CATA and was tasked with introducing financial self-sufficiency through greater commercialization of airports. The move to financial self-sufficiency and ultimately to devolution progressed as traffic levels stabilized.

The devolution of airports was spurred by three key factors. First, the government did not have the necessary capital to invest in the system, while deregulation was leading to increased demands on the system by airlines and passengers. Second, the government wanted to have airports funded out from airport resources, because general revenues were under pressure from many other government services including health care. Third, airport expansion was becoming more difficult due to increased public sensitivity to environmental issues. The environmental review process lengthened the airport planning process. It also provided local constituents with a federal political power point.

Airports, when owned by the federal government in the late 1980s, had a value in excess of $10 billion Canadien dollars.[14] In the 1988-89 fiscal year, the Airports Authority Group spent approximately $247 million for expansion, restoration and rehabilitation of the aviation system. Yet total airport transportation and engineering construction remained at about 4 per cent of total transportation construction from 1978 through 1991.

The National Airport Program (NAP)

The genesis of the NAP in Canada really began with the policy directive *A Future Framework for the Management of Airports in Canada* (1988). This policy document contained two primary goals; the transfer of a subset of airports to local airport authorities (LAAs) and the transfer the remaining airports to ownership by local municipalities.[15] The presence of scheduled passenger traffic was the key criteria to be used in deciding each airport's designation.[16] The local control aspect of the NAP made a great deal of sense in that service levels for the airports would better reflect community needs and desires and would not be subject to national political pressures.

Four distinct groups of airports were created under NAP. First, a National Airports System of 26 airports was identified. These larger airports accounted for

---

[14] This excludes the value of the land.

[15] In the latter case, these transfers were often for a nominal fee.

[16] As we note below, such an approach completely ignores the dynamics of the industry and in particular the approach of discount carriers such as WestJet and CanJet in Canada and Southwest Airlines in the US to enter new markets and develop them.

over 90% of all scheduled and air-cargo traffic. Included in this category were all national, provincial and territorial capitals, as well as airports with annual traffic of 200,000 passengers or more.[17] The *operation* of these airports was to be devolved to LAAs with the Federal Government retaining ownership.

Regional or local airports constituted a second group of airports that were served by scheduled passenger carriers, but with fewer than the 200,000 threshold required for "NAS" (National Airport System) status. Under the NAP, these were to be offered to Provincial governments, airport commissions or other interests on an ownership basis. Smaller airports (used mainly for recreational flying) would be transferred to local interests or closed within two years. Finally, remote and Arctic airports would continue to be operated and supported by the Federal Government.

With pending devolution came the need to devise new ways for airports to meet their capital requirements. The federal government assumed the 26 airports in the NAS would have the fiscal capacity to attract the capital necessary for infrastructure investment and that they would have strong enough markets to generate revenues from airside and groundside activities.[18] Regional/local airports were to be provided with assistance from an internal capital market: the Airports Capital Assistance Program (ACAP). These funds were designated for safety-related airside investment projects - the funds were project specific - and the monies were derived from the lease payments from the NAS airports. Local operators were required to contribute to a maximum of 15 per cent of project costs.

One justification for this internal capital market was the role the regional/local airports played in the country's aviation network. In a hub-and-spoke system, hub airports derive benefit from spoke airports and the more spokes the greater the value of the network. Private markets would tend to under-invest in spoke airports unless there was some means of internalizing this network externality.

Airports, Airline Competition and Canadian Competition Policy

In February 2001, the Federal Competition Bureau in Canada published new draft enforcement guidelines on the abuse of dominance in the airline industry. Chapter 4 of this document catalogues various forms of anti-competitive behavior in the airline industry and in section 4.2 (which focuses on exclusionary practices) the draft guidelines specify the pre-emption of take-off and landing slots separate from other forms of pre-emption relating to airport facilities. The reason for this is that slots can be regulated. Specifically, the draft guidelines state the following:

> A dominant carrier's pre-emption of slots would entail acquiring control of slots that it had no immediate use for, but that it wished to hold in order to keep entrants out of the market. If the carrier had to use the slots in order to maintain

---

[17] This traffic level was to have been sustained over a three-year period. No reason was ever provided for the figure of 200,000 nor was there any consideration that a new NAP would lead to a more entrepreneurial approach to airport management.

[18] Fiscal capacity refers to the ability of an airport to achieve a particular level of revenue and/or capital access (bonds) because of the markets it serves and traffic level it attracts.

> control of them, it might be able to schedule some service in the slots just to occupy them (even if the service operates at a loss). Pre-emption of the latter type could be referred to as pre-emptive scheduling. It involves the expansion of capacity in the market at a time before it can generate at least a competitive rate of return on a flow basis. In the absence of potential entry by a new carrier into the market, the incumbent carrier would have no incentive to expand capacity prematurely because its overall profits would be higher by delaying the increase in service until market growth justified it. It is the threat of new entry that drives the incumbent to expand its capacity, and the capacity expansion acts as an entry barrier.[19]

In the presence of a "use it or lose it" slot allocation policy, the Bureau determines whether a dominant carrier has pre-empted take-off and landing slots on the basis of whether the carrier is covering the avoidable cost of offering the service in the slots for which pre-emption is alleged. It should be noted that for pre-emption of take-off or landing slots to be an anti-competitive act, it must be done with the objective of withholding the take-off or landing slots from a market. Pre-emption of slots could adversely affect competition at airports where the pre-empted slots are arrivals or departures during the peak travel periods, or at airports that are slot constrained.

The draft guidelines therefore make the important distinction between overt hoarding of slots (slots held but not used) and the more likely case of pre-emptive scheduling. The question then arises as to the correct measure of avoidable costs for provision of passenger air travel for a given landing or take-off slot. The document also outlines anti-competitive acts by airlines in relation to airport facilities. In particular, pre-emptive use of airport facilities is defined to occur when: "…a dominant carrier obtains access to and control of certain airport facilities or services (e.g., gate space, counter space, baggage handling facilities) before a competing carrier has an opportunity to enter into or expand in the market" (p18).

Importantly, the Bureaus guidelines do not make the same distinction between overt hoarding and pre-emptive scheduling of facilities as it does with pre-emptive control of slots. However, pre-emptive scheduling is the more likely action of an incumbent trying to discourage entry or expansion by a rival. An incumbent airline in possession of desk slots will use them to reduce the wait time for its passengers and could argue that such behavior reflects a valid strategic move to compete on service quality.

Airport Policy and Domestic Airline Competition in Canada

The role of competition policy should be to protect competition rather than competitors. That is, the Government should not undertake to ensure the financial future of any particular competitor to Air Canada, but rather should seek to create a competitive environment. In general this means ensuring access to airports for potential competitors and creating a set of institutions that enhance the role of

---

[19] Competition Bureau. "Enforcement Guidelines on the Abuse of Dominance in the Airline Industry", pp. 19-20, February 2001

airports in defining a competitive environment in the domestic air travel market. In particular, Canada would benefit from the creation of an auction mechanism for take-off and landing slots, and the re-assignment of property rights for all gates and ticketing desks to airports.

The case for slot auctions is not limited to the Canadian context. We know that with an auction market, peak-demand slots will command a higher price than other slots, reflecting their higher value to airlines and their customers. Market pricing mechanisms will generate an efficient allocation of scarce airport facilities during peak-demand hours to users who value them most.

Importantly, a dominant incumbent airline might not relinquish control of available slots but would have to pay market prices for them, thereby raising the cost of anti-competitive behaviour. Note that the creation of an auctioning institution would result in efficient peak-load pricing at *all* airports in the system, not just those administratively defined as "slot-constrained". The practicalities of implementation of a slot auction would not be easy; however, there are emerging models that consider the associated complexities.[20] Note that revenues from slot auctions could be dedicated to capital spending requirements across the system, particularly at smaller airports in order to maintain the value of the network.

The transfer of property rights with respect to gates and ticketing desks from dominant airlines to airports would allow for similar efficient pricing of these resources, thereby diluting any strategic use of passenger throughput infrastructure by a dominant carrier.

The Role of Dominant Carriers in Financing Airport Capital Investment

In the current Canadian system, Air Canada plays a prominent role in the financing of capital infrastructure projects of airports. In one respect this might seem desirable given the economics of strategic investment and the role of co-investment in specific assets in strengthening long-term contracts by preventing hold-up problems. It is well accepted that an over-investment in dedicated capacity generates hold-up problems, so from an airport's perspective, current Air Canada business represents a portion of the overall capacity that places the airport in a strategically vulnerable position. By ensuring that Air Canada co-invests in the airport's infrastructure, the airport can help to mitigate hold-up problems.

From Air Canada's perspective, it can recognize that co-investment in airport infrastructure is strategically important; however, the airline is placed in a difficult position if it is the only airline to co-invest in capacity (while new competitors do not have similar requirements). There is no easy solution to this problem, given the current governance structure. If a per-passenger airside charge were applied, the effect would be disproportionate between Air Canada and its domestic competitors, given the different price-elasticities represented by the business travel market (dominated by Air Canada) and the discretionary travel market served by discount carriers. However, to the extent that new competitors may successfully obtain

---

[20] For example, see Ewers et al (2001) "Possibilities for Better use of Airport Slots in Germany and the EU", WIP Infrastructure Economics and Economic Policy Study, Berlin, January 2001.

some market share in business travel, they would be more able to absorb an airside AIF charge by passing the fee along to business travelers.

Should Canadian Airports be Regulated?

The preceding section has argued that, in addition to market pricing of peak demand slots via an auction mechanism, airports should be in control of, and free to set, market prices for the infrastructure associated with passenger throughput. The question is do these recommendations change our perspective of benefits and costs of regulating airports? Firstly, to the extent that airside prices would fall at airports in response to regulation (in particular for the single till case), one might think that this would lower the costs of entry for new competitors in the airline industry. However, such pricing creates a problem from the perspective of competition policy, since a natural reaction to lower airside prices by a dominant incumbent airline is to add capacity and/or lower fares. That is, the price effects of airport regulation provide a defense against strategic entry deterrence in the airline industry. Secondly, if airports are constrained via regulation in the pricing of infrastructure relating to passenger throughput (gates and ticketing desks), then the costs of pre-emptive scheduling of facilities by incumbents are made artificially low. Thirdly, the problem of gold plating as a strategic response to regulation (particularly in the case of dual till regulation) is likely to result in relative over-investment in retail infrastructure rather than capital spending on facilities that promote passenger throughput. In summary, the role of airports in fostering airline competition strengthens the case against regulation of any kind.

Currently, in Canada's airport system, the "no-profit" status of airport authorities for national (tier I) airports combined with the rental agreements between these airport authorities and the federal government create similar problems to those associated with price-cap regulation. Under these rental agreements, once certain levels of revenue generation are reached (above a benchmarked cost calculation), the airport authorities have little incentive to price or invest efficiently. Instead, airports and are left with an incentive to cut costs below the benchmark calculation or to engage in gold plating investments. To this extent the Canadian government should consider privatization of national airports, and replacement of the current rental agreements with a profit that does not distort incentives for efficient pricing and investment.[21] Note that private shareholders would provide private discipline against gold plating investment activities. Furthermore, privatization would help to separate the co-investment (contract) motive for airline investment in airport infrastructure from mere reliance on the dominant airline for capital funds. That is, private ownership and "for profit" status would significantly enhance the ability of airports to raise capital from non-airline private sources.

Finally, in the context of Canadian airport and airline policy, it is worth mentioning the ongoing debate as to whether North American airline fifth freedom

---

[21] Given the diversity within the group of national airports, a profit tax could be adjusted for passenger volumes or some similar measure of growth and economic activity.

rights with EU states are the same as cabotage rights. We should not exclude from consideration, the possibility that Canada and the US (or Canada, Mexico and the US) could successfully formulate an agreement for exchange of cabotage rights under the auspices of a trade-area agreement similar to that of the EU.

Another possible liberalization that has been considered would be for Canada to offer consecutive cabotage rights either unilaterally or bilaterally with other countries. Under such an agreement, international flights would be able to land at a primary destination in Canada and then continue to a second destination. For example a flight from Tokyo could land in Vancouver and continue (with some domestic passengers) on to Calgary. Such developments would clearly enhance the level of domestic airline competition in Canada.

Nevertheless, this does not alter our central argument that the welfare gains from efficient pricing and investments by airports extend beyond those usually considered to the gains associated with greater airline competition. A competitive environment is not the same thing as increased competition and although both are desirable, the former should be the focus of airport policy in Canada. Consequently, the future of Canada's airport system lies in privatization without direct regulation.

References

Civil Aviation Authority, *The 'Single Till' and the'Dual Till' Approach to the Price Regulation of Airports*, Consultation paper, December 2000.

Competition Bureau (Industry Canada), *Enforcement Guidelines on the Abuse of Dominance in the Airline Industry*, pp. 19-20, February 2001.

DAFFE Competition Policy Roundtable, *Competition Policy and International Airport Services*, #16, p. 4, OECD, 1998.

Ewers, H.-J. et al. *Possibilities for Better use of Airport Slots in Germany and the EU*, WIP Infrastructure Economics and Economic Policy Study, Berlin, January 2001.

Forsyth P., *Privatization and Regulation of Australian and New Zealand Airports,* Paper presented at the Fourth Hamburg Aviation Conference: Hamburg, Germany, 2001.

Hooper P., Cain R. & White S., *The Privatization of Australia's Airports*, Transportation Research (Part E) 36, 181-204, 2000.

National Research Council: Transportation Research Board, *Entry Conditions in the US Airline Industry: Issues and Opportunities*, August 1999.

Parker D., The Performance of BAA Before and After Privatization, *Journal of Transport Economics and Policy*, 33(2), 133-45,1999.

Starkie D., *A new deal for airports?*, Lectures on Regulation Series IX, Institute of Economic Affairs, 1999.

Starkie, D., Airport Regulation and Competition, *Journal of Air Transport Management*, 8 (2002) 63-72.

Starkie, D., The US Department of Transportation's Statement on Predatory Conduct in the Airline Industry: An Alternative Proposal, *European Competition Law Review*, 20(5), 1999.

Starkie D., and Yarrow G., *The single-till approach to the price regulation of airports*, mimeo, 2000.

Transport Canada, *A New Policy Concerning a Future Management Framework For Airports in Canada*, 1988.

Tretheway M., *Airport Ownership, Management and Price Regulation*, Report to the Canadian Transportation Act review Committee, April 2001.

US General Accounting Office, *Airport Privatization: Issues Related to the Sale or Lease of U.S. Commercial Airports* [GAO/T-RCED-96-82]. Washington, DC, 1996.

Chapter 4

The Regulation of US Airports

Anne Graham

Introduction

There are a number of distinctive features that differentiate US airports from many other airports, such as in the UK, Ireland, Germany, Australia and New Zealand, where there have been recent developments concerning airport regulation. These have a major impact on how the airports are operated and so need to be considered before legislative and policy issues related to airport revenues and privatisation are discussed. These differences can be divided into four categories, namely ownership; finance sources; the airport-airline relationship; and the provision of facilities and services (Graham, 2002).

Ownership

Most US airports are owned by cities or counties, although a few are not operated directly by the government body but by a separate public organisation such as a multipurpose port authority (an example is the Port Authority of New York and New Jersey) or an airport authority such as Metropolitan Washington Airports Authority. The degree of airport privatisation which has occurred (and is discussed later in the fourth section) is minimal compared with countries such as the UK, Germany, Italy, Australia, New Zealand, South Africa, Mexico and Argentina. US airports have no share capital, do not pay dividends and are not liable for corporate taxes. By contrast, there are a number of European airports which, although under public ownership, pay taxes such as Oslo and the Irish and Paris airports, and dividends, as at Manchester and Amsterdam airport.

Sources of Finance

The main sources of external finance are:

- Commercial bonds, which are exempt from federal income tax on interest paid to bond-holders because of the airports' public ownership. The life of the bonds is relatively long-term, with a maturity generally greater than 20 years. The majority of the bond finance comes from general airport revenue bonds (GARBs), which are secured by the future total revenues of the airports, but lease or special facility bonds (SRBs) which are secured by future rental or lease payments on particular facilities, such as terminals or cargo hangars, are also used.

- Airport Improvement Program (AIP) grants from the Airport and Airways Trust Fund which is financed by user taxes on various sectors of the aviation community (e.g. passenger tickets, cargo and fuel) and disbursed by the Federal Aviation Administration (FAA). In 2002, US$3,222 million of AIP grant funds were distributed to airports (General Accounting Office, 2002). A major issue related to this funding is that, over the years, less money has been given out for aviation projects than is obtained from the taxes because of the need to balance the Federal Budget.
- Passenger Facility Charges (PFCs) of up to $4.50 per passenger, which have to be approved by the FAA for identifiable projects. These funds go directly to the airports rather into central federal funds as with the AIP taxes. In 2002, it has been estimated that around US $2,019 million was collected from PFCs.

The importance of different funding sources varies from airport to airport. In 2000, 40 per cent of external funding for large hub airports came from bonds, 33 per cent from PFCs and only 12 per cent from AIP grants. By contrast, at small hub airports 39 per cent came from bonds, 16 per cent from PFCs but 37 per cent from AIP grants (ACI-North America, 2002a). This is clearly very different from the situation for major European airports, for example, where most investment finance typically comes from loans and, if applicable, share capital.

Relationship with the Airlines

US airports enter into legally binding contracts with airlines, known as airport use and lease agreements, which detail the fees and rental rates which an airline has to pay; the method by which these are to be calculated; and the conditions for the use of both airfield and terminal facilities. The life of the airport commercial bonds is typically tied to these use agreements and such contracts often guarantee that certain airlines play a significant role in the making of airport capital investment decisions This is specified in the Majority-in-Interest (MII) clauses of the agreements, so-called because they involve 'signatory' airlines which together carry the majority of the airport's traffic. The signatory airlines often pay lower levels of landing charges. There are two basic approaches to establishing the airport charges, namely residual and compensatory, which are discussed under 'Residual and compensatory approaches'.

Provision of Facilities and Services

The airport operator normally provides the basic aeronautical facilities and services. This excludes air traffic control, which is provided by the FAA, handling, which is provided by the airlines and agencies, and security, which used to be provided by third parties but has become the responsibility of the Federal Government as a result of the events of September 11. At many of the airports the airlines will lease or rent terminal space or gates on an exclusive- or joint-use basis or may even own and operate whole terminals, as at JFK airport in New York. This minimal involvement by airport operators in all but the basic airport facilities is one of the major factors that helps explain the typically lower unit costs at US airports compared, for example, with European airports (Graham, 2002).

The Existing Legislative and Policy Framework

The generation of revenues at US airports is subject to a number of statutory requirements determined by Congress and policy statements issued by the FAA/Department of Transportation. These primarily focus on the Federal Government requirement for 'reasonable' aeronautical fees at the airport and the prohibited use of airport revenues for non-airport purposes.

The Setting of Airport Fees and Charges

There are two major pieces of legislation that cover the setting of airport charges. The 1982 Airport and Airways Improvement Act states that, on accepting federal AIP grants, an airport is under an obligation to charge 'reasonable' fees to its aeronautical users. Similarly, the 1973 Anti-Head Tax Act allows publicly-owned airports to collect 'reasonable' charges from the airlines that are using the airport facilities. This 'reasonableness' requirement in these two Acts only applies to aeronautical users and does not require the Department of Transportation to regulate the reasonableness of non-aeronautical charges and rents.

In 1996, the Department of Transportation/FAA issued its Final Policy Regarding Airport Rates and Charges as required by the 1994 FAA Authorization Act, which incorporated all the statutory obligations (Federal Aviation Administration/Department of Transportation, 1996). This states that fees for the use of the airfield and public-use roads should be established on the basis of costs and it provides detailed guidance on how costs are to be determined. Assets must be considered at their historic cost value. The policy reconfirms that the fees should be 'fair and reasonable' and not 'unjustly discriminatory'.

For other facilities there is a more flexible approach, with the policy permitting fees to be set by 'any reasonable method'. In addition, it restates the principle, required in the 1994 FAA Authorization Act, that airports should set charges that make the airport as self-sustaining as possible, given the specific circumstances of the airport.

Use of Airport Revenues

There are a number of statutory requirements related to the use of airport revenues. The 1982 Airport and Airways Improvement Act established the rule that all revenues generated at a publicly owned airport receiving federal AIP grants must be used to cover capital or operating costs of that airport or local airport system or other local facilities which are owned or operated by the owner or operator of the airport and directly related to the actual air transportation of passengers or property. This is known as the 'revenue retention' requirement. There is a 'grandfather' exception which allows airport revenue to be used for non-airport costs if the debt is pre-1982. Grandfathered airports include Boston, New York and San Francisco. The 1987

Airport and Airways Safety and Capacity Act set further limits on the use of airport revenues by, for example, considering how taxes from aviation fuel could be spent.

In 1994 and 1996 Congress enacted additional statutes (the 1994 and 1996 FAA Authorization and Reauthorization Acts) which supplemented the original 1982 requirements. These focused on the identification of revenue diversion and the enforcement process for revenues which are unlawfully diverted. As mentioned above the 1994 Act also required that airports should set charges that makes the airport as self-sustaining as possible, given the airport specific circumstances (the 'self-sustaining' requirement). The 1996 Act extended the revenue use rules to any federally assisted airport.

In 1999 the Department of Transportation/FAA issued its Final Policy on Airport Revenue Diversion (as required by the 1994 Authorization Act) which incorporated the revenue retention, self sustaining and all the other relevant statutory obligations (Federal Aviation Administration/Department of Transportation, 1999). This policy lists the permitted uses of airport revenues such as destination marketing (if the airport is mentioned); co-operative airline-airport marketing; reimbursements to the state or local government for actual airport services and a portion of the costs of general government under certain circumstances; attorney/lobbying fees to support airport activities; community activities related to the airport; and certain airport ground access projects. Prohibited uses of airport revenues include payments which are not based on appropriate cost allocation methods; costs associated with general economic development and marketing activities; payments in lieu of taxes that exceed the values of services provided; payments to compensate government bodies for lost tax revenues; loans to government agencies at less than the prevailing interest rate; and the direct subsidy of an airline service.

As regards the self-sustaining requirement, the policy states that the airport operator must generally charge a fair market rental rate for non-aeronautical facilities (except for transit facilities and for property for community and recreational purposes in certain circumstances). Aeronautical charges should cover airport costs. The policy also describes the reporting and auditing requirements (such as the requirement for airports to submit annual financial reports) and explains the action which the FAA may take if the revenue is unlawfully diverted (such as withholding AIP grants or withholding the approval of PFC applications) (Federal Aviation Administration, 1999).

Legal Challenges

These statutory requirements and policy statements related to airport revenues have been strongly influenced by the outcome of legal action at particular airports. For example, back in 1988, the Massport Authority implemented a Program for Airport Capacity Efficiency (PACE) in an attempt to tackle the capacity problem at Boston Logan airport with a change in pricing policy. This introduced a movement charge for runway use as well as a weight-based charge, and had the effect of significantly increasing the landing fees for smaller aircraft. However, in response to complaints from airlines and other affected parties, the US Department of Transportation ruled that Logan airport had violated federal law since its landing fee structure unjustly discriminated against smaller aircraft and represented an unscientific approach to airfield cost allocation.

As a result of this, the airport resorted to its former pricing structure. Had it not done so it would have ceased to be eligible for its $10 million federal AIP grants in 1989 (Graham, 1992). As a result of this legal case, the Department of Transportation's policy regarding peak pricing was established – namely that under certain conditions, a properly structured peak pricing system could be found to be reasonable and would not be considered unjustly discriminatory. The airports argue, however, that this policy is somewhat unclear. An interestingly related development is the proposal that peak pricing should be used with a new runway planned for Boston (ACI-North America, 2002b).

In the 1990s, legal action brought about by airport users concerning the interpretation of the statutory requirement for 'reasonable' fees and the diversion of airport revenues, particularly at Grand Rapids airport in Kent County and at Los Angeles airport, played an important role in prompting Congress and the FAA to re-examine the existing airport charging policy which led to the passing of the 1994 and 1996 FAA Authorization Acts and the establishment of the 1996 and 1999 FAA Policy Statements.

At Los Angeles for example, landing charges were tripled in 1993 and it was proposed that $30 million of these airport revenues would be used for general municipal purposes. This led to a series of legal challenges by the airlines who claimed that the fees were based on market rather than historic cost asset values and could not be diverted to other uses. Eventually, in 2000, the US Supreme Court agreed with the Department of Transportation's conclusion that the fees had been based on an improper cost calculation method.

Residual and Compensatory Approaches

There are two basic approaches to establishing airport charges and fees: residual and compensatory. With the residual approach the airlines pay the net costs of running the airport after taking account of commercial and other non-airline sources of revenue. The airlines provide a guarantee that the level of charges and rents will be such that the airport will always break even and so take a considerable risk.

By contrast with the compensatory approach, the airlines pay agreed charges and rates based on recovery of costs allocated to the facilities and services that they occupy or use. The risk of running the airport is left to the airport operator. The residual approach, therefore, is more akin to the 'single till' practice when revenues from all airport activities (both aeronautical and non-aeronautical) are taken into account when setting the aeronautical charges. The compensatory approach is more similar to the dual till when just the aeronautical aspects of the airport are considered when the aeronautical charges are set.

Airports have applied these two different approaches in various ways to suit their particular needs and some have adopted a hybrid approach, combining elements of both the residual and compensatory methodologies. A study in 1998 showed that for the large US airports the residual and compensatory approaches were each used by 41 per cent of the airports with the remaining 18 per cent of airport using some kind of hybrid model. For medium sized airports the relative shares were residual (38 per cent), compensatory (19 per cent), and hybrid (43 per cent) (Federal Aviation Authority/Department of Transportation, 1999). Airport such as Los Angeles, San

Francisco, Dallas Fort Worth and Miami use a residual approach, Chicago, Newark and JFK in New York use a compensatory approach and examples of the hybrid methodology can be found at the Washington airports and Orlando airport.

Privatisation of US Airports

As in many other parts of the world, airport privatisation has been considered in the US, It should be noted, however, that the private sector already has considerable influence at the airports because of commercial bond financing and because most of the airport's functions are provided by airlines and other private organisations. In addition, some small airports such as Albany, Burbank, Teterboro and Atlantic City have been operated by a private management contract.

In 1995, BAA won a 10 year management contract for operating the much larger airport at Indianapolis. Under the scheme, BAA was not to receive any fixed management fee but to share in the savings it generates. The company guaranteed average annual savings of more than $3 million ($32 million over a ten-year agreement) and was not to be paid any fees until after it produced average annual savings of nearly $6 million ($58 million over the ten-year agreement). BAA expected to save the airport $100 million during the 10-year contract by increasing non-aviation revenue and reducing expenditure from energy supply, equipment and payroll costs.

The airport board was to continue to set policy and control rates and charges. In 1998, an amended new 10 year contract was signed. BAA also has commercial management contracts at Boston and Pittsburgh and it did have a general management contract at Harrisburg airport, but this was terminated in 2001 against BAA's wishes just three years into a 10 year contract.

In another development, in 1997, the financing, construction and operation of the international arrivals building at JFK New York airport was handed over to a private consortium (which includes Amsterdam Schiphol airport) for 25 years. This is first such BOT (Build, Operate and Transfer) project at a US airport. With all these developments, the legislative and regulatory framework within which the airports operate remains the same.

Various issues would have to be resolved if more radical privatisation moves, such as the total transfer of the assets to a private sector company, were to take place (American Association of Airport Executives, 1992; Mew, 2001) For example, would private airports survive if they could not use AIP, PFC or tax-exempt debt financing? Would they have to pay back AIP grants? Would private airports have to pay property taxes? At many of the airports, the use agreements with the airlines may mean that the airports can only be privatised as the agreements expire or that privatisation will have to be limited within the bounds of the agreement.

In 1995, the full privatisation of John Wayne Airport in California's Orange County was discussed as part of the solution to the county's bankruptcy. However, the likelihood of litigation by the airlines who would have claimed that this was an unlawful use of airport revenues for non-airport purposes led to the conclusion that airport privatisation was not feasible. This revenue diversion issue, namely the inability of local and state governments to reap the financial benefits of the airport sale, is seen as one of the key obstacles to airport privatisation in the US.

In 1996, an airport privatisation pilot programme was established by the FAA in order to explore privatisation as a means of generating access to sources of private capital for airport improvement and development. This made provision for five airports to be exempt from some of the legal requirements that impeded their sale to private entities.

At least one of airports had to be a general aviation (GA) airport and no more that one could be a large hub air carrier airport. The GA airports could be sold or leased whereas the hub airport could only be leased. Five airports could be chosen, at least one had to be a GA and no more that one a large hub air carrier airport. GA airports could be sold or leased whilst hubs could only be leased (General Accounting Office, 1996).

Under this programme the airports are exempt for repaying federal grants or returning property acquired with federal assistance. The restrictions on prohibiting the proceeds of the sale or lease to be used exclusively for airport purposes have also been waived. Such privatisations do, however, need approval of the majority of the airlines using the airport (65 per cent of the airport's airlines in terms of landed weight). The airport can apply for AIP funds, or to levy PFCs and it is still subject to the requirement to set 'reasonable' fees (Federal Aviation Administration/Department of Transportation, 1997).

There has been only limited interest in this scheme, particularly because of slow and rather complex approval procedures and the majority airline consensus rule. The first airport to be approved under the scheme was Stewart International Airport in New York, which was given a 99 year lease to the British company, National Express. The airport transferred management in April 2000 (Federal Aviation Administration, 2000; McCormick, 2000). Other airports which have been involved with the scheme and are at various stages of approval are Brown Field (a GA facility in San Diego); Niagra Falls, Aguadilla in Puerto Rico and New Orleans Lakefront.

Future Developments

The events of 11 September 2001 in the short-term have shifted much of the focus away from issues of airport capacity and congestion, or airport charging and funding for investment to more immediate concerns such as the provision and financing of security services.

However there have been two developments in the last year or so which have indicated that the basic principle that airport charges must be determined by strict cost formulas is beginning to be questioned and that a more market-based approach could have a role to play in coping with the congestion problems that exist at many airports.

The first development was when the Department of Transportation issued a 'Notice of Market Based Actions to Reduce Airport Congestion and Delay'. (Federal Aviation Administration/Department of Transportation, 2001a). This discussed market-based approaches to charging at airports such as peak pricing, minimum landing fees (which in fact have already existed at airports such as New York, Los Angeles, Boston and San Francisco) and slot auctions. Airlines and other interested parties were asked to comment on this notice by July 2002 before any changes are suggested.

Generally, the airport industry is much more in favour of market-based options than the airline industry, which wants to keep the current system (ACI-North America, 2002b; Air Transport Association of America, 2002). Clearly, any shift away from cost-based and towards a market-based methodology would require significant changes in the statutory requirements and policy statements that have been described in this paper and could also have implications for other legislation, such as the Airline Deregulation Act of 1978, which prohibits local regulation of routes and services and states that proprietary powers must be reasonable, non-arbitrary and non-discriminatory.

The second related development is specifically concerned with JFK's La Guardia airport. This is one of four 'high density' airports in the US where slots have been restricted, co-ordination of schedules by airlines has been allowed and where a certain degree of slot trading has been permitted. However the Aviation Investment and Reform Act (AIR21) of 2000 made substantial changes to the slot rules at these four airports. At La Guardia, all restrictions are to be eliminated by 2007. In the interim, new long-haul entrant carriers and airlines operating regional jets were given slot restriction exemption. This led to major overscheduling and congestion in La Guardia in 2000 and so the Port Authority of New York and New Jersey imposed a moratorium on peak hour flights.

However, the FAA claimed that the airport authority did not have a legal right to impose this moratorium and instead it was agreed that the number of new flights would be capped and a slot lottery would be undertaken. This took place in December 2000. This temporary solution was due to end in October 2002 but has been extended until October 2004. In the meantime, the industry has been consulted about more longer-term solutions (Federal Aviation Administration/Department of Transportation, 2001b). These include market-based initiatives such as congestion-based pricing or slot auctions or administrative processes such as favouring operations with larger aircraft.

The implementation of a market-based solution could potentially raise another problem at La Guardia airport related to revenue diversion. Long standing financial arrangements of the Port Authority of New York and New Jersey means that this airport has grandfathered status as regards the diversion of revenues for non-airport uses. A market-based pricing system might produce a large volume of revenues well in excess of the airport costs and some industry bodies that this could be diverted off-airport rather than used to reduce the congestion problems (Reason Foundation, 2002).

Conclusions

This paper has shown that the regulatory and legislative environment within which US airports have traditionally operated has been very different from airports elsewhere. A consequence of this situation is that airports are viewed, at least by airlines and institutionally, much more as public infrastructure than in many other parts of the world. The unique financing system which exists has also led to an entrenchment of the airline-airport relationship rather than an evolution of more strategic relationships which have developed in other regions.

No doubt airport privatisation will continue to be an option that is considered, but primarily as a result of pressure from carriers to keep rates and charges down rather than in any sense to increase efficiency. Market-based pricing will remain a significant issue for discussion but, as long as airports continue to be thought of as public utilities and also maintain their close relationships with the airlines, it seems unlikely in the near future that there will be any major changes in how airports are regulated or in the way in which they levy their revenues.

References

ACI-North America (2002a) *Annual Economic Report*

ACI-North America (2002b) *Comments re: Notice of Market-based Actions to Relieve Airport Congestion and Delay*

Air Transport Association of America (2002) *Comments re: Notice of Market-based Actions to Relieve Airport Congestion and Delay*

American Association of Airport Executives (1992) *Airport Privatization*, Alexandria, AAAE

Ashford N. and Moore C. (1999) *Airport Finance*, Second Edition, Loughborough, Loughborough Airport Consultancy

Federal Aviation Administration (1999) *Fact Sheet: FAA Policy and Procedures Regarding Use of Airport Revenue*, 10 February

Federal Aviation Administration (2000) *Fact Sheet: Stewart International Airport Privatization,* 21 March

Federal Aviation Administration/Department of Transportation (1996a) *Policy Regarding Airport Rates and Charges*, Docket No 27782, Washington DC, FAA/DOT

Federal Aviation Administration/Department of Transportation, (1996b) *Policy and Procedures Regarding Use of Airport Revenue*, Docket No 28472, Washington DC, FAA/DOT

Federal Aviation Administration/Department of Transportation (1997) *Airport Privatisation Pilot Program: Application Procedures*, Docket No 28895, Washington DC, FAA/DOT

Federal Aviation Administration/Department of Transportation (1999) *Airport Business Practices and their Impact on Airline Competition*, Washington DC, FAA/DOT

Federal Aviation Administration/Department of Transportation (2001a) *Notice of Market-based Actions to Relieve Airport Congestion and Delay*, Docket No 2001-9849, Washington DC, FAA/DOT

Federal Aviation Administration/Department of Transportation (2001b) *Alternative Policy Options for Managing Capacity at La Guardia Airport*, Docket No 2001-9854, Washington DC, FAA/DOT

Graham A. (1992) Airports in the United States, chapter in Doganis R *The Airport Business,* London: Routledge

Graham A. (2001) *Managing Airports: An International Perspective*, Oxford, Butterworth-Heinemann

Graham A. (2002) The US Experience, *University of Westminster/Cranfield University Airport Economics and Finance Symposium*, London, March

General Accounting Office (1996) *Airport Privatization: Issues Related to the Sale or Lease of US Commercial Airports*, Washington DC, GAO.

General Accounting Office (2002) *Using Airport Grant Funds for Security Projects has affected some Development Projects*, Washington DC, GAO.

Mew K. (2001) Barriers to Airport Privatization in the United States, *Aviation Management Education and Research Conference*, Montreal, July

McCormick C. (2000) Breaking the Success Barriers, *Airports International*, June, 16-20

Reason Foundation (2002) *Comments re: Notice of Market-based Actions to Relieve Airport Congestion and Delay.*

Part C
Europe

Chapter 5

Calculating the Short-Run Marginal Infrastructure Costs of Runway Use: An Application to Dublin Airport

Oliver Hogan and David Starkie

Introduction

The airport industry has been slow to adopt a structure of charges based on economic principles such as marginal cost pricing. There are two particular reasons for this. First, motivation on the part of the traditional public sector airport companies, which have often lacked a commercial drive, has been absent. Second, such an approach has been viewed, perhaps mistakenly, as contrary to the principles on charging set out in Article 15 of the Chicago Convention. That Article has encouraged the setting of charges to reflect average accounting costs.

The world has now moved on. In the 21st century, a number of significant airports have been privatised and many others have been transformed into commercial enterprises with an incentive to make an efficient use of their assets. In recognition of these pressures, new text has now been added to the ICAO Airport Economics Manual (DOC 9562) and the Manual of Air Navigational Services Economics (DOC 9161), which permits airport and air navigational charges to reflect economic principles, providing their application is non-discriminatory.

The focus of this paper is on the application of economic principles to derive the (short run) marginal infrastructure costs of runway use. Central to these costs are the costs of damage or wear and tear imposed on runways and related taxiways by the movement of aircraft. Such costs have taken on added significance in recent times because of the growing practice of airports to encourage the development of new routes, by offering discounted airport charges. These discounted charges should, at a minimum, cover the specific cost of wear and tear caused by each aircraft movement. The cost calculations in this paper are based on data for Dublin Airport, Ireland and form the basis of a schedule of charges introduced as part of the Irish Commission for Aviation Regulations' statutory Determination of charges.[1]

By focusing on damage costs, the analysis differs from the few previous applications to airports of marginal cost pricing principles. These latter applications have emphasised the need for peak charges at congested airports at, or nearing,

[1] Because of the specifics of the Irish legislation, the schedule of damage related charges form the basis of an off-peak charge only.

capacity and have given less attention to the issue of an efficient level of charge reflecting the wear and tear imposed on runway infrastructure. Although other studies have considered charging principles at non-congested airports, their pre-occupation has been to design a structure of prices for the efficient recovery of capital and other fixed costs (see, for example, Morrison, 1982). One exception to this general picture was a study of Birmingham airport in the UK by Littlechild and Thompson (1977). Although its focus remained one of efficient recovery of capital and other fixed costs (using a game theoretical approach) it, nevertheless, did consider runway maintenance costs and their allocation to different types of aircraft.

The Marginal Cost Approach

Runway, taxiway and apron pavements sustain damage from the pressure imposed by the combined weight and speed of aircraft landing, taking off, taxiing and parking at an airport. The resulting cracks and damage to the sealing of joints require "routine" repair and maintenance to maintain the quality of the assets and it is this expenditure that forms the initial measure of the costs of use.

These routine expenditures do not, however, capture all of the damage costs associated with additional aircraft movements. There is also damage to the basic structure of runways, taxiways and aprons that leads eventually to their reconstruction[2]. This gradual loss of structural load-carrying capacity over time is the fundamental principle underpinning pavement design. With concrete pavements, the chief structural failure is through fatigue cracking of the concrete, which is induced by many repetitions of the loading and unloading cycle as aircraft move towards, over and away from the point of (un)loading.

Once the sum of both the 'routine' and the structural damage costs has been determined, a methodology is required for allocating this total damage cost across different aircraft types on a causation basis. Aircraft weight is one factor contributing to pavement damage, but it is not the only factor; configuration of the aircraft landing gear and tyre pressures also play a significant part. All these factors are summarised in an ICAO rating called an Aircraft Classification Number (ACN). A higher ACN indicates a more damaging aircraft and, for the same gross weight, more wheels and lower tyre pressures usually result in a lower ACN. The ACN value also varies according to ground conditions and according to whether pavements are rigid (concrete) or flexible (bitumen).

In the following analysis, we have combined aircraft ratings based on their ACN with estimates of routine maintenance expenditure, together with estimates of

[2] Literature relating to the economics of road infrastructure (see, for example, Small et al. (1988) and Newbery (1988)) has drawn attention to a cost externality that might be of relevance here: pavement infrastructure, once damaged, increases vehicle or, in this current context, aircraft operating costs (through an increase in tyre wear and stresses placed on landing gear for example) and thus increased operating costs, which are borne by the aircraft operators, should perhaps be taken into account. However, we believe that this externality can be ignored in the runway context because safety considerations require surfaces to be maintained in a reasonably steady state condition. We are grateful to Ken Button for drawing our attention to this issue.

structural damage costs, to derive a cost-related set of charges that reflect the principles of marginal cost pricing.

To represent structural damage costs, we used the annualised cost of the airport operators' planned airfield upgrade projects over the ten years, 2001-2010, which included apron reconstruction and runway and taxiway overlays[3]. For the analysis, it was assumed that Dublin's pavements were rigid and that the sub-grade classification was C.[4]

Analysis

Based on the most recent year for which all aircraft movements (number and aircraft type) were available (calendar year 2000), aircraft were grouped according to the damage that they impose (represented by ACN numbers) with aircraft in each group inducing a similar amount of damage per landing. The results are presented in Table 5.1.

To calculate the proportion of damage attributable to each of the 18 aircraft-damage categories, the following formula was used:

$$P_j = (\Sigma_{i \in j} [(ACN_i / ACN_d)^4.L_i])/(\Sigma_i [(ACN_i / ACN_d)^4.L_i]$$

where $i \in \mathrm{I} = \{1,\ldots,n\}$, which is the set of aircraft types that landed at Dublin airport during the calendar year 2000; and $\mathrm{j} \in \mathbf{J} = \{1,\ldots,18\}$, which is the set of 18 aircraft damage categories. Note that each j is a subset of **I**. This formula and its constituent parts can be explained and interpreted in the following way. The 4th power law for pavements states that the damage induced by aircraft A relative to aircraft B is the ratio of the ACN of aircraft A to the ACN of aircraft B, all raised to the 4th power. By selecting a 'design' aircraft with a specified ACN (ACN_d) and calculating the damage induced by each aircraft type relative to the design aircraft, we established a consistent basis for the allocation of damage costs.

---

[3] Details of the phased expenditure on these projects were not available, so the present value of the estimated costs were calculated based on the assumption that the capital expenditure would be averaged over the period. The assumed rate of interest was taken as Aer Rianta's pre-tax cost of capital (calculated at 7%). Dividing by the relevant annuity factors gave the annualised cost of projects planned for each of the periods 2001-2006 and 2007-2010.

[4] The sub-grade classification at Dublin varies between B (medium) and D (very low). The main runway (10/28), associated taxiways and new aprons are generally B. Most other taxiways have a C classification, while older runways (16/34 and 11/29) have a D classification. Newer pavements, such as runway 10/28, its associated taxiways and aprons are rigid. Most other pavements are composite (originally rigid and subsequently overlaid with bituminous layers). Rigid pavements are considered to be representative of the majority of pavements at Dublin airport.

Table 5.1 Aircraft Damage Categories and ACN. Ranges

Aircraft damage category	*Aircraft types*	*Minimum*	*Maximum*
1	< 10t	2	7
2	10 - 20t	7	12
3	20 - 30t	12	12
4	CRJ; FK70; BAe146; BA11; RJ85; TU134	16	28
5	FK100; RJ100; B717; B737-200, 500	31	35
6	TU154; B757	32	38
7	B737-300, 600; DC9	36	39
8	A319; AN12; B737-400, 700, 800	41	46
9	A320; B727; MD80	48	49
10	A321; MD90	52	58
11	A300; A310	52	58
12	B747-100, -200	59	66
13	B767-200, 300; DC8	61	63
14	B727-200	63	63
15	A330; B777; L1011	63	66
16	A340; DC10	67	68
17	B747-400	75	75
18	MD11	79	79

For each aircraft type *i*, the relative damage factor was multiplied by the corresponding number of landings to give the equivalent number of landings of the design aircraft. The proportion of damage attributable to each damage category, *j*, was then calculated as the sum (over the subset of aircraft types contained in that damage category, that is, all $i \in j$) of the equivalent number of landings of the design aircraft, divided by the total equivalent number of those landings (summed over all aircraft types). Table 5.2 presents the proportion of damage attributable to each of the aircraft damage categories. Although the resulting schedule of 18 levels of marginal cost (one for each damage category) provided the basis for a relatively simple and more practical charging schedule, it was decided that in view of the traditional approach of charging aircraft on the basis of their weight, the administrative burden on the airport operator could be further reduced by converting the schedule based on damage categories into a per-tonne-schedule.

For each aircraft type i, the marginal damage cost per landing of the relevant damage category j (where $i \in j$) was divided by the MTOW tonnage to give a marginal cost per tonne. That is,

$$MC^{t}_{i} = MC^{1}_{j} / MTOW_{i}$$

where MC^{t}_{i} is the marginal cost per tonne for aircraft type i, MC^{1}_{j} is the marginal cost per landing of aircraft in the relevant damage category j, and $MTOW_i$ is the Maximum Take-Off Weight of aircraft type i. It can be seen from this equation that if two aircraft types, for example, $i = 1,2$ form part of the same damage category j (such that the marginal cost per landing is the same) but have different weights, such that $MTOW_1 > MTOW_2$, the heavier aircraft has a lower marginal cost per tonne, $MC^{t}_{1} < MC^{t}_{2}$.

Table 5.2 Proportion of Damage to Rigid Pavements Attributable to each of the 18 Aircraft Damage Categories

Aircraft damage category	*Aircraft types*	*% damage to rigid pavements*
1	< 10t or similar	0.00
2	10 - 20t or similar	0.04
3	20 - 30t or similar	0.02
4	CRJ; FK70; BAe146; BA11; RJ85; TU134 or similar	2.08
5	FK100; RJ100; B717; B737-200, 500 or similar	11.98
6	TU154; B757 or similar	1.09
7	B737-300, 600; DC9 or similar	1.25
8	A319; AN12; B737-400, 700, 800 or similar	10.62
9	A320; B727; MD80 or similar	7.69
10	A321; MD90 or similar	36.74
11	A300; A310 or similar	1.00
12	B747-100, -200 or similar	0.14
13	B767-200, 300; DC8 or similar	4.71
14	B727-200 or similar	2.38
15	A330; B777; L1011 or similar	17.83
16	A340; DC10 or similar	0.32
17	B747-400 or similar	0.01
18	MD11 or similar	2.15

Significant increments in marginal cost per tonne were identified to establish a suitable set of bands for the purpose of categorising aircraft according to the per tonne cost that they impose (called aircraft cost categories). The result was five cost categories and a weighted marginal cost per tonne was found for each of these by dividing the total cost of landings of all aircraft within each of the categories by the total weight of those landings. That is,

$$MC^{t}_{k} = (\Sigma_{i \in k} [MC^{1}_{j} . L_i])/(\Sigma_{i \in k} [MTOW_i . L_i])$$

where $k \in \mathbf{K} = \{1,\ldots,5\}$ is the set of aircraft cost categories.

The schedule of tariffs adopted by the Commission for Aviation Regulation therefore consisted of five charges, one for each of the five cost categories (see Table 5.3). The movement charge is half of the landing charge, which is based on the assumption that each landing has a corresponding departure.

Table 5.3 The weighted per tonne marginal cost per landing and per movement

Aircraft Cost Category (k)	*Weighted per tonne marginal cost per landing*	*Weighted per tonne marginal cost per movement*
1	€ 0.50	€ 0.25
2	€ 1.59	€ 0.79
3	€ 2.52	€ 1.26
4	€ 3.88	€ 1.94
5	€ 5.38	€ 2.69

Is MTOW an Accurate Reflection of Damage Costs?

Most of the worlds' airports have a weight-related landing charge based on the MTOW of the aircraft concerned. This relationship is usually expressed as a constant charge per unit weight although, as at Dublin, it is frequently subject to a minimum threshold so that smaller aircraft pay a fixed sum. Graham (2001) notes that some airports have a charging rate that declines or increases with the weight of the aircraft. Various reasons have been given for this weight-based approach. It is argued that it reflects both willingness-to-pay (and is, therefore, a form of Ramsay Pricing) and the damage that individual aircraft impose on airfield infrastructure. It is worthwhile, therefore, to reflect on the relationship between MTOW and damage costs on the basis of the Dublin data.

Figure 5.1 provides an overall picture from which it can be seen that the relationship is imprecise with notable outliers. To take a specific example, a DC8-62 freighter with a quoted ACN of 64 and MTOW of 152 metric tonnes causes approximately the same amount of damage per movement as an A321-200 with an ACN of 62 and a considerably smaller MTOW of 79. Application of traditional weight-related charging would result in a charge for the DC8-62 that was twice that for the A321-200. However, for the purposes of a cost-related charging schedule, the greater tonnage of the DC8-62 requires the per tonne charge for that aircraft to be less than that of the A321-200. The tariff structure and aircraft categorization for Dublin has been designed to effect this. The A321-200 lies in cost category 4 with a charge per tonne per landing of €3.88, approximately twice that of the DC8-62 which lies in Aircraft Cost Category 2 and incurs a charge of €1.59. Therefore, the aircraft that is twice as heavy but causes the same damage pays a charge per tonne about half that of the lighter aircraft.

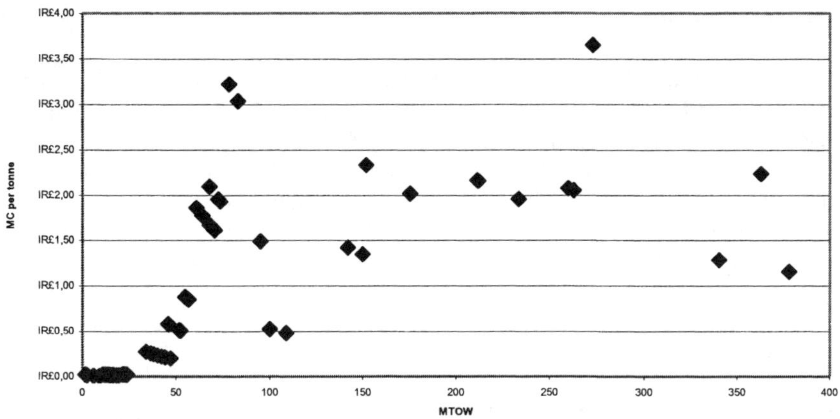

Figure 5.1 Relationship between aircraft weight and calculated marginal cost per tonne

Conclusion

The approach set out in this paper is based on the premise that each aircraft movement should pay for the damage it causes to pavement infrastructure, while maintaining weight-based charging rules for administrative convenience. In pursuing this approach, the analysis illustrated that runway damage reflects a range of factors, of which weight (MTOW) is only one. Indeed, Figure 5.1 illustrates that there is a rather tenuous relationship between the marginal cost per tonne and MTOW.

In a marginal cost-based approach, damage-related charges would normally complement peak period charges that take into account either congestion costs or the long-run costs of expanded infrastructure. However, calculating the marginal costs for peak period use can be complex and the introduction of separate off-peak charges based on the marginal costs of damage to runway/taxiway infrastructure might provide a means of accelerating the introduction of peak/off-peak differentials at congested airports generally, allowing time for the more difficult task of calculating peak period marginal congestion costs.

Making airport charges reflect aircraft specific marginal damage costs should encourage, with the passage of time, the use of aircraft that cause less pavement damage, at the expense of those that cause more. Currently, the situation remains very much as it did a decade ago when Doganis (1992) pointed out that airport charging systems provided no inducement to aircraft manufacturers to develop aircraft requiring runways of lower load-bearing strength. Consequently, if the approach outlined in this paper was to be adopted more widely, aircraft manufacturers would face appropriate design incentives and airport operators should benefit from a reduction in annual maintenance and repair expenditure and from an extension to the lives of runway, taxiway and apron pavements.

Acknowledgements

The authors would like to thank Dr. Kieran Feighan of Pavement Management Services Limited for assistance with the determination of ACN values, the corresponding damage allocation and the relevant costs.

Thanks are also due to Cathal Guiomard (Head of Economic Affairs, Commission for Aviation Regulation) and Jorge Gonzalez (Infrastructure Management Group Inc.) for useful comments during drafting and to the Commissioner, William Prasifka for permission to publish this piece.

References

Doganis, R. (1992) *The Airport Business*, Routledge.

Graham, A. (2001) *Managing Airports: an International Perspective*, Butterworth Heinemann, Oxford.

International Civil Aviation Organisation (ICAO) (1997) *Airport Planning Manual, Part 1: Master Planning,* Second Edition, Doc 9184-AN/902 Part 1.

Littlechild, S.C. and Thompson, G.F. (1977) "Aircraft Landing Fees: A Game Theory Approach", *The Bell Journal of Economics,* Vol. 8. No.1, pp. 186-204

Morrison, S.A. (1982) "Landing Fees at Uncongested Airports", *Journal of Transport Economics & Policy,* Vol. XVI. No.2, pp 151-160.

Newbery, D.M. (1988) "Road Damage Externalities and Road User Charges", *Econometrica*, Vol.56. No.2, pp. 295-316

Small, K.A., Winston, C. and Evans, C.A. (1988) *Road Work: A New Highway Policy*, Brookings, Washington D.C.

Chapter 6

Privatisation and Regulation of Amsterdam Airport

Jaap de Wit

Introduction

When the discussion in the Netherlands about the viability of an offshore airport in the North Sea finally came to an end, the Dutch cabinet decided in 1999 to resume preparations for the privatisation of Amsterdam airport Schiphol. These preparations had already been started in 1995, at the request of the Dutch parliament, but they had been postponed for a few years to give society full opportunity to arrive at the conclusion that the existing location of the national airport will do for another few decades. During the years 2000-2002, the details for an Initial Public Offering (IPO) of Amsterdam airport were further elaborated. After a period of political turmoil, a decision in parliament is now expected to be forthcoming in 2004.

In general, the major driving forces behind airport governance reform are adequately described elsewhere (cf. Ashford and Moores, 1999; Carney and Mew, 2003; and Graham, 2001). Political considerations in the Netherlands concerning privatisation of Amsterdam airport primarily focused on the argument that public ownership should not be continued if it is not indispensable for safeguarding public interests. In other words, if public policy measures effectively cover these interests, these measures should be preferred to private ownership. This appears to be the more urgent since, these days, the state, as a shareholder, is left with very little influence in the limited company that is Amsterdam airport.[1]

During the preparations for privatisation three public interest issues were identified that require adequate legal ruling:

- the need for a well-equipped national airport operating to up-to-date standards to generate optimal forward and backward linkages in the national economy;
- an efficient market for airport services;
- environmental interests, notably noise and safety interests.

---

1 Other arguments are, for example, better access to capital markets, efficiency improvements, and a better position for Schiphol airport to participate in international airport tenders.

A new legal framework for noise measurement as well as noise and safety contours has been put in place recently, and therefore the further preparations concentrated on the two other interests. Here we discuss primarily the development of a regulatory framework for the airport charges.

The choice between a more heavy-handed and a light-handed regulatory system is mainly determined by the deemed monopoly power of the airport involved. This depends on the relevant markets in which the airport provides services. We successively discuss here the market delineation of Amsterdam airport services and the related question of airport competition, the controversy between single, 'middle' and dual till, and negotiated access principles. Finally, we analyse the instruments that have been developed to guarantee the availability of a well-equipped national airport.[2]

The Relevant Markets for the Airport Services of Amsterdam Airport

Starkie (2002) clearly articulates that the raison d'être of economic regulation is to try to encourage the 'natural monopolist' to be cost efficient and to increase output to a level that maximises economic welfare. Conventional wisdom views the airports as an example of a natural monopoly industry.

The Segmented Airport's Customer Base

This issue played an important role in the development of a regulatory framework for Amsterdam airport. In an early stage of the preparations for the new framework, the Dutch Competition Authority (NMa) was requested to review the then current airport charges in the context of the general competition law. The NMa (2001) concluded in its answer that Amsterdam airport is a monopolist in the relevant geographical market, which was restricted by the NMa to the Schiphol airport area.[3] To arrive at this conclusion, the NMa more or less ignored the characteristics of the relevant product market. The main criterion used to define the relevant product market is demand substitutability, if we follow the definition proposed by the European Commission (Larouche, 2000). This brings us to the question as to who is the airport's customer? The identification of the customers of the airport services is not so obvious, because an airport operates mainly upstream in the supply-chain. Consequently, a multi-stage approach is required that places

---

[2] In the Netherlands this is called the 'main port' interest. The question may arise, however, whether this interest actually is a public interest, i.e. a social interest for which the public authorities take the final responsibility to look after. For example, what to do if KLM and Air France decide to choose Paris as their main hub? Or, what about a high-speed rail link from Amsterdam to Brussels airport that changes Zaventem into a relevant alternative?

[3] This conclusion surprisingly indicates that the NMa may have misunderstood the concept of the geographical market. The relevant geographical market does not necessarily comprise the location where the relevant services are produced and (inevitably) consumed, but it concerns the area in which the conditions of competition are sufficiently homogeneous. Therefore, for airport services, the concept of the catchment area for an airport answers much better the relevant geographical market definition.

the demand for airport services at Amsterdam airport in the context of the substitution possibilities throughout the supply-chain, as Frontier Economics (2000) reported to the NMa. It is not only the demand from airline operators that is relevant here. This demand ultimately derives from passengers and cargo shippers. Substitutability in the context of the SSNIP-test approach[4] has to be analysed in relation to the demand behaviour of (categories of) airline operators, (categories of) passengers and cargo users at Amsterdam airport. This may imply more segmented product markets for airport services of Amsterdam airport than was assumed by the NMa. Before analysing the relevant markets in more detail, we first have to address the question which products are provided by an airport and which customers are involved. The next question is whether the supply of (a subset of) these products at Amsterdam airport is a natural monopoly.

The Airport Products

An airport nowadays is a multi-product firm that provides a growing range of services and products to an increasing number of customers.[5] Actually, the growing customer base of larger airports is one of the attractive characteristics to private investors. Real estate developments (hotels, restaurants, business centres, landside shopping malls, etc) at the airport site and in the neighbouring region focus on an increasing variety of customers. Selling duty free articles to the air travellers has become an important profit generator. Car parking lots are operated for visitors and travellers. Cargo sheds are provided to cargo handling companies and forwarders.

Irrespective of this increasing diversity of products and customers, the essential role of an airport remains the interface between the air transport mode and surface transport modes.

This primarily boils down to the accommodation of aircraft movements, i.e. services for safe landings, take-offs, taxiing and parking of aircraft, and the throughput of passengers, baggage and cargo via this multi-modal interface. These core activities are also the airport services that have to be taken into account within the context of market power. Hotels, car parking shopping malls etc may benefit

---

4 The Small but Significant, Non-transitory Increase in Price (SSNIP) is the most common approach to relevant market delineation. This test should answer the question, whether the consumers of the product for which a hypothetical small (5-10%) but permanent price increase is introduced would substitute other products or other suppliers established within the same area studied. If this is the case and the substitution compensates the price increase, the substitutes and the area belong to the same relevant market.

5 An intriguing question in this context is, whether the joint production of the essential air traffic and passenger services on the one side and for example duty free sales to passengers at the other side is an example of joint production in the Marshallian sense. Are some of the production factors public inputs in the sense that once they are acquired for the use in producing one good, they are available costlessly for use in the production of others? This opinion is more or less reflected in KLM's justification for a single till by stating that the runways and terminal make duty free sales possible. It seems however more likely to assume a more flexible relationship, i.e. economies of scope and quasi public, sharable inputs.

from a locational rent at the airport site, but these services actually compete with comparable services downtown or in the wider airport region.

Runways and terminals, however, cannot be duplicated in the same area by a competing new entrant. We therefore focus on the prices of these airport services, i.e. landing and take-off charges for aircraft movements, aircraft parking charges, passenger charges for the terminal throughput[6] of passengers and baggage.[7]

A Natural Monopoly?

Although the concept of the natural monopoly may well apply to the network component of most network industries (gas, electricity, water, railroads etc), it can be questioned whether this is the case for airports. A natural monopoly requires the firm's cost function to be subadditive *over the entire range of outputs.* Actually, this is quite a demanding condition, since we have to determine whether single-firm production of y is cheaper than its production by *any* combination of smaller firms. That is, we must know $C(y^*)$ for every $y^* \leq y$ (Baumol et al, 1982). This requires a constantly decreasing long-run average cost curve. For airports however, this characteristic is unlikely. Doganis (1992), for example, indicates that, beyond a level of about three million passengers, unit costs flatten out and do not seem to vary much with airport size. As pointed out by Starkie (2002), it is even more likely that the cost curve will increase for larger airports, due to the increasing scarcity of one input factor, i.e. land in the neighbouring area of the airport. Thus, competitive entry is not frustrated by returns to scale but rather by other entry barriers, especially the availability of land. Also, other factors may stimulate the airport's market power, such as the lock-in effects for airline operators. This will be addressed in the analysis of relevant markets for airport services of Amsterdam airport.

If we apply the multi-stage approach to the various customers in the supply-chain, the primary customers are the airline operators.

Market Power and Airline Captivity

An airport's market power is reflected in the level of captivity of the various airline operators at that airport. Captivity is created by entry and exit barriers. If the airport is the home base of a carrier, sunk costs will be involved in operational facilities, buildings, maintenance, etc. Branding of the airport with the national airline also creates exit barriers. These sunk costs make it costly to station aircraft at other airports if the home-based operator increases the airport charges. The reluctance of Dutch charter airlines to station aircraft at the regional airports in the

---

[6] Usually passenger terminals in Europe are owned and operated by the airport company. Due to the high transaction costs between the airport and the airline, home-based carriers may prefer to rent or even own dedicated piers and gates. The new Lufthansa terminal in Munich is the current exception.

[7] Since most cargo handlers and forwarders own or rent their cargo terminals at the ramp, the terminal costs are included in the handling and forwarder fees. This explains the absence of cargo charges in the overview of official airport user charges at most European airports.

Netherlands is partly explained by this operational argument. They prefer to serve these regional markets by so-called "W-flights" from Schiphol.

Another argument put forward to illustrate the airline's captivity refers to the slot scarcity at alternative airports. This argument however has a limited impact. First, slot availability varies strongly between airports. Secondly, a limited reallocation of flights can already be an effective demand reaction if the airport operator raises its charges above competitive levels (see Greenhut et al, 1987).

The regulation of international air transport markets also stimulates captivity. In particular, older types of bilateral air service agreements specify the routes to be served by the designated carrier. As a consequence, KLM is obliged to operate from Amsterdam airport to benefit from a number of Air Servive Agreements (ASA). This captivity has further increased due to the fact that the third and fourth freedom traffic rights based on ASAs have been combined with sixth freedom operations via the home base Schiphol during the last 25 years. This has resulted in a large number of transfer passengers via the home base. This connectivity got an extra boost by the intensified hubbing process after the liberalisation of the internal market in 1993. Nowadays, KLM's radial network heavily depends on transfer passengers (probably more than 70%) and, as a consequence, the transfer share in the total traffic volume of Amsterdam airport is also quite substantial (about 40-45%). If, however, Schiphol airport increases its charges, KLM could not respond adequately. A reallocation of flights to other airports would more than proportionally damage the KLM network synergy.[8] Consequently, KLM is a captive customer at Amsterdam airport due to aeropolitical as well as operational conditions.

One should realize, however, that this situation can rapidly change. Since KLM has been taken over by Air France, the captivity will decrease.[9] In that case, an increase in airport charges might evoke a reallocation of flights from Amsterdam to Paris, using the high-speed rail link Amsterdam-Paris as a feeder line.

For the time being, captivity of airline operators at Amsterdam airport strongly depends on the type of carrier: KLM's captivity was high but is decreasing, whereas the captivity level of the home-based charter airlines and short-haul foreign airlines is lower. Long-haul foreign airlines and cargo airline operators probably show the lowest level of captivity. Both types of carriers can easily choose a different large airport as their hub to serve Europe if aeronautical charges become relatively too high.[10]

---

8 Recent analysis reveals that KLM's intercontinental network is almost completely dependent on the transfer volume. If this volume is eliminated, only daily flights to New York and Paramaribo (Surinam) could be maintained.

9 Until now EU Cross-border mergers have been frustrated by the nationality clauses in ASAs. Stepwise, these regulatory obstacles are disappearing. For example, the European Court of Justice decided in November 2002 that these nationality clauses are in conflict with EU-rules on the free establishment inside the EU. Furthermore, in May 2003, the EU Transport Council agreed on the EC mandate to negotiate a multilateral ASA with the USA.

10 An exemption has to be made for the alliance partners of the home-based carrier, which are almost as captive as the home-based airline.

Airports Competition in Different Relevant Product Markets

It is still premature to conclude definitely on the market power of Amsterdam airport based on these levels of captivity, which is what the NMa (2001) did. Such a conclusion requires a further analysis of the final stage in the supply-chain. The ability of Amsterdam airport to raise charges for its services to airlines ultimately depends on the willingness of the passengers (and cargo users) to pay for air transport services to and from Schiphol.[11] This willingness to pay is ultimately determined by the substitution possibilities in terms of alternative airports or transport modes.

Since, in general, the nature of transport demand is conditioned by the origin and destination of the trip, the individual route in air transport is also the starting point for the relevant product market.[12] In other words, in principle, route A-B is not a substitute for route C-D. Even a further segmentation should not be surprising within this narrow definition. The reason is that the criterion of demand substitutability implies that the same physical product (a transport service for route A-B) can be supplied in different relevant product markets, if two or more distinct classes of customers whose preferences differ buy it. For example, the differences in time- and price-elasticity between business and leisure passengers may require a split into two distinct relevant product markets within route A-B.

The body of case law on relevant markets as developed under the European Commission's legislation not only points towards more segmentation and fragmentation of relevant product markets for airport services. More aggregate relevant product markets can be found as well (Larouche, 2000). For example, indirect transfer flights A-H-B via each relevant hub H have to be included in the A-B market of direct flights.[13] Furthermore, high-speed trains can be included in the A-B market if they are an adequate substitute in the eyes of the customer (Paris-London, Paris-Brussels, London-Brussels).

Mediterranean holiday-package tours are another example of a more aggregate relevant market. According to the Commission, these trips are sufficiently substitutable from the demand side to include them in the same relevant market.[14] In this view, many Mediterranean airports compete in the holiday package-tour market.

It is similar for air cargo. In the eyes of the Commission, the relevant market for airport services in intercontinental air-cargo transport comprises many airports on the same continent, since indirect routes as well as multi-modal transport chains are now taken into consideration.[15] Consequently, many West European airports

---

[11] One should realise that passenger charges are directly transferred to the passenger, without further airline interference. Every flight coupon shows the amount of airport 'tax' to be paid directly by the passenger. The question whether the airline will absorb a part of these airport charges is not relevant here.

[12] See also the ECJ Judgement of 11 April 1989, case 66/86, Ahmed Saeed Flugreisen v. Zentrale zur Bekämpfung unlauteren Wettbewerbs (1989) ECR 803 at Rec. 40-41.

[13] See for example Decision of 11 August 1999, Case COMP/JV.19, *KLM/Alitalia* (2000) OJ C 96/5, CELEX number 399J0019 at Rec. 22.

[14] See for example the Air tours-First Choice case (Case no IV/M.1524 of 22.09.1999).

[15] *KLM/Alitalia*, supra, note 25 at Rec. 23-25.

are potential competitors of Amsterdam airport in the relevant product market for air cargo.

As already indicated, other relevant product markets based on the principle of demand substitutability are the indirect routes A-H-B in the city-pair market A-B. In intercontinental city-pair markets the relevant product market can also comprise hubs in the other continent. For example, in the Warsaw-Detroit market not only Amsterdam and Frankfurt are competing hubs but possibly also New York. From the point of view of demand substitutability, these indirect markets are competitive, and the level of competition as reflected in the cross elasticities depends on the number of alternative indirect routes and the number of carriers serving these routes. The share of these indirect transfer markets in the passenger volume of Amsterdam airport is substantial: 40-45% of total passengers. This concerns non-captive product markets since most of these passengers can choose between different indirect routes and their intermediate hubs.

In 1997, the Commission included the following airports as competitors in the West-European transfer market: Frankfurt, Munich, Copenhagen, London, Amsterdam, Brussels, Paris, Zurich and Vienna. Perhaps today Milan Malpensa should also be included, whereas Brussels and Zurich should be excluded.

The NMa's opinion on the role of Amsterdam airport in this category of relevant product markets is peculiar. The exclusive concentration on supply-side (non)substitutability brings the NMa (2000) to the conclusion that competition in these markets only exists in theory, based on the argument that airlines in Europe cannot easily move their operations to another hub. Apparently, this approach enables the NMa to ignore fully the increasing probability that the price-sensitive transfer passengers will choose other hub airports and other carriers if aeronautical charges substantially increase.[16]

All in all, Starkie (2002) concludes that the market power of an airport with respect to its aeronautical charges is likely to vary between the different relevant product markets. As Starkie also illustrates, the final conclusions about monopoly power of airports also require a further analysis of the spatial setting of each relevant product market. This is about catchment areas and the availability of proximate airports as sufficient substitutes to the passenger: the relevant geographical markets.

[16] Most hub airports in Europe apply a kind of Ramsey pricing based on different levels of price elasticity in the various market segments. Transfer passenger charges are for example substantially lower (or nil) than charges for departing passengers. It is possible, however, that a difference in terminal costs is involved as well, since departing passengers use both the land- and airside of the terminal, and transfer passengers only use the airside.

Airport Competition in Different Relevant Geographical Markets

It is not unusual to apply the distance to the airport as a simplification to determine the radius of the catchment area.[17] Within the overlapping part of the various circular catchment areas, the airports involved are expected to compete.[18] This may, however, result in an oversimplification of one variable, i.e. distance. Airport-choice models can be more helpful to delineate relevant geographical markets for airports. Important variables in these models for example as developed by Harvey (1987), Ashford et al. (1987), Furuichi and Koppelman (1994) and Veldhuis and Pelger (2003), are the airline ticket prices offered in the relevant product market at each competing airport, and the various travel times in the transport chain, especially access time and flight frequencies. In each separate product market the demand elasticities of these variables can vary substantially. Long-haul flight passengers show smaller elasticities with respect to travel time than do short-haul passengers. Business passengers show higher elasticities as to travel time and lower elasticities as to airline ticket prices than do leisure passengers.

It is also important to realise the impact of trade-offs between these variables. A cheap airline ticket will compensate for longer access times. Regional airports, for example, that accommodate low-cost carriers, are covering much larger catchment areas with respect to the air routes served. In addition, higher flight frequencies compensate for longer access times. For example, in 1995, about 40% of the airline passengers from the Rotterdam region to London were captured by Amsterdam airport instead of being served by Rotterdam airport (De Wit, 1996). Differences in flight frequencies and more competitive airline ticket prices explain this airport choice.

Obviously, changes in the aeronautical charges are expressed in the ticket prices. The more expensive the airport, the smaller the catchment areas for the various relevant product markets owing to higher ticket prices. The popularity of more distant cheap airports served by low cost carriers provides further evidence of this point.

It is important to realize that a catchment area analysis is a snapshot situation. The delineation of geographical relevant markets can rapidly change over time. For example, access times may change due to new infrastructure. The high-speed rail link Amsterdam-Brussels will relocate an important part of the Belgian market into the overlapping catchment areas of Paris and Amsterdam airports. At the same

---

17 See for example the Commission's approach: a 100 km radius around the airport for regional flights and a 300 km radius for direct intercontinental flights, in Commission Decision of 21 May 1999, Case No IV/M.1255 – Flughafen Berlin; Commission Decision 98/190/EC of 14 January 1998, FAG-Flughafen Frankfurt/Main AG. It should be noted, however, that the Commission also points to other factors, like access mode time.

18 A misinterpretation of these EC distance standards may also have played a role in NMa's opinion on the market power of Amsterdam airport: it appeared that only those airports situated within a distance of 300 km from Schiphol have been identified as Schiphol competitors. However, these standards are about overlapping catchment areas, *each of them* with a radius of 300 km (Frontier Economics, 2000). Therefore, one cannot ignore Frankfurt and Paris if EC standards are applied correctly.

time, the catchment area of Amsterdam airport may further shrink due to diminishing accessibility by road and rail as a consequence of increasing congestion and decreased rail punctuality.

It is obvious that the captivity of passengers will increase with decreasing distance between the place of origin in the catchment area and the airport. If the highest population density is found in the proximity of the airport, the major part of the originating passengers will be generated from this limited area. As a matter of fact, 70% of Amsterdam airport's non-transfer passengers originate from the three surrounding provinces (North Holland, South Holland and Utrecht). It is likely that a relatively low percentage of airline passengers from this area would choose a different airport. Outside this core of the catchment area the average captivity will diminish and the percentage of passengers that choose a competing airport will increase.[19] Apparently, the border provinces belong to the overlapping part of different catchment areas of various competing airports. These border provinces show a lower population density and a lower propensity to fly than do the three core provinces. As a consequence, only a relatively small share of Amsterdam airport's total non-transfer passenger volume originates from these border provinces. However, this small share of non- or less- captive passengers in the catchment area does not confirm in advance the market power of Amsterdam airport in the various geographical relevant markets. Starkie's (2002) reference to Greenhut et al (1987) is highly relevant here: competition at the boundary points is often sufficient to transmit price changes over the whole of the market. This is also illustrated by the fact that Amsterdam airport recently (2002) became more anxious about this part of market.

The analysis of the relevant geographical markets of Amsterdam airport indicates that demand substitutability of airport services at Amsterdam airport can be based on overlapping catchment areas of other European airports. The number of competing airports and the level of competition depends on the individual relevant product market.

Based on these findings, we conclude that a light-handed regulatory regime for the aeronautical charges of Schiphol airport would be the most obvious solution, if any regulatory regime should be introduced. The conclusions of the NMa (2001) on the monopoly power of Amsterdam airport pointed in a different direction. This probably at least partly explains the rather heavy-handed regulatory framework that has been developed.

Elements in the New Regulatory Regime for Amsterdam Airport

The "Old" Regulation

The aeronautical charges of all international airports in the Netherlands have been subject to a legal approval procedure of the Minister of Transport for many years. The authorities originally intended to implement the non-discrimination article 15

---

[19] This impression was confirmed after matching the data of the passenger surveys of a number of German airports and the Schiphol passengers survey.

of the Chicago Convention through this approval procedure. In this Convention, contracting states agreed not to apply discriminatory aeronautical charges to foreign versus national aircraft. This origin of the approval procedure in the Netherlands explains why even very small general aviation airstrips were subject to this procedure: very small aircraft from abroad could land and take-off at them and might be discriminated by the airport charges. To underline the general interest of this procedure, each approval is still crowned by a Royal Decree.[20]

This procedure was also developed to comply with other international obligations, such as various ASAs, which usually require that the airport charges reflect the principles on user charges recommended by ICAO. These principles broadly refer to cost-relatedness, transparency and non-discrimination.

In the second half of the 1990s the procedure described came under pressure. The explanation is obvious, since the only reason for this procedure was to prevent possible discrimination between aircraft of different states. Furthermore, the criteria for approval were vague. The tension between airport users and airport operators built up, especially at Amsterdam airport and the larger regional airports of Eelde, Rotterdam and Maastricht. This can be attributed partly to the absence of rules concerning a consultation procedure and the information to be provided by the airport operator to the users. The basic explanation for this tension, however, was the increased competition in the liberalised internal air-transport market, which forced airlines to implement continuous cost reduction programmes. At the same time, Amsterdam airport continued to increase the aeronautical charges and succeeded in staying profitable by expanding its commercial activities.

In 1998, Dutch competition law was implemented, together with the establishment of the new competition authority NMa. Airline complaints about airport charges increasingly started to point towards the abuse of monopoly power. This was followed by several court cases in which the state was accused of approving alleged abuse of monopoly power by the airport. It was obvious that this procedure required a fundamental revision. When, at the end of 1999, the Dutch minister of transport decided to resume the preparations for the privatisation for Amsterdam airport, the efficiency of the airport services market of Amsterdam airport was identified as a public interest that should be safeguarded by new procedures before actual privatisation could take place. The NMa (2001) report further underlined the importance to replace the existing approval procedure by explicit regulation, in order to cope with the alleged monopoly power.

[20] To date, Dutch citizens are informed about five times a year through official announcements in the Dutch newspapers, that it pleased Her Majesty to approve the new airport charges of for example Texel, Midden-Zeeland, Hoogeveen, Hilversum, Budel, Teuge, Maastricht, Eelde, Rotterdam or Amsterdam. An approval procedure for Eindhoven and Twente airport was never implemented, since their status as military airports with civil co-use created a problem between the ministry of transport and the ministry of defence about the designated civil area of the airport.

Negotiated or Regulated Access

The experience with the introduction of new regulatory regimes in other network industries inspired the Ministry of Economic Affairs[21] to introduce the so-called negotiated access model as a new component in the regulatory regime on aeronautical charges at Amsterdam airport (Ministry of Economic Affairs, 1999). Network industries like gas, water, electricity, telecommunications and railroads have been involved in a process of vertical separation in recent years to isolate the monopoly component (the network infrastructure) from the competitive component (the service providers). In such a situation, network access is conditional to create competition between service providers.

This access can be realised either in a relatively light-handed or in a heavy-handed approach. In a so-called negotiated (third party) access approach (Engel, 2002), only minimum network access conditions are specified ex ante. Market parties themselves determine the tariffs for the use of the network and disputes are settled in court.

The regulated (third party) access approach is more heavy-handed (Bier, 2001). The public authorities influence the tariffs directly, via either a price cap or a rate of return regulation. Access conditions are determined ex ante and disputes are primarily settled by the regulator.

One may wonder, however, whether market access to the network infrastructure should be the key issue in the regulation of airport services. In air transport, the issue of market access has been regulated for many years already in an international setting. Bilateral air service agreements between states or EU competition rules for the internal market explicitly address the issue of market access. Congested EU airports can be earmarked as slot-coordinated airports based on objective criteria. For these airports, slot scarcity is regulated by uniform EU slot allocation rules. These rules explicitly address the interests of new entrants by the creation of a separate slots pool.[22]

All in all, the history of the air transport industry is different from other network industries in that it has operated in a strictly vertically integrated way for a long time. It justifies the conclusion that market access should not require much attention in a new regulatory framework for Amsterdam airport. The basic idea of the negotiated access model corresponds with the findings from the relevant market analysis for Amsterdam airport: a light-handed regulatory model without direct regulatory interference in the tariffs.

However, the regulatory system that was ultimately developed for Amsterdam airport only bears the name 'negotiated access'; in actual reality it became a full-fledged regulated access system. The tariffs and conditions are not primarily negotiated by the market parties but almost completely fixed ex ante by detailed rules. For example:

---

[21] The new regulation of Schiphol airport was developed in a working group consisting of members from the ministry of transport, the ministry of economic affairs, the NMa and the ministry of finance.

[22] The slot allocation rules are now being reconsidered, to look for more market-oriented approaches.

- Airport charges will be based on the dual-till principle. This principle requires a cost allocation system to handle the common costs of aeronautical and commercial activities and to determine the regulatory asset base. This cost allocation system has to be proposed by the airport operator and to be approved ex ante by the NMa.
- The NMa is the regulator that has to enforce the rules and settle disputes in the first instance.
- Rate of Return regulation will be applied to the aeronautical charges. A specified and NMa approved Weighted Average Cost of Capital (WACC) will be applied to the regulatory asset base.[23]
- Charges and service levels as negotiated between an individual user and the airport have to made available to all other users, given the international obligations of non-discrimination.
- The airport operator must consult users about the proposed charges and service levels. The consultation procedure is specified as well as the information to be provided by the airport in the consultation. After the consultation the airport operator establishes the new tariffs. The resulting charges and service levels, as well as the arguments for not following individual user requests, must be published.
- Users have the right to request the NMa to test the established charges ex post on the criteria of transparency, cost-relatedness and reasonableness.
- The NMa can also take the initiative to test the new charges on these criteria. The cost-relatedness is only tested on the total of airport charges, i.e. the revenue yield. The NMa can further test the reasonableness of individual charges by benchmarking them with the charges at other airports in Europe.

The resulting detailed regulation is partly based on ex ante rules and partly on ex post procedures. However, the details do not correspond with the negotiated access model concept. Irrespective of this confusing terminology, the main question remains unanswered: what determines the choice for a negotiated or a regulated access model? Bier (2001) has tried to derive these conditions under social welfare considerations for the electricity market. If the monopoly power of the airport appears to be moderate, the regulatory incentives should be moderate as well, keeping in mind Starkie's (2002) warning that there is a trade-off between living with imperfect regulation or imperfect markets. If the relevant market analysis and the resulting level of monopoly power of Amsterdam airport is adequately taken into account, it is obvious that the characteristics of a true negotiated access model make this approach more appropriate for the regulation of Amsterdam airport.

---

[23] Actually, the choice for RoR regulation of the aviation till was not the result of a more fundamental discussion about the well-known pros and cons of price cap regulation and RoR regulation. RoR regulation was introduced as a more or less inevitable component of the envisaged 'negotiated access' model.

Single Till, Middle Till and Dual Till

During the preparations for the new regulatory regime of Amsterdam airport, the single - dual till controversy also played a role. All over the world, and also in the Netherlands, airlines intuitively advocate a single till, whereas airports intuitively opt for a dual till. Airlines underline the common-good characteristics of airport activities: "runways serve to develop commercial activities" (See also footnote 5). However, airports underline the need for a reasonable rate of return on aeronautical activities and the entrepreneurial freedom to develop new commercial activities.

The consequences of these two approaches for the aeronautical charges are illustrated by Amsterdam airport's financial figures (2003) which are specified in four individual business units: aviation, consumers, real estate and alliances/participations. The unit "aviation" comes close to the aeronautical activities, and the other business units together more or less cover the non-aeronautical/commercial activities (see Table 6.1).

Table 6.1 Financial performance of individual business units within Amsterdam airport

Amounts in millions Euro	*Aviation*	*Consumers*	*Real Estate*	*Alliances and Participations*	*Total*
RONA before tax	5.9%	26.9%	8.3% (10.2%)*	-/- 6.4%	9.1%
RONA after tax	3.9%	17.6%	5.4% (6.7%)*	-/- 4.2%	6.0%
Total revenues	399	242	114	35	790
EBITDA	147	133	80	-/- 4	356
Operating result	78	108	76	-/- 9	253
Fixed assets (av.)	1,322	402	915	137	2,776
Investments	258	12	65	10	345

* After changes in value
Source: annual financial report Schiphol Group 2002

According to the NMa (2001), an interval of 6.5-9.2% for the overall WACC before tax is reasonable, as is an aviation-specific WACC of 7.9%. The contrast between the consequences of a dual-till and a single-till is clear: a dual till requires a substantial increase in airport charges to boost the aviation Return On Net Assets (RONA) from 5.9 to 7.9%. A single till, however, allows for a substantial reduction in airport charges as long as the overall RONA remains in the range 6.5-9.2%.

The Dutch version of the 'till' problem is a little more complicated, however: a choice had to be made between three options. This is because in a public hearing on the privatisation of Amsterdam airport, the NMa introduced the third option of a so-called 'middle till'. The NMa arguments for this option ran as follows. Locational rents play a major role in the profits of commercial activities. These locational rents should be partly redistributed to the benefit of the airport users. Therefore, the land at the airport site and even around the airport should be included in the regulatory asset base. If this land were hired for commercial activities, the aviation till should benefit from the locational rents by applying market-oriented square-metre prices that could be derived from comparable sites elsewhere, like the Central Business District. Some considerations have to be taken into account concerning this middle till option. Forsyth (2003) for example clearly indicates that locational rents are not due to the abuse of market power like monopoly rents, which reflect market inefficiencies. Locational rents are difficult to separate from monopoly rents at an airport, but as such they arise from the premium paid for preferred locations. The better the landside accessibility of the airport region, the lower the locational rents. Not only the airport operator gets these rents. Also owners of the surrounding land enjoy these locational rents by virtue of their proximity.[24]

From the point of view of allocative efficiency, however, the middle till is not fundamentally different from the single till, since both of them intend to cross-subsidise the aeronautical activities. The allocative efficiency of the single till has been disputed in the case of capacity-constrained airports (CAA, 2000; Starkie and Yarrow, 2000), since it reduces the incentives for the optimal use of airport facilities. Since Amsterdam airport will remain a slot-coordinated airport after the opening of the fifth runway, slots remain scarce during substantial periods of the day. Under these circumstances, the expected economic inefficiency of a single till has resulted in the decision to implement the dual till system.

The Public Interest of the Availability of Adequate Airport Infrastructure

Although it can be contested whether the interest of the 'main port' availability is a public interest, it was identified as such in the preparations for the privatisation of Amsterdam airport. As a consequence, specific instruments were developed to safeguard this interest. Since there are some interrelations with the 'main port' interest and the efficient market interest, it is necessary to discuss the safeguards for this main port interest here in more detail.

Amsterdam airport was corporatised as a limited company in the early 1950s. Public ownership for a long time corresponded with the public utility interest of the airport. However, commercialisation, privatisation and internationalisation of the airport sector have been strong incentives to develop new commercial interests as an airport company. New opportunities emerged at the Schiphol site, in the wider airport region, at other Dutch airports, and abroad at foreign airports. The single public utility interest issue of a well-equipped home base for the national airline KLM is less self-evident anymore in that stage of development.

---

[24] An IPO of Amsterdam airport enables the selling shareholder, in this case the state, to cream at least a part of the capitalised future locational rents.

Parallel to these developments, another development was important: the disappearance of state commissioners in the supervisory board of publicly owned enterprises.[25] Under these circumstances it became evident that the influence of the state as a shareholder in Amsterdam airport is not so different from the position of any other shareholder in a Dutch limited company.[26] In the existing corporate governance structure, this influence is very limited nowadays.

If the state was to pass on to privatisation of Amsterdam airport, this would trigger new commercial activities, productivity improvements, higher cost efficiency, international participations, etc. However, the core business – i.e. the aeronautical activities at Schiphol – will never show high rates of return (see the table above). Politicians therefore suspected the danger that Amsterdam airport, after privatisation, would neglect its core business and put big efforts in other more profitable commercial activities.[27]

To cover the interest of the core business for the Dutch economy, a separate instrument is intended to be introduced; specifically, an operating licence for an unlimited period of time. If the airport operator were to neglect this interest in a substantial way, the Minister of Transport could withdraw the licence if the airport's viability is endangered. The problem is, however, that it would take years to remove the operator. In other words, the licence would be almost ineffective. To be able to change the operator immediately (if necessary), the legal ownership of the land at the airport will be transferred to the state just before the actual IPO is started. At the same time, the land is leased back to the airport operator for zero ground rent.[28] Substantial negligence of the core business, to an extent that the continuity of the airport is endangered, is an explicit condition to immediately end the land lease. This land lease also enables the immediate expropriation of the infrastructure and real estate on the leased land.[29] All in all, an important incentive has been created to influence the behaviour of the airport operator according to the public interest of the 'main port'.

A final comment concerns the enforcement of this licence. Enforcement criteria should be specified before the introduction of the policy measure. However, a 'well equipped airport' is not a standard concept. It will change in the course of time. To grasp the key issues in a monitoring system is difficult, and too much focus on the short run in this system could result in direct public interference

---

[25] A state commissioner has always been a contradiction in terms. Each member of the supervisory board shall only serve the company's interest, independently, without any order or consultation. As long as the public interest and company interests point in the same direction, the potential conflict of interests remains hidden. At the same time, the impression is created that the state is able to influence a company's policy and to safeguard the public interest through its state commissioners. But this is an illusion.

[26] The so-called Structuur NV.

[27] This danger is rather small if one realises that the profitable commercial activities are more or less rooted in the aviation activities. Neglecting the aviation activities will inevitably have a strong negative impact on commercial activities.

[28] The balance sheet will not be affected by these changes, since it only refers to the bare legal ownership. The airport operator keeps all possibilities to exploit the land as he intended to do.

[29] Various financial compensation principles have been developed for different situations.

with private investment policies of the airport operator. However, the regulatory principles of dual till and rate of return regulation as such are already sufficient incentives to guarantee adequate investments in the aeronautical facilities. Therefore, withdrawal criteria for the operating licence can only be seen in the context of an ultimum remedium; otherwise a combination of a heavy-handed economic regulation and an operational licence could develop into a substantial degree of regulatory overkill.

Starkie's trade-off between living with imperfect regulation or with imperfect markets will probably show whether a light-handed system based on negotiations between market parties is preferable for Amsterdam's Schiphol airport.

References

Ashford, N. and Moore, C.A. (1999) *Airport Finance*, Woodhouse Eaves.

Ashford, N. and Benchemam, M. (1987) "Passengers' choice of airport: an application of the multinomial logit model", *Transportation Research Record*, 1147, 1-5.

Baumol, W.J., Panzar, J.C. And Willig, R.D. (1982) *Contestable Markets and the Theory of Industry Structure*, Harcourt Brace Jovanovitch.

Bier, C. (2001) "Network Access in the Deregulated European Electricity Market: Negotiated Third Party Access vs. Single Buyer", *German Working Papers in Law and Economics*, Vol. 2001, Article 17.

Carney, M. and Mew, K. (2003), "Airport governance reform: a strategic management perspective", *Journal of Air Transport Management*, 9, 221-232.

Civil Aviation Authority (2000), *The "Single Till" and the "dual till" Approach to the Price Regulation of Airports*, Consultation paper, London.

Doganis, R. (1992) *The Airport Business*, Routledge, London.

Engel, C. (2002) Verhandelter Netzzugang, (Negotiated Access), *Gemeinschaftsgüter: Recht, Politik und Ökonomie, Preprints aus der Max-Planck-Projektgruppe, Recht der Gemeinschaftsgüter*, 2002/4, Bonn.

Forsyth, P. (2003) *Creating and Shifting Locational and Monopoly Rents at Airports*, presentation at the Hamburg Aviation Conference 2003.

Frontier Economics (2000) *Schiphol Airport: Market Definition Study*, A report prepared for NMa, London.

Furuichi, M. and Koppelman, F.S. (1995) "An analysis of air travellers' departure airport and destination choice behaviour", *Transportation Research A*, 28A, No. 3, 187-195.

Graham, A. (2001), *Managing Airports, an International Perspective*, Butterworth/ Heinemann.

Greenhut, M.L., Norman, G. And Hung, C. (1987), *The Economics of Imperfect Competition: A Spatial Approach*, Cambridge University Press, Cambridge.

Harvey, G. (1987), "Airport choice in a multiple airport region", *Transportation Research* A, 21, No. 6, 439-449.

Larouche, P. (2000) "Relevant market definition in network industries: air transport and telecommunication", *Journal of Network Industries*, 1, 407-445.

Ministry of Economic Affairs (1999) Publieke belangen en marktordening, Liberalisering en privatisering in netwerksectoren (Public interests and market structure, Liberalisation and privatisation in network industries), The Hague.

NMa (2001) *Rapportage Luchthaventarieven Schiphol* (Report airport charges Schiphol), The Hague.

Schiphol Group (2003) *Annual Financial Report 2002.*

Starkie, D. (2002) "Airport regulation and competition", *Journal of Air Transport Management,* 8, 63-72.

Starkie, D. and Yarrow, G. (2000) *The Single Till Approach to the Price Regulation of Airports*, CAA, London.

Veldhuis, J.G. and Pelger, M. (2003) "Airport competition and changing landside accessibility", paper to be presented at the ATRS Conference, Toulouse.

Wit, J.G. de (1996) "De kwetsbaarheid van meervoudige airportsystemen; lessen voor nieuwe luchthavenplanners, (The vulnerability of multiple airport systems; lessons for new airport planners)", *Tijdschrift voor Vervoerwetenschap*, No. 4, 355-370.

Chapter 7

Airport Regulation in the UK

Nienke Hendriks[1] and Doug Andrew

Introduction

Aviation is often regarded as the first of the major regulatory reforms in Western economies. Unlike the US where airlines were already privately owned, in the UK de-regulation and privatisation were closely linked. The main reasons for privatisation were a reassessment of the role of government, budget constraints and greater awareness of the relationship between ownership structure and governance.

In the UK aviation market, privatisation started with the privatisation and deregulation of British Airways. The benefits of airline deregulation are seen to be substantial in terms of efficiency gains, innovation and consumer welfare. In the US, Steven Morrison and Cliff Winston's recent work estimated a 27% reduction in airfares due to de-regulation.[2] They also stress the benefits of competition or the threat thereof. In the UK, competition has resulted in the introduction of innovative business models by the low frills carriers, which has led to major benefits for European travellers.

Going beyond the US practice, the UK extended the reform model to infrastructure with the privatisation of BAA in 1987, following the British Telecom privatisation in 1984. Given the large market share of the BAA London airports, they were made subject to price cap regulation. The airport services market was liberalised and gradually many airports were put onto a more commercial footing. At the time, price cap regulation was seen by experts as a temporary measure: sector-specific economic regulation was introduced to protect consumers "until competition arrived".

One of the main problems faced by the downstream market is the lack of responsiveness in the upstream infrastructure market. The downstream market in the UK is highly competitive in the sense of few or no government-imposed economic entry barriers. The upstream market is still characterised by monopolies in the South East. This raises issues about the impact of market structure, ownership structure and regulation.

---

[1] The views presented in this paper are these of the authors and do not necessarily represent the views of their respective organisations.

[2] Steven Morrison and Clifford Winston (2000), "The Remaining role for Government policy in the de-regulated airline industry" in *Deregulation of Network Industries*, AEI-Brookings.

Public Policy Framework

In developing a public policy framework, it is desirable to adopt a comparative institutional approach where market failures and government/regulatory failures are taken into account in designing optimal policy responses in a world where perfect competition (e.g. no fixed, let alone, sunk costs) is merely a pedagogical tool and information asymmetries are inherent.

The two main types of models available are the traditional de-centralised market approach on the one hand and public sector management models on the other hand. There are a range of variants in-between; Buchanan's user clubs, franchise bidding and not-for-profit models, for example.

The market model is based on the fact that commercial firms, aiming as they generally are at maximising shareholder value, have strong incentives to define and price outputs. However, theoretically when a commercial firm has market power it might restrict output as a corollary to increasing its prices. Its incentive to invest optimally (from a social perspective) is therefore weakened and it is likely to invest late, even when accounting for real option values.[3] This becomes even more of an issue when dealing with lumpy investments.

The traditional critique of the market approach to infrastructure was highlighted by Dupuit's case of a proposed bridge: high fixed and sunk costs, zero marginal costs. Private provision funded by user charges would lead to under-utilisation as prices would exceed marginal costs, once the bridge was built. This results in a loss of economic efficiency. Private provision may be later than ideal as the private developer may not be able to price discriminate sufficiently to obtain all the consumer surplus that would feature in the social cost benefit. However, a tax-funded subsidy could address this problem, although taxes themselves also impose costs to the economy which must be accounted for.

The public sector model is built around the premise that governments act in the public interest and are therefore more likely to achieve economic efficiency, i.e. ensuring best use of scarce capacity, least cost production and optimal investment levels, the aim being for projects to proceed as long as their marginal social costs equate to marginal social benefits. Under public provision the publicly interested government would undertake a cost benefit analysis, trying to judge the expected demand "schedule" for the bridge and assess the costs through to implementation, all against the next best alternative. If the bridge was built, no charge would be levied, achieving best use.

However, this is based on three key assumptions. Firstly, it assumes that the government is able to obtain the best information on demand and costs. However, the problem of asymmetric information is a considerable obstacle in doing so. Secondly, it assumes that the government would be able to remain "public interested". Public choice theory suggests that interest group capture of public policy diverts governments from this goal: local construction interests for example.

---

[3] A real option is the right but not the obligation to take an action that might consist of deferring, expanding, downsizing or abandoning the project at a pre-determined price for a pre-determined period of time. This flexibility is valuable and should therefore be taken into account in the cost of the project last sent. For example, a cost of undertaking a mutually exclusive project at time t is not being able to undertake it at time $t+1$.

Niskanen's model of bureaucratic behaviour[4] suggests that empire building is an important motive explaining government behaviour: the bridge building agency for example. And thirdly there is the issue of the deadweight costs of taxation to finance the bridge.

Public Policy Objectives

From a public policy view, the objective of economic regulation should be economic efficiency: the aim being to maximise the size of the national pie in standards of living terms. Practically, this suggests that the policy problem is how to ensure:

- Least-cost production: productive efficiency.
- Best use of scarce outputs: allocative efficiency (including environmental costs).
- Optimal investment: projects only proceeding when the expected net present value exceeds zero and costs include option values.

The main policy issue then becomes having sufficient instruments to address each of the targets and, where competition is seriously limited, the trade-off between market failure versus regulatory failure. This raises the question of how far is regulation more likely to achieve the public policy objectives compared with relying on competition law.

Economic Regulatory Models

Economic regulatory models can be distinguished by the degree to which they rely on the use of incentives as the regulatory equation shows:

$$P = k + \beta C$$

P is the maximum price allowed by the regulator, k are costs independent from the regulated firm's own costs and C represents the firm's own costs. β represents the cost pass-through coefficient.

On one side of the spectrum there are the so-called Cost-of-Service (CoS) regulation models (β=1 and k=0). On the other side of the spectrum, there are the high-powered pure incentive regulation models (β=0). Clearly, there is a continuum of options in between ($0<\beta<1$).

Cost-of-Service Regulation

Under the pure Cost-of-Service model (i.e. rate of return regulation) all the firm's costs are remunerated. The firm is ensured a fair rate of return ex-post: the firm

[4] Niskanen, W. (1971) *Bureaucracy and Representative Government*, Chicago: Aldine.

will ultimately be able to pass all its costs to its customers. This has the advantage of protecting the firm's investment from the risk of expropriation, respecting private property rights. However this also raises issues with respect to efficiency. The firm knows that all its investment, no matter whether profitable, or desirable from a customer's point of view, will ultimately end up in its cost-base on which it will be allowed to earn a fair rate of return. This might result in 'gold-plating': the firm might act as if its cost of capital is lower than it really is.

In the US, regulators have spent considerable resources examining investment programmes to address the resulting adverse selection problem ex ante. At the extreme is the state regulation of investment decisions by hospitals in the US. Certificate of Need programmes require a hospital to obtain approval before undertaking certain investment programmes.[5]

Thus, although in theory the firm will recoup all its costs as long as the regulatory cost of capital is equal or greater than the firm's actual cost of capital, in practice CoS regulation seldom allows an automatic cost pass-through of all operating expenditure and capital expenditure. In practice, this tends to be subject to prudency tests, which might result in certain investments being disallowed ex post. Given the regulatory lag, depending on the period for which the regulator sets the rate of return, regulatory risk such as the exclusion of some investment from the allowed regulatory cost base ex post may force regulated firms to behave more prudently or excessively risk-adversely. This might result in sub-optimal investment decisions.

RPI-X Regulation

The dominant economic regulation model in the UK is RPI-X regulation. This form of regulation, pioneered by Stephen Littlechild in the 1980s, is based on the premise that prices rather than profits should be regulated.

RPI-X regulation allows the firm to adjust its prices by the retail price index (which measures consumer price inflation) plus/minus an ex ante determined X-factor. The maximum prices are determined ex ante for a set period (e.g. five years in the case of UK airports) and not meant to be adjusted until the next control period.[6] This implies that if the firm is able to outperform the regulator's expectations, the firm keeps the efficiency gains until the next price review.

Given the information asymmetry between regulator and regulatee, one of the key objectives is to incentivise the firm to reveal its true costs by allowing the firm to keep efficiency gains within the price control period. The next period's prices are adjusted for inflation and the X-factor. 'X' depends on how the regulator assesses the trade-offs under her objectives given the cost and demand climate in which the firm operates. A high positive X-factor (i.e. RPI-X, resulting in lower real prices) might indicate that the firm revealed substantial cost savings in the past or it may indicate that the regulator sees considerable scope for (further) efficiency improvements during the next control period. A high negative X-factor (i.e.

---

[5] W Kip Viscusi, John M. Vernon and Joseph E. Harrington (2000) *Economics of Regulation and Antitrust*, 3rd edition, p. 310

[6] In practice only the regulated firms can seek an interim review.

RPI+X, enabling a real price increase) is an indicator that the regulator might be placing more emphasis on the firm's planned investments and the firm facing rising incremental costs.

The degree to which an RPI-X regime provides strong incentives depends on the objectives of the regulated firm and the credibility and the duration of the control period, and the risk sharing specified in the price cap. A high level of cost pass-through results in a regulatory regime with weaker incentives, close to CoS regulation, whereas a credible regime that allows significantly less automatic cost pass-through could be more high powered. If a regulator is particularly concerned about rents then pass-throughs allow tighter caps without risking the viability of the firm. Generally speaking, RPI-X price cap regulation in the UK tends to a large extent to be cost-based, i.e. like CoS regulation it is mainly based on inputs rather than outputs. Low quality output specification, including service quality dimensions, is often a constraint.

High Powered Incentive Regulation

The more the focus shifts to outputs, the more high powered the regulatory approach could become. One of the main reasons why regulators might be reluctant to use high powered incentives is the limited insight they have in the firm's true cost structure together with the concern about rents being earned.

By setting a price cap solely based on the 'most efficient' firm in the same or similar industry without taking the firm's own costs into account, the firm faces maximum incentives to operate as cost-efficiently as possible during the control period. However, if the firm cannot achieve the predicted efficiencies it might get into financial difficulties and approach the regulator for an interim review. This raises the issue of regulatory credibility.

One of the main issues when setting a price cap is the trade-off between the risk of bankruptcy if the cap is set too low and the risk of high rents if it is set too high. If the firm were to earn abnormal returns there might be (political) pressure on the regulator to intervene, and similarly if the firm were to get into financial difficulty the regulator might be pressured to intervene, especially when security of supply is perceived to be an issue.

The main problem is therefore asymmetric information between regulator and regulatee, which gives rise to considerable scope for gaming. Where the regulator positions herself will clearly depend on her main objectives. Where the regulator sets the cost pass-through coefficient will depend on how much she focuses on economic rents rather than incentives. This will at least in part be determined by the regulator's main objective given the statutory framework.

If cost reduction is the prime concern then it is often argued that the price cap might be tight, whereas if investment is the main concern the price cap is likely to be looser. If the level of cost-pass through is relatively low then a tight price cap might increase the risk faced by the firm as part of the profit curve is chopped off compared with the profit curve of an unregulated firm. This would potentially result in a higher cost of capital (and thus potentially looser cap). However, even a looser price cap might not necessarily provide the right incentives for investment. The main risk if the firm was to make excess profits is regulatory intervention during a control period. This gives rise to regulatory uncertainty for the regulatee and its financiers (potentially increasing the cost of capital if this risk is regarded as being non-diversifiable), it might also deter potential new entrants, given the potential regulatory threat.

Regulatory Credibility and Commitment

Regulatory credibility and commitment are key determining factors of the firm's behaviour. The length of the period for which the price cap is set is therefore of importance. The shorter the interval between the setting of price caps, the closer RPI-X becomes to CoS regulation.

Long-term regulatory commitment increases incentives. The longer the control period, the stronger the incentives, because the firm will be able to benefit for a longer time from its cost savings. This especially applies when dealing with long-term assets.

The risk with relatively frequent resetting of the price cap is ex-post opportunism of the regulator. Future regulators might ex-post decide to disallow certain capital investments and thus exclude them from the Regulatory Asset Base (RAB). In a situation with high sunk costs, this is likely to result in the firm investing below the socially optimal level. In situations where infrastructure investment is seen as one of the prime objectives, a long-term price cap commitment is therefore desirable.

However, it is difficult for the present regulator to indicate her commitment to a long-term cap, especially considering that she might not be able to commit her successors. Regulatory commitments can never be as strong as contractual obligations. The time inconsistency problem is an issue, but one that is addressed by the establishment of regulators independent of day-to-day political control.

Institutional Framework: The Issue of Governance

The forgoing stresses the importance of the institutional framework in which the regulator operates. The institutional framework will depend on how the government defines its role, the implementation of this definition and its perceived sustainability.

The relation between the regulator and the government should be transparent and set out in statute, ensuring the regulator's independence whilst also ensuring that the regulator can be held accountable. The government appoints the regulators and determines how much discretion the regulators have (by statute and/or other means).

Critically, the UK regulators, generally as single persons, were statutorily independent of the Government, although appointed and with budgets controlled by the Government. On the surface this was seen as important to reduce the risk of dominant market positions being abused but there was also the objective of reducing the risk of the Government intervening post-privatisation to keep prices too low and so at least partially expropriate the investment by private investors.

The idea behind the UK model is that as long as the regulator is given a clear statute she can be held accountable against her statutory objectives without compromising her independence. This enables the Government (which is the regulator's 'owner') to hold the regulator accountable against its statute. However, the other side of the coin is that the regulator is given considerable operating autonomy in carrying out her duty under the Act.

Regulatory governance can be regarded as the degree of the regulator's discretion and therefore the extent to which the regulator can be held accountable. Best practice in the UK is evolving with the operation of monetary policy via the Monetary Policy Committee perhaps leading the way in implementation while Ofcom represents current policy thinking, e.g. separation of the Chair from the Chief Executive Officer.

In how far the regulator is able to impose an effective incentive structure on the regulatee on behalf of society overall, will depend to a great extent on the institutional framework, including market structure, in which both operate. Incentive compatibility is the objective. Management of private firms, which aim at maximising shareholder value, face stronger incentives to improve performance than managers of state-owned firms. However, a new type of firm has been (re)-emerging at the interface between the public and the private sector: the so-called not-for-profit/not-for-dividend firms.

These types of firms are likely to face considerably fewer incentives even when operating in the private sector.[7] These types of firms are tending to be highly geared which, when subject to economic regulation and other on-going "government involvement", gives rise to a whole range of issues. For the remainder of this chapter the focus is on "for profit" firms when referring to privately owned firms.

In order to design and implement a regulatory framework based on high-powered incentives, regulatory credibility is essential. However, regulatory credibility will, to a large extent, depend on how far the regulator can pre-commit and this will depend on the institutional framework and the approach to regulation from the government and regulator alike (i.e. how far is the ultimate aim the phasing out of economic regulation, duration of the control period, etc).

The UK Framework

Like other UK regulators, the CAA (Civil Aviation Authority) is an autonomous body, set up by the UK government with all its board members appointed by the Secretary of State. The CAA consists of four groups: the safety regulatory group, economic regulatory group, directorate of airspace policy and the consumer protection group. The CAA only sets a price cap on airport charges at airports that have been designated by the Secretary of State. These are the three BAA-owned London airports and local government owned Manchester airport. The CAA can investigate complaints about the conduct of other UK airports (if their annual

---

[7] E.L. Glaeser (2002) "The Governance of Not-for-Profit Firms", Harvard Institute of Economic Research, Discussion Paper Number 1954, April

turnover exceeds £1 million) but cannot set caps on airport charges. It also manages the licence with NATS including the price control arrangements.

Under the Airports Act (1986), the CAA is required to set price caps for a five-year period, extendible by one year. The CAA formulates proposals for price caps but then has to refer the airports to the Competition Commission. The Competition Commission then reports back to the CAA with its recommendations. The final decision is made by the CAA, after consultation with interested parties.

The main weakness in this process is that there is no appeal against the CAA decision apart from resorting to judicial review. It potentially introduces greater regulatory uncertainty as two regulatory bodies are dealing with the one problem, which they might approach in a rather different way. This is not surprising given their different statutory objectives. The Government policy is to change this arrangement into the conventional one whereby the Commission is the appeal body that the regulatee can appeal to over a regulator's decision.

In determining the price cap the CAA is subject to its objectives under the Transport and Airports Acts. The CAA's statutory objectives in the case of airport regulation are as follows:

- Further the reasonable interest of users.
- Promote the efficient, economic and profitable airport operation.
- Encourage timely investment in new airport facilities.
- Impose minimum restrictions.

The CAA has also to take account of international obligations advised to the CAA by the Government.

A key difference with the Competition Commission is that whereas the Competition Commission can come with public interest findings, this is not in the remit of the CAA. If in the view of the Competition Commission the designated airports have acted against the public interest, it can come with a public interest finding under which the CAA has to take action to remedy the situation.

This process is rather different compared with that followed by the UK utility regulators (OFWAT, OFGEM, OFTEL[8]). These regulators determine the price cap without referring to the Competition Commission, as the latter is the appellate body. This process is more transparent. The expectation is that in the near future the Airports Act will be amended in line with the Utilities Act, thus bringing airport regulation more in line with utility regulation.

Airport Infrastructure in the UK: The Problems

The provision of airport services in the South East of the UK is dominated by the BAA London airports (Heathrow, Gatwick and Stansted). In 1987, BAA was sold with a dominant position in two regions (Scotland also) and a golden share, making

---

[8] Office of Water Services (OFWAT), Office of Gas and Electricity Markets (OFGEM), Office of Telecommunications (OFTEL).

hostile take-overs more difficult. The BAA London airports serve approximately 90% of the South East market.[9] Local-government owned Manchester Airport (MA) also has a considerable degree of local market power.

In both cases, market power seems to be the main rationale for subjecting these airports to economic regulation. Privately owned BAA, operating with a profit motive, and having considerable market power, might be expected to engage in monopolistic behaviour, i.e. increasing prices as a corollary to restricting output. How far this applies to local-government owned MA is debatable, as MA shareholders probably operate with public sector objectives. If, for example, regulation allowed MA to monopoly price, would MA's shareholders not intervene to address such pricing following airline complaints given its adverse effects on local/regional business and travellers?

In both cases, market structure is clearly an issue and ownership structure is potentially an issue as well. For a considerable time now, Heathrow, and to a lesser extent, Gatwick, have been characterised by excess demand. It might be argued that given the lumpiness of aviation infrastructure, the lack of seemingly adequate levels of capacity is not necessarily always inefficient. When real option costs are allowed for, it might be efficient for the market to undertake the investments "late" compared with the timing that a benevolent social planner would prefer. So some excess demand is probably optimal with efficient prices.

However, especially in the case of Heathrow, the persistence of excess demand is likely to come at considerable welfare costs. In a competitive market, the price mechanism not only ensures best use of scarce capacity but also functions as a signal to where and when new investment is needed. On the other hand, firms with market power, which operate under a profit motive, might want to restrict output and increase prices as a corollary. The firm's objectives are of importance in this context and hence its governance structure should be taken into account when defining the problem. The situation with respect to local-government owned MA is rather different compared with privately owned BAA, as MA operates under public sector objectives. It might therefore not be surprising that whereas BAA seems to invest too late, MA might have been investing too early, which is too costly given that it now has considerable excess capacity.

The key problems in relation to airport infrastructure in the UK are:

- Persistent excess demand in the South East of England: potential inefficient use of scarce capacity and sub-optimal investment levels.
- BAA market power (market structure).
- Manchester airport: excess capacity (investment too early? Too costly?).
- Manchester Airport: public sector objective (ownership structure).
- Service quality issues.
- Inefficient slot allocation.

---

[9] The South East market being defined as Heathrow, Gatwick, Stansted, London City and Luton.

Given the variety of problems, it should be noted that the regulator has only one instrument: the price cap.

This raises the question of how far price cap regulation is the best available mechanism to address these problems. Price cap regulation limits price adjustment, preventing best use of scarce capacity and potentially distorting investment signals. The inefficient functioning slot market further exacerbates the problem. The lack of clear property rights with respect to slots is the key obstacle to more efficient slot allocation systems, such as slot trading. The current system prevents best use of scarce slot capacity.

Price Cap Regulation of UK Airports

The Regulatory Asset Base (RAB)

Airport regulation in the UK is based on the single till RAB-based approach. The starting point of this approach is the regulated firm's projected cost base. The price cap is set to ensure that the expected return of the firm covers all its projected (and, by the regulator, allowed) costs (including the regulatory cost of capital) over the duration of the control period. A key issue for the regulator is therefore to determine the firm's RAB.

The valuation of the RAB is a key factor in determining:

- The (maximum) level of price to the users;
- Economic returns to the regulatee.

Initial valuations of the asset base have generally been made by reference to market values at privatisation, as a proxy for value in use. Another way of determining initial valuations has been to use the present values of future cash flows assuming a pre-existing price regime, based on incremental or benchmarked costs. Optimised depreciated replacement costs would be another option.

However, valuation of the asset base is not just a one-off issue, in all successive price reviews the regulator will again have to establish the starting value of the RAB. In addition, the regulator will have to decide how to treat depreciation and how to deal with capital expenditure. The regulator will also have to determine the regulatory cost of capital.

In the case of previously regulated firms, the issue for the regulator is how to roll the regulatory asset base forward. In the UK, regulators use the real value of financial net investment as the basis for rolling forward asset base valuations. The starting RAB consists of assets rolled forward from the previous control period, i.e. the opening book value plus allowed capital expenditure minus depreciation for the period in question maintained in real terms.

The key advantage of using the real[10] value of financial net investment is that prospective returns on investment will be driven by the cost of capital assessment

[10] Hence the RPI component in the pricing formula.

and the incentive mechanisms put in place by the regulator. This implies that the users (or more generally the consumers) carry the inflation risk as the RAB will be maintained in real terms. It also implies that the cost of capital applied is in real terms. This approach ensures greater certainty over future valuations of the asset base and hence should aid investor confidence. Therefore, whenever firms are privately or part-privately owned, this approach is likely to be preferable over a current cost approach. The latter approach is based on the replacement cost of assets. From an investor point of view this implies that investors are penalised for technological advancements where incremental costs are lower than average costs. From a regulator's point of view, this could result in perverse incentives with respect to innovation, and dynamic efficiency, as financing new investment might become more costly under such an approach.

Depreciation

The CAA has adopted an approach based on projected rather than actual depreciation. If actual depreciation is adopted the airport might have an incentive to adjust its capital expenditure plans, or engage in accounting 'gaming', in order to maximise the RAB at the next review. Since depreciation is an accounting construct rather than related to any actual economic costs, the CAA considers this undesirable.

Using actual depreciation also provides an added incentive to reduce capital expenditure between reviews, which is inconsistent with the CAA's general view that investment incentives are the critical challenge faced by the South East airports.

However, in practice, price controls are often based on a combination of economic data (i.e. future cash flows) and accounting data. Initial RABs are adjusted in part by accounting depreciation. Future cash flows include projected operating expenditure and capital expenditure.

Single Till RAB-based Approach

Airport regulation in the UK is currently based on a single till RAB based approach. In this approach not only the aeronautical but also the commercial revenues and costs of the airport are taken into account when determining the price cap for airport charges. The RAB therefore incorporates all airport assets regardless of their function and characteristics. The objective under the single till is to determine the level of airport charges so that the expected return across all activities reflects the regulatory cost of capital.

In practice, this involves costs and volume projections being translated into a multi-year price cap that is re-set periodically (five yearly) on the basis of newer information. The single till operates to offset the costs of monopoly airport services by the projected net profits on retail activities (less losses on certain public transport schemes). Depending on the level of commercial profits, this approach may result in the commercial activities bearing a substantial share of an airport's common costs. It potentially results in cross-subsidisation of the aeronautical activities if these fail to cover their incremental costs. However, it does not address excessive retail pricing.

The key drivers in the single till RAB- based approach are projected to be:

- capital expenditure:
- operating expenditure;
- passenger volumes for the whole business;
- revenue from sources other than airport charges; and
- the regulatory cost of capital.

The charges are set to allow the airport to earn its regulatory cost of capital and thus depend on the difference between the total revenue required to do so and the projected revenue from sources other than airport charges. Under the single till RAB-based approach, the price cap does not only apply to revenues of monopoly activities but also to the revenue of commercial activities. This mixing of aeronautical activities with commercial activities could potentially result in distorted decisions not only in relation to the monopoly activity but also in relation to the commercial activities: investments in the latter have the same policies applied to them over the long-term as aeronautical investments.

The regulated airport in its investment analysis will allow for the single till RAB-based regulated price plus the expected net profits from the unregulated activities over the first five years multiplied by projected volumes. The investment and operating costs are a cost to the firm as in the commercial model in the first period. In second and subsequent periods, the single till RAB approach "takes away" any excess earnings including profits from non-regulated activities and sets regulated prices relevant to the project to allow on-going operating expenditure and sunk capital expenditure to be recovered.

One critical point is that this approach distorts investment incentives because it turns costs into benefits, in taking away any super profits. The price cap increases incentives for regulatory gaming with regulated firms having incentives to under-spend projected capital programmes to gain the cash-flow and hence business value benefit within the control period, thus managing the regulator's response at the next review.

It is therefore in the interest of the firm to ensure that its projected cost base is as high as possible when the regulator sets the price cap. As a result, the firm is likely to enter in gaming to present its projected costs and its projected cost of capital as high as possible as the firm will be able to keep the difference between its regulatory cost of capital and its true cost of capital during the control period.

This regime has generated real price reductions but has provided weak incentives for allocative efficiency and weak investment incentives compared to a situation where prices reflect much higher short or long-run social marginal costs and values that are likely actually to prevail.

Assets in the Course of Construction

Given the fact that airport infrastructure projects tend to be lumpy, one of the key issues is how to treat assets in the course of construction (AICC) under a RAB approach. The two main options are either to account for these costs when these assets become operational as indicated by an output focus or to remunerate them while still in construction. In the former case, prices would be lower while the assets are still in construction: the incentives for the airport to ensure that the assets come on stream as soon as possible are clearly strong. However, from an economic perspective it would be counterintuitive as prices should be relatively higher during the periods of congestion and vice versa.

The other approach is to remunerate the assets while still in construction. This implies that airlines would at least in part pre-fund the assets. Remunerating AICC might reduce the need for price hikes when new capacity comes on stream, although it might not eliminate the need for price increases altogether. From an economic perspective, it is more sensible that prices are higher when resources are scarce (i.e. situation of excess demand).

Price Profiling

The second issue for the regulator to address when dealing with large and costly infrastructure projects is whether profiling should be used in determining the price caps. Profiling might entail revenue advancement from a later price control period to an earlier control period. The advantage of profiling is that it results in more stable prices and gives some assurance about regulatory crediblility and risk. Without profiling, the regulator would have to commit herself to large price increases when the new assets become operational. This is potentially an obstacle to raising funds for these types of investments, given the fact that nothing is known about what the world looks like at that point in time, and the investment is substantially sunk.

Airlines are likely to exert maximum pressure on the regulator to limit price increases, thus preventing the regulatee and its financiers from recouping their costs. Given the fact that control periods are set for a relatively short-term (5 years in the UK), in relation to the economic lives of the assets, this is a real issue when dealing with long-lived assets. The risk of such an approach is that investment becomes either very costly (financiers might view the project as very risky and might want to be remunerated if they expect that this type of regulatory risk is not diversifiable) or it might not proceed at all (which is likely to result in considerable welfare losses), because under the UK regime the regulator cannot commit her successor.

In order to raise finance for major and potentially risky infrastructure projects with long-lead times, regulatory credibility and regulatory commitment are of utmost importance. Profiling therefore aids the sustainability of a regulatory regime.

Price Path Commitment

In its price cap review, the CAA recognised that the application of single till cost-based price caps at the congested Heathrow and Gatwick airports has become increasingly problematic, forcing prices down and seriously out of line with the value of that capacity (as indicated by slot values) and the costs of new capacity.

However, setting caps to allow market-clearing prices, while permitting better use of scarce capacity, would provide weak incentives for development by the dominant BAA. The resulting rent transfers would be substantial, raising questions about the sustainability of such a policy.

In February 2002, the CAA proposed a compromise. The CAA proposed to maintain (modified) cost-based pricing for existing outputs at Heathrow and Gatwick while introducing more powerful incremental cost incentives for the delivery of new capacity. This would allow real prices to rise at the congested airports, reflecting the economic fundamentals and the long-term user interest. Nevertheless, although real prices would be allowed to rise, even under the proposed new regulatory regime, prices would have remained below (marginal) costs/values. Price profiling was to be used to prevent very large price hikes. Instead, over time, prices were to rise until in line with (marginal) costs.

The idea was to minimise regulatory risk through a simple and transparent foundation for the major investment programme planned, by bridging the gap between investment projects with long lead times and pay back periods and price caps that are fixed for only five years.

The price path commitment would have entailed a 20 year commitment on the price caps linked to current capacity and to Terminal 5, with arrangements for incentives for new investments, such as runways, to be considered separately and added on to the proposed commitment in a similar manner. The price path commitment was to be based on a dual till approach in order to provide headroom against negative shocks.

The objective was to give strong incentives to BAA to improve service quality and address the capacity-demand imbalance; however, the CAA was well aware of the regulatory risk involved. As the CAA set out in its original proposals, a move to a more high powered regulatory regime would hinge on regulatory commitment and hence on regulatory credibility. The move away from the single till was part of this commitment.

The fact that the Competition Commission has not recommended the dual till and has not recommended the price path commitment to be adopted and the fact that the current regulator cannot bind her successors, would have made the price path commitment less credible, which would have severely weakened its incentive properties. This has resulted in the CAA continuing with the RAB-based single till approach in line with the Competition Commission's recommendation. However, the CAA considers that the case for moving to a higher powered incentive regime in future would be substantially stronger if the airports were better able to demonstrate the potential benefits that it could bring, and considers that a range of possible mechanisms for providing enhanced investment incentives, and superior alternatives to both the single till or dual till, could be considered.

Conclusion

Regulation is a means to an end, not an end in itself. At the over-arching public policy level it is therefore important periodically to examine the trade-off between market failure and regulatory/government failure. Given the variety of problems regulation might seek to address, it should be noted that the regulator has only one instrument: the price cap.

Regulation is always second best to competition. Price cap regulation tends to limit price adjustment. The regulated price might not be consistent with long-run incremental costs, over the long-run. This might result in inefficient capacity levels resulting in excess demand and deteriorating service quality (e.g. delays). This would not only result in a loss of allocative efficiency but also of dynamic efficiency. Therefore, market structure options, while respecting property rights, should be used to the maximum extent if economic regulation can be avoided as a consequence.

Commercial firms, operating under a 'for profit' motive, face strong incentives to define and price outputs. However, if they have market power, they might restrict outputs with increased prices as a corollary. However, first best solutions may be unobtainable, but the potential downsides of economic regulation are significant. Regulated firms might spend a considerable amount of time and effort gaming the regulator rather than responding to the preferences of their customers.

In order to design and implement a regulatory framework based on high-powered incentives, regulatory credibility is essential. However, regulatory credibility will, to a large extent depend, on how far the regulator can pre-commit and this will depend on the institutional framework and the approach to regulation from the government and regulator alike.

Thus, when looking at the social loss function, regulation might not necessarily be the preferred option. It might be worthwhile to consider the potential for contracting between the airport and other parties. This would allow for risk (and return) sharing. Airlines would be an obvious contract counter-party for a major airport terminal development. It is well known that in US airports airlines often own terminals. Retailers would be other potential contractors with whom to lay off the project and volume risk.

Chapter 8

UK-Regulation from the Perspective of the BAA plc

Mike Toms

Airports Act

The first structured system for the economic regulation of airports was established by the UK Government in the 1986 Airports Act. Although the system was designed to be workable for both publicly and privately owned airports, its political context was a clear intention by the then Conservative government to privatise airports wherever possible. The intention of the regulation system was to capture the best features of private ownership and management, whilst ensuring that airports did not unreasonably exploit their market power. An appreciation of this philosophical framework is important to understanding why the system operates as it does.

The system is not intended simply to prevent airports making excessive profits; it aims to encourage cost efficiency in operations, and innovation in management and business development. The regulatory framework was built upon the structures previously created for the two major preceding privatisations, British Telecom (BT) and British Gas (BG). In both cases the emphasis was on 'light-touch' regulation, where having set a price formula for five years, the regulator would leave the company alone between reviews. (In practice, this deteriorated rapidly, and both industries were subjected to regular and increasing intervention.)

The key elements of the airport system were:

(1) The retention of BAA plc as the single owner of three London and four Scottish Airports (just as BT and BG had been privatised intact). This reflected the view that competition between airports was likely to be weak, and any benefits would be more than offset by the disbenefits of loss of economies of scale, dispersion of expertise, and fragmentation of the financial strength of BAA.

(2) The distinction between smaller regional airports, which were not felt to have sufficient market power to merit direct control of their prices, and larger airports (Heathrow, Gatwick, Stansted and Manchester) which were to be subject to direct price regulation.

(3) The adoption of price control, through a five year RPI-X type formula; using the model originally devised by Professor Stephen Littlechild for BT.
(4) The establishment of a statutory procedure for complaints about monopolistic behaviour by airports generally, with binding remedies.
(5) The absence of any formal incorporation of the delivery of service quality, or agreed capital investment, in the system.
(6) The identification of a sector regulator - the Civil Aviation Authority - but with the requirement to take advice from a general trading regulator - the Competition Commission - when the price formula was reset every five years.

The decision to create a single separate specific sector regulator for each privatised industry was in itself an interesting step. The Government had had the option of using pre-existing legislation (the Fair Trading Act and the Treaty of Rome), and existing regulatory bodies, to control the industry. These laws and institutions are powerful bodies, so why create another set of controls? The reasoning was never full articulated, but with the benefit of hindsight, it appears that:

(1) the Government wanted to provide each industry with a regulator having specialist expertise in that sector; and
(2) the general regulatory agencies (the Office of Fair Trading and the then Monopolies and Mergers Commission) operated in a highly autonomous way, and are not obliged to adopt any particular approach to regulation. The Government however wanted its political choice of RPI-X to be locked into the system.

So has the system stood the test of time? Have the five pillars of regulation remained standing over 15 years?

Airport Ownership

The decision not to break up BAA and introduce 'competition' between the London Airports was controversial, and has re-emerged at regular intervals. (Interestingly, the demand for break-up has tended to come from academics, political sources, and potential investors, rather than from airlines. With the exception of Virgin, British airlines have remained conspicuously neutral on the subject of airport ownership.) The notion of competing airports has a superficial attraction, particularly to free market economists in the 'think tanks'. It has been tested again periodically.

In 1991, the Monopolies and Mergers Commission (the predecessor to the Competition Commission) investigated the possibility of a "break up" in its five-yearly review of charges. It rejected the notion, albeit with a dissenting note from the Commissioner associated with right wing political and economic thinking.

In 1996, the Commission again considered requests that BAA be broken up, but concluded that BAA had not been guilty of any misconduct that justified this drastic action.

In 1999, the Chancellor, Gordon Brown, announced that the scope for competition between airports would be investigated, by a team led by the Deputy Prime Minister. Given the Chancellor's pro-competition views, it was expected that break-up was a real possibility.

However, having taken evidence from the Civil Aviation Authority, a joint team of the Departments of Transport, Trade and Industry and the Treasury, concluded that break-up would not offer benefits to consumers that outweighed the damage. It therefore concluded that break-up should not be pursued *at that time.* (This qualification is interesting, since if left in the air the possibility of break-up sometime in the future. This can be interpreted as a Sword of Damocles, designed to ensure the good conduct of the company; as such it is an effective piece of shadow regulation.)

Most recently, the Competition Commission again considered airport ownership, as part of its 2002 investigation. Again the notion was rejected, although the Commission suggested that the issue might need to be reopened after the Government has published its plans for the development of the airports in a policy statement (or 'White Paper') expected in late 2003.

These repeated debates have illustrated a number of clear themes;

(1) the notion of effective competition between airports at different locations, and with different networks, is seriously flawed. In practice this is not so important where airports are geographically closer, and transfer networks are not important, as in the case of the competing airports at Belfast.
(2) In London, Heathrow would enjoy a dominant position, which would fatally undermine the benefits of competition.
(3) Fragmentation of BAA would involve the loss of economies of scale, and dissipate centres of excellence in areas such as airport planning and security.
(4) Joint ownership of the three airports would provide a stronger financial structure, in which the investment troughs and peaks at individual airports could be absorbed within the larger group balance sheet.

The question of break-up and competition will therefore no doubt re-emerge in the future, and the threat provides a useful constraint on any inclination by the airport operator to abuse any dominant position it may enjoy.

Two Tier Regulation

Since 1986 there have been three attempts to extend direct price control to smaller regional airports.

In 1994, the Government investigated whether BAA's Scottish Airports should be subjected to RPI-X. BAA made a strong case against price control, and offered a voluntary package of measures, including a three year RPI-3 formula, to head off the threat. The Government accepted these undertakings and decided against any action.

In 1994, Easyjet sought price controls at Luton airport to prevent substantial price increases. The Government rejected this request on grounds that the airport was not profitable (!) and, interestingly, on the grounds that Easyjet could, if it wished, transfer its operation to Stansted.

Conversely, in 2001, the Government's Better Regulation Task Force recommended that the Government consider the lifting of price controls on BAA's airports to encourage direct negotiation with airlines and eliminate regulatory gaming. The increased general power to remedy monopoly abuse contained in the 1998 Competition Act could provide an effective backstop. Unfortunately, the Government did not act on this recommendation.

This position can be set against the decision of the Australian Government, to abandon RPI-X type price control at the major airports, for a trial period of five years, to test whether normal commercial negotiation will produce a more effective outcome. In doing so, they had recognised an important feature of airports, which is the countervailing economical and political power of small groups of highly organised and litigious customers.

RPI-X

The RPI-X approach to regulation was first adopted for airports as an extension of the principle originally devised as a temporary method of regulating telephone charges levied by British Telecom, until competitors emerged in the telecoms industry.

When RPI-X was imposed on airports it was initially opposed by airlines, who preferred Rate of Return, or Cost Plus regulation. Subsequently airlines have learned to support RPI-X for the benefits it brings in terms of cost control and guaranteed prices. RPI-X is now solidly established as the preferred basis of regulation by all sides of the industry.

However, in the course of the 1991 and 1996 Reviews, the application of RPI -X has tended to deteriorate into a strict single-till Rate of Return based formula, with protracted arguments about the cost of capital, the definition of the asset base and financial protections.

The formula itself has become progressively more complex, with somewhat spurious precision replacing simplicity and transparency. The latest manifestation of this is the proposed incorporation of triggers in the formula, linking the value of *X* in individual years to delivery of individual elements of capital projects.

Complaints Procedure

The Airports Act 1986 introduced a complaints procedure in which airport users could complain to the CAA about airport conduct that might be predatory, discriminatory or an otherwise unreasonable exploitation of monopoly. In addition, the Competition Commission was required to consider all public interest complaints at each five-yearly review.

Given the tendency of airlines to denigrate airport conduct, it is remarkable that there have been only 11 complaints to the CAA in the last 15 years. Complaints to the Commission have been made at each review, but with only minor consequences. Interestingly, while the flow of complaints dried up completely over the past five years, in the current (2002) review, the Commission received 87 separate complaints. Of these only two were upheld.

Airlines have argued that the CAA Complaints Process is too expensive, time consuming and bureaucratic, but an alternative interpretation is that the process has simply demonstrated that airlines have little confidence in the strength of their own complaints. It may be concluded that the existence of the complaints process has itself been an effective deterrent to unreasonable conduct by airports.

It is certainly true that the CAA has not encouraged airlines to complain, and the BAA has now stepped in to propose its own informal fast track internal complaints process. This provides an interesting example of self-regulation superseding imposed structures.

Service Quality

Interestingly, when the system of airports regulation was first established, little attention was given to service quality, and the issue did not even emerge in the first review in 1991. Paradoxically, at the next review, the Mergers and Monopolies Commission noted that the level of service quality had improved, but also bemoaned the absence of formal quality regulation as a structural weakness in the system. It therefore put the BAA on clear notice to engage with airlines on a voluntary system of Service Level Agreements with airlines, to avoid more formal regulation at the next review.

BAA did indeed discharge this obligation in full. However, at the current review, ever though the Commission has found service quality to be generally satisfactory, it has decided to implement a complex system of penalties for performance failure. It is not immediately clear how this reconciles with light touch regulation. It is however clear that it is a move towards the kind of interventionist quality regime that has served the railway industry so badly.

The Two-Regulator Model

The two-regulator model, with the CAA taking decisions, advised by the Competition Commission, contrasted with other sectors in the UK in which the single-sector regulator prevails, with the Competition Commission used only on appeal. The airports model originally had two purposes:

1) to provide a check on any wilful or extreme act intended by one regulator; and

2) to combine detailed knowledge of the aviation industry (held by the CAA) with the high level regulatory expertise on technical issues, such as cost of capital, held by the Competition Commission.

This has been possibly the most interesting area of the regulatory structure. At face value it should have led to a fine complementary. In practice, the result has been quite different. In the 1991 Review, the CAA rejected the Commission's use of an 8 per cent cost of capital, giving RPI-3, and proposed 7 per cent, equivalent to RPI-8. In the end, middle ground was found at 7½ per cent, equivalent to RPI-4.5. In this instance the CAA had usurped the Commission's expertise on Cost of Capital.

In the 1996 Review, there was a broad consensus around 7½ per cent, leading to RPI-3, although the CAA did float options on the phasing of charges that had been rejected by the Commission.

In the current review, at the time of writing, large-scale differences of approach appear to be emerging between the two regulators. The CAA approached the review from first economic principles - normally the remit of the Commission - whilst the Commission appears to be intent on simply defending the existing regulatory model with the aim of protecting the precedent it sets for all the industries it has to regulate. Differences have included such fundamental issues as:

- Dual or single-till
- System or stand-alone pricing
- Treatment of airport security
- Regulation of service quality

This is resulting in a long and intensive process with a highly uncertain outcome.

The situation points to some rules for regulation;

- Ideally, there should be a single regulator, but sufficiently accountable to avoid regulation by whimsy.
- If there are to be two regulators, their respective roles need to be closely and precisely defined.
- The relationship between the regulator of the specific sector, and regulatory precedent overall needs to be fully clarified. If not, there is the danger that decisions made in, say, water industry disputes, will drive airport regulation.

In undertaking analytical work, both regulators should have a mind to the fact that the rigour and quality of their analysis should be sufficient to satisfy not just themselves, but also the other regulator. The adoption of this principle by the CAA would certainly have eased the current review.

Where two regulators can differ as much as the CAA and Competition Commission appear to, the credibility of regulation itself is open to question. This is not helped when both regulators adopt confrontational styles, and engage in a manifest contest of academic arm wrestling. In that context, regulators could learn from the commercial companies they regulate, who have to manage their own business partner relationships towards agreement, not victory.

Conclusion

The regulation of airports in the UK was originally devised to create a climate in which airports act responsibly and commercially, and negotiate directly with strong and organised airlines within a fixed price ceiling, and without the distortions created by continuous regulatory interference. To this end, there was a simple price formula, reviewed through a simple review every five years.

What happened?

The first review, in 1991 took 12 months.
The second review in 1996, took 21 months.
The current 2002 review has taken 32 months.

The first formula was a simple value of *X*.
The current proposed formula is a value of *X*, with six trigger points, and a service quality scheme covering a dozen parameters. In addition, the BAA operates under a web of agreements and undertakings which has grown at each review.

So much for light touch regulation.

Chapter 9

New Approaches in Airline/Airport Relations: The Charges Framework of Frankfurt Airport

Michael Klenk

Current Economic and Political Background and its Effects on Air Traffic Business

Airlines have long been used to the cyclical nature of their industry given that economic upswings and downswings in world economy have increased in both frequency and amplitude while at the same time air traffic demand has tripled in the last 35 years. Current trends and developments seem to indicate that the route will become even more turbulent. In the year 2002 we have seen two major US carriers - United Airlines and US Airways - having to undergo Chapter 11 procedures. Taking a look at the performance of European Airlines in 2002 is also sobering. Passenger kilometres of AEA[1] Airlines was 4.6 per cent below the disastrous 2001[2] levels - although some like Air France, Lufthansa and in continental Europe Ryan Air were able to deliver satisfactory results. European tour operators (Thomas Cook, TUI, My Travel etc.) are facing their biggest crises ever with turnovers and customers down by 8-10 per cent compared with 2001. The tourist sector is especially suffering from weakening economies - headed by Germany - in some of the member states of the European Union, as well as international conflicts.

The increasingly globalised world seems to have entered an apparently longer period of political instability with war and terror risks becoming an almost "daily" and very burdensome "routine" on a worldwide scale; burdensome especially for enterprises involved in aviation. The instability is reflected in a second Gulf War, military action in Afghanistan, conflicts between Pakistan/India, North Korea/US, and the politically destabilised countries in South America such as Venezuela, Bolivia and Argentina, the loss of major destinations for many tour operators due to terrorist threats in Indonesia, Tunisia, Morocco and Egypt have shattered the industry's global perspective tremendously. On top of these, the outbreak of the SARS virus has lead to an almost complete breakdown of international air traffic from and to China.

---

[1] Association of European Airlines (AEA).

[2] Association of European Airlines official press release, February 5, 2003.

Airlines in the European Union are not only facing these above-mentioned challenges but also a regulatory policy, promoted strongly by the European Commission, in the environmental and security sector that has two effects: higher costs and lower productivity for airlines as well as airports.[3]

Furthermore, the airline market has become increasingly competitive, with Low Cost Carriers successfully entering and expanding in the domestic markets of established network carriers such as British Airways and Lufthansa. With their point-to-point operations in geographically confined markets they are obviously less prone to global economical and political distortions. Whereas many airports by and large still seem profitable and resilient to the overall industry sector's upheaval, the entrepreneurial survival of airlines has become more obvious than ever before with more than 30 airlines worldwide having to undergo insolvency procedures since September 2001.[4]

Overall, one can certainly argue that the air traffic sector as a whole is facing significantly higher risks with regard to the demand of its products and a substantial lower amount of planning reliability.

Incumbent Models of Setting Airport Charges

In light of the given economic, political and specific market background, the question arises as to whether the commercial relations between airports and airlines need to be adapted to the changing environment. Such a change may be necessary in order to provide a long-term sustainable business strategy for both. The significance of the question becomes apparent when taking a closer look at the nature of this relationship as not being one of an ordinary supplier and its customer. What is different in comparison to other commercial relations is the high mutual dependence on each other - one cannot exist without the other and each produces an indispensable "upstream" or "downstream" product for the other's business activity: The airport is providing the necessary infrastructure for the operation of an aircraft, which cannot be operated outside an airport's facilities, and it is the airlines' aircraft which deliver the essence - dare one say the spirit - to almost 100 per cent single purpose sites. And it is without doubt that the airlines' schedules shape the corporate position of most airports - a fact that holds true for Low Cost Carriers and even more for the networking carriers. Together the airports' and the airlines' respective services - basically infrastructure on one side, and air transport on the other - are actually combined to the joint product "air travel". The relation may as well be characterised as a "System Partnership".[5]

---

[3] White Book of the European Commission on Transport, 2000.

[4] United Airlines and US Airways are currently undergoing Chapter 11 procedures; American Airlines, the world largest airline, is still jeopardized to be subjected to Chapter 11 procedures. Air Canada, the largest Canadian airline, also faces similar procedures at the moment.

[5] P. Gerber, *Journal of Air Transport Management* 8 (2002) p. 29-36 (36).

Another specific trait of their co-existential link is that both are living from the same primary revenue source - which is the passenger.[6] The revenue stemming from a passenger's purchase of a ticket has inter alia of course to cover a flight's operational expenses, amongst which airport charges play an important role. Being significant costs for airlines on one side, charges deliver a crucial income source for the airport on the other side. But it is also the departing or landing passenger who provides for an airport's non-aviation revenues when spending money at retail shops - thus stimulating concession fees - or using an airport's parking sites for example.

However, delivering a joint product and living from the same revenue source does not mean that airports and airlines gain their proceeds under the same conditions. Actually the conditions differ considerably.

With regard to the airports - at least when referring to the most common charges regulated in European Countries - it is evident that they are entitled to calculate their aviation revenues according to the cost-plus-regime. Cost plus is understood as a method to calculate prices solely on the basis of cost incurred plus a certain amount of return on the capital employed without the need to set prices according to competitive influences. Basically, in most regulatory systems there is no incentive for airports to conduct any target costing approach in the process of setting charges.[7]

On the other hand, airlines are facing growing and intensive competition and have to earn their revenues under full market conditions. It is the market which defines the ticket prices (= revenues) and establishes what is affordable. As aircraft capacity will be operated where the best cost/revenue ratio can be found and with airport costs having a decisive impact on this ratio, competitive airport costs have become more relevant for the entrepreneurial survival of both airlines and airports.[8] However, since the mid 1990s, steadily declining yields and a continuous increase in airport charges have been shown to be a critical path for airlines (see Figure 9.1).

Hence, commonly applied airport pricing schemes not only seem to fail to provide for a balanced mitigation of interests, but they also constrain the ability of the whole aviation system to respond to the ever increasing ups and downs of the economic cycle. These business cycle fluctuations will become even more important in the future. In the long run this does not follow the idea of a sustainable partnership. Therefore, an alignment of the commercial relations seems to be due. New models for risk- and profit-sharing have to be found.

---

[6] Cargo provides revenue to airports and passenger airlines but the proportions are relatively low in comparison to passenger revenue.

[7] H.M. Niemeier, *Journal of Air Transport Management* 8 (2002) p. 37-48 (42).

[8] Airport charges which are subject to § 43 LufVZO and equivalently comprised of the Frankfurt charges model account for up to 16 per cent of direct operational costs of a domestic flight and 6 to 10 per cent of intra-European and international flights. Taking into account total turn around costs at an airport (airport charges, charges for centralised infrastructures, handling fees, security fees; see footnote 13) including ATC charges, the ratio would be the following: total turnaround costs on domestic flights: up to 40 per cent; intra-European and domestic: between 18 to 30 per cent. All figures refer to Lufthansa traffic in the year 2002.

Future Elements of a New Approach

We have argued above that the incumbent systems fail in delivering balanced results for both system partners and they especially lack the necessary flexibility to adapt to the changing market requirements. As the degree of exposure to market forces is different between airports and airlines, one conclusion might be to bring in more market-based elements in the commercial relationship.

The most significant market element we know is the demand for air travel, expressed as the number of enplaning/deplaning passengers using an airport.[9] This provides an opportunity for an airport to shift from solely cost-based airport charges to more market oriented ones. The natural linkage is to the development of the number of passengers. Today, in most cases, airport charges are already linked to the number of passengers being on board the departing or landing aircraft. At the same time, many airports also levy charges according to a fixed aircraft weight - the so-called Maximum Take Off Weight (MTOW) which is laid down in the aircraft's certificate. However, it is questionable, if the current structure of charges adequately reflects the market conditions. The following example may illustrate this.

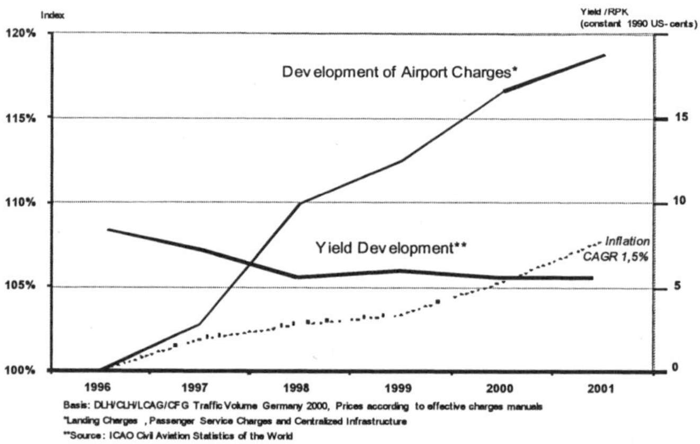

Figure 9.1 Cost/Yield – development

In Germany, the average ratio between passenger-related charges and fixed MTOW related charges accounts for 50:50.[10] Admittedly this is simplified but in the end it is still true: This means that 50 per cent of the revenues could still be earned by the airport even if not a single passenger was on board the departing or landing aircraft in a respective period and given no schedule adjustments were

---

[9] Other measurements of demand could be movements of aircraft, take off weight or cargo transported. However, the author chose the measurement of passengers using an airport since this is still the most important economic value driver for airlines as well as for airports.

[10] Aircraft parking charges are not specifically taken into account but treated as MTOW charges. As aircraft parking charges do not correlate to the number of passengers their economic effects are the same as MTOW charges: they are fixed and not variable.

made by the airline. In other words: Whereas an airline would operate without any revenue an airport may be relatively lucky to obtain at least half of what was expected. In a state of growing fluctuations and on a long term scale, even more extreme volatility of air travel demand adjustments seem to be appropriate in order to find a new balance.

Therefore, one element of a new approach might be to design the structure of charges schemes to be more variable, i.e. more on a per passenger base. Of course, some may argue that this simply means economically shifting market risks onto the airports. It certainly cannot be denied that a greater participation of an airport in the market risk would be the case. But would the only consequence of such a change be to make airports more susceptible to an economy's downturn effects? Or could there even be benefits for both airports and airlines, a so-called win-win situation?

Without in-depth discussion a more variable design of charges might have the following features.

(a) First, with a more variable charging scheme, some objectives that usually are attributed to a formal economic regulation,[11] such as cost efficiency and adequate incentives for investments, increasing the productivity of the airport etc, could be achieved naturally. Passengers are not only the "life-spending" income source of an airline they are also the most important value driver for an airport, being "responsible" not only for a significant portion of aviation revenues, but also for the increasingly more important non-aviation revenues. Moreover, passenger-related charges make an airport reflect market demands all along the value chain of its services and products. Thus, proper managerial decisions in terms of cost, investments and allocation of labour forces are, in principle, ensured as every decision is taken under market impact – a prerequisite to enhance economic welfare. Apart from this, viewing the issue more practically, the above outlined idea of airports and airlines delivering a joint product is also better reflected in their commercial relationship.

(b) Secondly, some variability of charges provides a promising and fair commercial perspective for airports and airlines at the same time. By linking the level of charges to the passenger development, airlines could be rewarded with declining charges if a target growth number is reached. This would take into account that passenger growth is owed to airlines' prior investments in sales and distribution channels, of which airports benefit. On the other hand, given an extraordinary decline of traffic, airports could be entitled to increase charges to a limited degree above average if a parallel decrease of fixed charges was introduced at the same time. Both, the benefits of growth and the negative effects of a passenger downturn could be "shared" in a fairer way than before as airports and airlines are subject to a stronger obligation to reflect and to communicate to each other their expectation of market developments.[12]

(c) Thirdly, a more-passenger focused design could contribute to specific revenue prospects for airports while reducing unit costs for airlines (see Figure 9.2). At German airports from 1996 until 2000 the average yearly growth rate of

[11] H.M. Niemeier, *Journal of Air Transport Management* 8 (2002) p. 37–48 (38).

[12] Ideally airports and airlines agree on a risk and profit sharing model. This is what the "Frankfurt Charges Model" comes close to.

passengers was 6 per cent, whereas the increase of MTOW was only 3.9per cent p.a., meaning higher load factors. This ratio is not only likely to be a realistic projection for the future but is expected to develop even more in favour of passenger growth for two reasons: new large aircraft offering more seat capacity, such as for example the A330 or A380, are to replace smaller aircraft. And low cost carriers are operating their aircraft with higher seating density. Figure 9.2 shows how greater proportionate airport revenues may be created, if the ratio of fixed (MTOW) to variable (passenger-related) charges were changed from 60:40 to 40:60. At the same time airlines have the opportunity to reduce their fixed unit flight costs since - within given elasticities and dimensions of competition - passenger related charges can be directly passed through to the passenger in the ticket prices ("tax box effect").[13] Consequently, airlines are, to a larger extent, only then due to pay charges and deliver revenue to an airport when they themselves are able to rely upon revenue.

(d) Fourthly, flexible, transparent and efficient options for environmental charges in the field of noise and gaseous emissions are provided with a charges scheme that refers to the passenger using the respective airport.

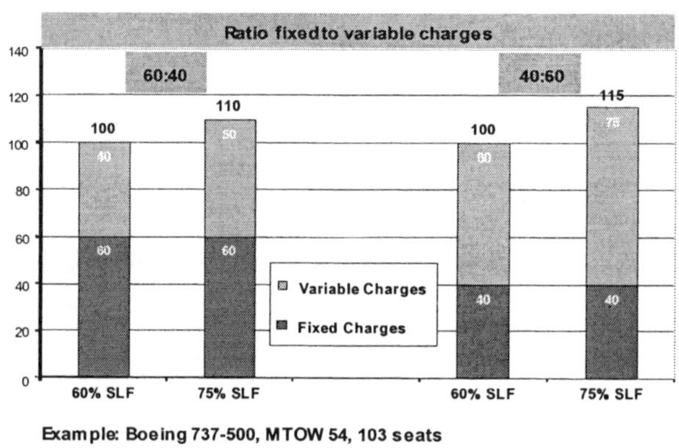

Figure 9.2 Commercial perspectives of more variable charges

[13] It has to be stated clearly that in competition among airlines, respectively between airline alliances - especially when competing for transfer passengers – the total cost of an aircraft's turn around at an airport are decisive. Total turnaround costs consist of all costs incurred when an aircraft lands at an airport, picks up passengers and departs. Total turn around costs include: airport charges, charges for centralised infrastructures, handling fees, security fees, rents. Therefore, passenger charges can not "endlessly" be passed through to the passenger without producing a competitive disadvantage in the composition of the ticket price. Actually there are clear hints that even small differences in the ticket price between competing airlines influence a passenger's choice for an airline and can only to a limited extent be compensated by an airline's "premium" (Frequent Flyer Programmes, reputation etc).

Passenger-related environmental airport charges - especially if they are made visible in airline tickets or even in catalogues of tour operators - could accomplish numerous effects; they make the external costs of air travel visible to those who demand travel - thus following the often-postulated concept of polluter pays environmental cost pricing.

This would be in contrast to concepts currently discussed on a European Union level,[14] which propose inter alia to introduce in addition to already existing environmental charges, en route charges for CO_2-emissions[15] and link noise charges exclusively to engine performance, and fixed charges.

In contrast to these ideas a more variable system for environmental charges would have several advantages:

- It would keep transaction costs low, as it is incorporated in a existing accounting system.
- It is transparent as it avoids strenuous (pseudo) scientific attempts to find a fair and just measure to determine and implement environmental costs in a pricing scheme for modes of transport.
- Due to competition among airlines, and between airlines and other modes of transport, for low prices such charges maintain their function to provide an incentive for environmentally friendly behaviour. Either competitive price advantages result in internal cost savings, which have a natural limit, or they are due to better environmental performance.

It goes without saying that such a concept is not to be misunderstood as simply another source of tax revenue. Given the current business environment it would, from an airline perspective, only be feasible and acceptable, if the implementation was revenue (cost) neutral with regard to the individual airport concerned. The fault critics often seem to find with this approach is a clear incentive function. This is not convincing as airlines - due to competition - have a natural business habit to keep operating expenses as low as possible and are therefore interested in a good environmental performance. This holds true for all costs, whether they are fixed or variable. The decisive difference in the current widespread concepts of fixed environmental charges is that, in a variable system, airlines are only burdened if a corresponding revenue exists.

Although not being perfect and certainly to be developed further, a concept of variable environmental charges seems at least to be a feasible approach in reconciling environmental objectives with economic interests - which is not often

---

[14] *White Book of the European Commission on Transport,* 2000, p. 45. To avoid misunderstandings: the criteria for defining the exact level of a passenger-related environmental charge and a necessary differentiation would still have to be found (long haul versus short haul aircraft, gaseous emissions during take off and landing cycle etc). Once such criteria are set up the author proposes to express and levy the price on a per passenger base.

[15] These are to be administered by a European body - perhaps Eurocontrol.

accomplished nowadays.[16] The latter - self-explanatory - is in the mutual interest of airports and airlines, both being confronted more and more with regulatory issues in the environmental sector.

Summing up the basic features of a more variable approach to charges schemes one may draw the following conclusions.

(a) Such an approach would incorporate market conditions within the pricing scheme of an airport and mitigate the commonly estimated shortcomings of a simple cost-based system.
(b) A structural shift to more variable charges does not only lead to a greater participation in market risks by an airport but also provides a set of options that enables airports as well as airlines to reap beneficial effects they otherwise were not able to gather.

It may therefore be a worthwhile approach to be taken in the commercial relations between airports and airlines.

The New Charges Framework of Frankfurt Airport

History

In April 2002, Frankfurt Airport (Fraport) and the Board of Airline Representatives in Germany (BARIG),[17] the German Air Carrier Association (ADL)[18] and Lufthansa signed a Memorandum of Understanding (MoU) on the future development of airport charges for the term between the year 2002 and 2006. The MoU concluded negotiations of more than one and a half years. These negotiations had been severely interrupted twice: first, when Fraport unilaterally suspended talks in early summer 2001 with regard to its ongoing Initial Public Offering (IPO) with roughly 30 per cent of the airport stake being transferred to private owners.[19] Second, only a couple of days after talks had been resumed, the events of 9/11 led to a suspension until January 2002. Those interruptions show that the genesis of the MoU was anything but a smooth one. The parties were able to finally conclude the MoU more than 8 months after 9/11, despite the substantial blurring of the economic perspective of air traffic from a clear growth scenario to a rather clouded

---

[16] It would be even conceivable that variable airport charges are used to recycle their revenue into environmental projects (noise insulation programmes, environmental protection measures etc), if certain criteria were cumulatively met, such as: competitive level of charges, transparent use of proceeds, equal financial participation of airport (with non-aviation revenues), means of last resort to avoid strict operational restrictions.

[17] BARIG represents 107 German and foreign air carriers that are operating services in Germany.

[18] ADL represents the German charter and leisure carriers.

[19] In fact the MoU was yet ready to be signed at the end of April 2001 when Fraport Executive Board decided not to sign the fully negotiated text of the agreement and suspended talks. As a result, relations between airlines and airport worsened substantially until talks were taken up again.

outlook.[20] The MoU has certainly been catalysed by the regulation of Hamburg Airport which was established in 2000 in the course of the privatisation process.[21] Similar to Hamburg, it was important to the airlines that along with privatisation of Frankfurt Airport a mechanism was established to prevent monopoly abuse and make privatisation acceptable.

Legal Construction

Legally the MoU can be perceived as a multilateral contract under private law. In Germany, the commercial relation between airports and their users is also subject to private law. Airport charges and the respective services connected to them hence share the same legal nature. Nevertheless, airport charges are subject to a formal approval by the local government.[22] In the case of Frankfurt, the responsible body is the state of Hessia's ministry of economic affairs.[23] The approval of charges by the local authority, in contrast to the commercial relation between airport and airlines, belongs to the public law regime. In consequence, the granted or missing approval of charges is only effective in the relationship between the authority and the airport and relates the question of supervision. The regulatory approval of airport charges legally is not constituent for their effectiveness in commercial relations between an airport and its users.[24]

Therefore, Fraport and the negotiating airlines first sought to settle matters in a private law contract, the MoU.[25] The contents of this contract subsequently have to be fully transferred - into an additional 5 year public law contract - to be concluded between the regulator and the airport. The public law contract replaces the formerly needed yearly governmental approval of the charges level for the duration of 5 years (2002- 2006).[26] The structure of charges is later subject to the consent of a special panel, called the Review Board, in which the airlines, the

---

[20] It deserves notion that the negotiating parties on behalf of the airport in the end managed to overcome scepticism towards the agreement within their own organisation.

[21] H.M. Niemeier, *Journal of Air Transport Management* 8 (2002) p. 37-48.

[22] H.M. Niemeier, *Journal of Air Transport Management* 8 (2002) p. 37-48 (40).

[23] It has to be noted that the state of Hessia owns a 31 per cent stake in Frankfurt airport and keeps the chair in the supervisory board of Frankfurt Airport - as do many other approval bodies for airport charges in Germany at other airports. German private corporate law obliges members of the supervisory board not to act against the interest of the represented company. From an airline perspective, this regulatory setting is an ambivalent one that cannot be perceived as independent and "neutral".

[24] It has to be conceded that the approval, despite the described legal implications does have a strong factual effect in a way that airports usually in Germany have so far not commercially implemented charges unless they had governmental approval.

[25] In Hamburg, the price cap regulation introduced in 2000 - the first ever in Germany - was nota bene established without prior civil law contract. As the acceptance of the price cap regulation was an obligatory requirement in the tender for Hamburg Airport's privatisation and hence strictly enforced by the Ministry of Economic Affairs, no prior contractual agreement between airport and airlines was necessary.

[26] The full text of both agreements, the public contract as well as the MoU, are published in the Journal "*Nachrichten für Luftfahrer*" Part I NfL 328/02, http://www.dfs.de/dfs/deutsch/inhalt/aviation_services_business.

government and the airport are represented. If no agreement between airport and airlines can be reached about structural changes, the airport can launch, as in the past, a formal request for approval to the local government (Figure 9.3).

Content

The key elements and, in many respects, new approaches of the Frankfurt Charges Framework are the following.

(a) The scope of the framework comprises all aviation revenues that the airport is entitled to levy according to the respective national legal stipulation which is § 43 Luftverkehrszulassungsordnung (§ 43 LuftVZO). Practically, it includes the fixed, the variable and the parking charges. However, it does not (yet) contain rules concerning the charges for centralised infrastructures according to the EC Directive 96/67 on the liberalisation of the ground handling market in the European Union.[27]

As their nature is a clear monopolistic one and they are not subject to any governmental approval it would have been desirable from an airline perspective to have them under the contract, too. So far, the parties have agreed to negotiate as to how to incorporate charges for centralised infrastructure into the contract. Explicitly not included are any potential additional costs of the airport's extension programme for a fourth runway and new terminal in Frankfurt.[28]

[27] Article 8 of EC Directive 96/67 defines Centralised Infrastructure Facilities as follows: *Official Journal of the European Communities*:
"1. Notwithstanding the application of Articles 6 and 7, Member States may reserve for the managing body of the airport or for another body the management of the centralised infrastructures used for the supply of groundhandling services whose complexity, cost or environmental impact does not allow of division or duplication, such as baggage sorting, de-icing, water purification and fuel-distribution systems. They may make it compulsory for suppliers of groundhandling services and self-handling airport users to use these infrastructures.
2. Member States shall ensure that the management of these infrastructures is transparent, objective an non-discriminatory and, in particular, that it does not hinder the access of suppliers of groundhandling services or selfhandling airport users within the limits provided for in this Directive".

[28] However, in the meantime the parties have already taken arrangements on how to handle costs incurred with the airport's necessary planning procedures and audits with the competent external agencies for the extension programme. They are considered to be preliminary costs that have to be regarded separately from financing the extension itself.

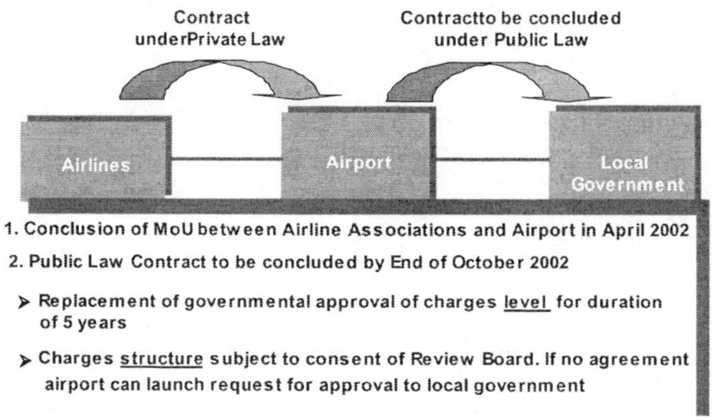

Figure 9.3 Frankfurt charges model: history and construction

Here, too, the opening of the scope of the agreement to such costs was agreed upon with the provision that the exact implementation is a matter for future negotiations at due time.

(b) The heart of the Frankfurt charges framework is the price setting formula. Unlike Hamburg, which has a CPI-x formula, the negotiating parties chose a risk-sharing model that strongly links the level of charges to the development of passenger demand. The basic characteristics are as follows.

- The formula was developed in a fixed revenue approach over the 5 years' period of the contract.
- The allowed maximum of total revenues granted within one calendar year to the airport is determined by a "referential quotient" (RQ). This means that all revenues in a period (n) are added to a total and then divided by the number of passengers. The referential quotient itself can only be derived through application of the formula in connection with the projected development of passenger demand. Deviations between the projected and the actual passenger volume - in terms of decline as well as unforeseen increases - are compensated in subsequent periods ($n + 2$).
- The risk sharing effects of the formula emerge as follows.

Airlines have a 33 per cent share in additional revenues generated due to extra passenger volume compared to the parties' projections. This amounts to a 67 per cent windfall profit for the airport. The other way round, i.e. in times of traffic decline, the airlines bear the risk of a passenger shortfall merely to the extent of 33 per cent, which limits the airport's right to compensate for loss of traffic through potential increases in charges.

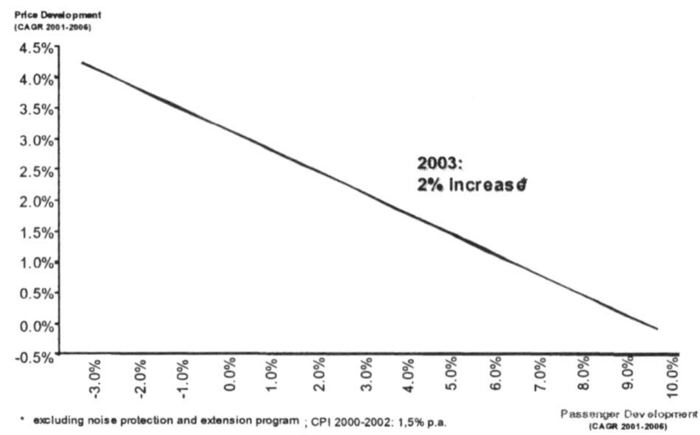

Figure 9.4 Frankfurt – Model

The effects of the formula are illustrated in Figure 9.4. In contrast to formulas at other places such as Hamburg or Vienna, which link the development of the charges level to the passenger volume only after certain thresholds are reached, the Frankfurt Model provides a continuous sliding scale.

(c) A special Review Board was established in which the negotiating airlines, the airport and the local government are represented. The Review Board meets regularly and has the task of providing in-depth, efficient and transparent consultation on the contract. All matters concerning the implementation of the agreement shall be discussed here such as, for example, possible structural shifts of charges or the application of the formula, and brought to a settlement. Special provisions are laid down to ensure that comprehensive data are provided by the airport with regard to development of traffic, productivity and investments in order to accomplish a meaningful consultation process.

(d) The framework also contains provisions for a noise protection fund which the local government obliged Fraport to establish effective 2002. The final settlement of this matter was preceded by bleak expectations on the funding and its conditions. Four months after 9/11 the airlines saw themselves economically incapable of bearing the full financial burden of the programme until certain conditions had been met. Among which, the conclusion of the MoU and the incorporation of the funding formula in the contract were the most important. The parties finally agreed upon the following conditions:

- The funding through charges is time and budgetary limited (for the duration of the contract and to a maximum sum of € 76 million).
- Separate and transparent monitoring of the fund employment is ensured with possible repayments of unemployed means at the end of term.

- The fund is largely financed through variable charges, specifically to a degree of 75 per cent.

(e) In addition, the framework contains a clause in which airlines are waiving any legal action against the level of charges. It has addressed the issue of quality with a commitment by Fraport to maintain and develop a competitive level of quality complying with the international standards of a hub airport, but leaves the definition of detailed parameters to a working group.

Assessment

The Frankfurt charges framework shall be briefly assessed from three different angles – from a regulatory, economic and political perspective.

(a) From a regulatory point of view the Frankfurt model shows that even within an entrenched legal environment new and future oriented solutions are possible. What is necessary is a common will of all parties involved and a mutual understanding of the overall benefits of the chosen approach. This definitely is easier said than done: if there had not been a certain bargaining momentum at the beginning of the talks between Frankfurt airport and the airlines, which gave the latter a certain wind of opportunity - triggered by a mixture of political issues simmering around the public discussions of the airport extension, some hard economic facts, legal disputes at other airports and the publicly well noticed privatisation process[29] - the Frankfurt framework would not have been possible. Once talks had started the local government - to the surprise of the airlines - began to support the conclusion of the MoU and finally acted as a facilitator in some matters. So the route to the charges agreement in Frankfurt was definitely not - unlike Hamburg - a well coordinated "top down" approach to establish a new mechanism of economic regulation. It was indeed a rather itinerant journey, which showed that a commonly accepted culture of such solutions was not yet existing. Therefore, discussion and promotion of models for independent regulation are still necessary and needed, given the fact that the Hamburg as well as the Frankfurt system are time limited.

(b) Evaluating the economic aspects of the Frankfurt framework in retrospect one can clearly see that Frankfurt is one step beyond Hamburg. Times have changed since the Hamburg contract was concluded at the beginning of 2000 and therefore the parties had to find a solution to cope with the effects of traffic decline. They actually dispensed with the famous CPI-x formula and found other ways to put their commercial relationship on a new platform. One year after implementation, it seems too early for an in-depth economic analysis of the framework, but some general remarks may be made.

---

[29] Adding to that, the privatisation of Amsterdam Schiphol, which Fraport is linked to in the so-called "Pantares" Alliance, was put off by parliament in the Netherlands. "Pantares" is the name for the alliance between Fraport and Schiphol; it was postponed.

- The model delivers a more controlled and foreseeable development of charges for both sides. Planning security in terms of costs for airlines and revenues for airports is enhanced - a not to be underestimated factor in the given economic environment. For the year 2003, the formula grants Fraport an increase of the RQ by 2.0 per cent, which seems to be a lot compared with the obligation of Hamburg airport to keep charges constant for more than two years. Yet it has to be kept in mind that this result reflects not only the described evolution of the Frankfurt model in its historical and political context but also the fact that Frankfurt, as the second largest airport in Europe, differs in its financial requirements from Hamburg.
- Having linked the charges development to the value driver passenger, market elements have been introduced in the price setting mechanism. This implies that one has moved one step away from simple cost-plus price setting, although strong elements can still be found as, in determining the formula, a fixed revenue approach was chosen. This shortcoming is partly outweighed by the risk sharing model which grants airlines, for the first time ever, that they receive a financial reward in reducing fees if they deliver growth. At the same time, the airport's possibilities to simply increase charges to compensate for lower traffic volumes are capped. Overall, it seems reasonable to state that the new price setting mechanism has substituted the formerly missing market elements and has hence achieved what is to be considered a foremost goal of economic regulation: to avoid monopoly pricing by setting incentives to correct "market failures" or create virtual market conditions when markets do not exist.

The depicted variable elements - also in the environmental sector - better reflect the idea of a joint product air travel than the old regime. They have largely facilitated the funding of the noise insulation programme and help airports and airlines to better mitigate environmental concerns with regard to the planned extension. The whole set of stipulations in their combination and mutual effects seem to provide for a - albeit not perfect - time adequate and certainly more comprehensive commercial approach. It remains to be seen whether the parties are able to reap the benefits to the sake of each other's prosperity.

(c) Assessing the political implications, a difference has to be made between an internal view, i.e. in a closer sense the psychological effects between the negotiating partners, and an external look at the matter, i.e. the significance of the Frankfurt model for the discussion at other airports in Europe and for air transport policy.

- From an internal perspective, the importance of the Review Board has to be emphasised. Already at this state it can be said that the consultation process has improved in terms of transparency and efficiency. Better consultation of the users enhances trust and finally leads to higher customer satisfaction. In addition, the Review Board has already adopted the features of a dispute settlement institution with the local government only then intervening if consensus cannot be reached by the parties. Finally, the MoU has without doubt appeased many difficult issues in the complex commercial relationship between airports and airlines. As the commercial relationship goes beyond charges (ground handling, lease arrangements etc) and is only the monetary reflection of complicated operational - and very often controversially discussed - ties between an airport and its users, the MoU disposed of some gravel lying on the path ahead.

- From an external perspective, it has been remarkable to observe that, in the meantime, some German airports have shown interest in a similar charges settlement.[30] Yet, initial negotiations have so far only been taken up with the airport of Hanover. As the European Commission recently has been said to revive the plans of a European Directive on airport charges - though explicitly on a much more light-handed and limited approach than the two failed efforts tried before - the Commission might give hints that a contractual agreement between airports and airlines could be an option for the member states to adopt some principles of economic regulation.

Summary and Outlook

Growing cyclical fluctuations in the air traffic sector in combination with the, to be expected, vast changes of the worldwide political agenda, demand - from airports, airlines and governmental authorities - more willingness and speed to adapt. This is essential if one is to sustain the economic welfare of air traffic for the economy as a whole and to acknowledge international mobility of people (and goods) as a fundamental and necessary principle in a globalised world. As recent developments are very likely to become long term trends, it seems high time to re-align commercial relations between airports and airlines according to current market demands. Although confronted with a difficult environment in Frankfurt a path has been chosen that seems to provide a setting of parameters that might be suited for the airport and its users to weather looming difficulties in their common stride ahead.

---

[30] Worth noticing in this context is the fact that some airports announced vigorously they were not to accept a "price cap" regulation but showed interest to conclude a MoU like the Frankfurt one.

Chapter 10

Privatization in Austria: Some Theoretical Reasons and First Results about the Privatization Proceeds in General and of Vienna Airport

Friedrich Schneider

1. Introduction

Privatization has been a key element of structural reforms in most European Union countries, including Austria, during the last decade. Governments undertaking privatization have pursued a variety of objectives: achieving gains in economic efficiency, given the extensive prevalence of poor economic performance of public enterprises in many countries and limited success with their reform; and improving the fiscal position, particularly in cases where governments have been unwilling or unable to continue to finance deficits in the public enterprise sector. In addition, budgetary-constrained governments, facing fiscal pressures have sometimes privatized mainly to finance fiscal deficit with the privatization proceeds.

The issues of privatization (and sometimes deregulation) have been reviewed in a large literature on the various aspects of privatization, and this literature has emphasized the potential efficiency gains.[1] The goal of this paper is twofold: firstly, to provide some theoretical reasoning why privatization is useful and has occurred and secondly, to illustrate the extent of privatization in Austria. First, in section 2, the reasons why privatization is necessary are elaborated. Second, in part 3, the privatization proceeds for Austria and the one of the Vienna Airport are presented. Finally, in part 4, a short summary of these findings is given.

2. Reasons for Privatizing Public Enterprises

For at least the last century, economists have employed a positive economic theory to explore the implications of wealth maximization by private firms operating in private property contexts. Only since the late 1960s have empirical studies dealing

[1] Surveys of the privatization literature is provided in Megginson and Netter (2001), Boes und Schneider (1996), Bartel und Schneider (1991) and a summary for the earlier discussion is given in Borcherding et al (1982).

with the behaviour of publicly operated firms been undertaken.[2] Since then, a large number of studies of a variety of activities now exists and their main focus is the question of how public firms differ from their private equivalents.

Basically two methods are employed. The first, explored in section 2.1, is the property rights approach. It concentrates on the differences in the ease of captureability of economic surplus of a resource and the rights to direct an asset's use, alter its form or transfer its claims among existent and potential owners. In short, this approach explores the differences in incentives between public and private agencies caused by variation in the ability of owners to monitor management and the problems that emerge when the goals of "owners" and their agents, "managers" diverge.[3] The second is "Public Choice approach" (elaborated in section 2.2) and concentrates on political coalitions and their effect on input usage and reward and/or product characteristics. The Public Choice approach also includes the theory of bureaucracy (see Niskanen, 1971, 1975).

2.1. The Property Rights Approach

The property rights approach points out one crucial difference between private and public firms, i.e. the practical difficulties in transferring ownership rights among individuals in the public sector and the relative ease of such transactions with private assets which includes, of course, the ability of owners (citizens) to monitor their agents' (elected officials' and bureaucrats') behaviour. By now, this approach pioneered by Armen Alchian is well known, but it is useful to recall his predictions: government managers will not organize the inputs under their direction in such a way as to maximize the wealth of the ultimate owners, the general citizenry. Alchian predicts, therefore, that public firms will be less efficient, their management will enjoy "quieter lives" and because of this the public will give them lower levels of discretion than their colleagues in private firms. To put it another way, the property rights approach is concerned with any type of cooperation in which ownership and management are separate. The emerging principal-agent problem may be prevalent in private enterprises as well, but to a much lesser extent. Numerous studies have been undertaken which have tested this proposition and the result that public enterprises are less efficient then private ones is confirmed in most of them.[4]

To sum up the results so far: the property rights approach seems to indicate that (1) private production is cheaper than production in publicly owned and managed firms and (2) given sufficient competition between public and private producers (and no discriminatory regulations and subsidies) the differences in unit cost turn out to be insignificant. From this, one may conclude that it is not so much the difference in the transferability of ownership but the lack of competition that leads to the often observed and less efficient production in public enterprises.

---

[2] Compare e.g. Borcherding, et al (1982) and Boes and Schneider (1996).

[3] The first approach has been developed by Alchian (1961, 1965) and more recently Baron and Myerson (1982), Grossman and Hardt (1983) and MasColell et al (1995).

[4] Compare the study by Boes and Schneider (1996), Schneider (1997, 2002), Schneider and Hofreither (1990). As these results are so well known, they are not reported here.

2.2. The Public Choice Approach

The public choice approach appears to provide a broader analysis than the property rights one. The public choice approach assumes that politicians, bureaucrats, managers of public enterprises are selfish utility maximizers subject to constraints.[5] In this approach it is, for example, assumed that a politician acts selfishly in order to reach his ideological or personal goals under constraint not to lose the next election. Since, for a politician, to stay in power is a most important constraint (or sometimes the only goal), he will also use public utilities for his own selfish goals. One reason for this is evidently the lack of incentives for politicians and tax payers to exert effective control of public enterprises or efficient use of resources in the economy. This argument seems especially valid for the case of public utilities. Public utilities offer excellent opportunities to reach the selfish re-election goals of governments, like additional employment and the stabilization of purchasing power of certain regions.[6] If such a "misuse" of public utilities or enterprises leads to full employment and higher income, at least for a certain time span, then it is easier for a government to win an election without such a "misuse" of public utilities. The cost of such a policy can be made invisible for several years (or even one or two legislative periods) as the deficit of the public enterprises can be hidden in the general budget deficit.

As the public choice approach is more concerned with micro-economic aspects, De Alessi claims that public managers are growth not wealth orientated. He argues, and finds supporting evidence, that this leads to larger staffs and, higher capital labour ratios since excess capital makes managers and their subordinates' productivity appear higher to their monitoring agents, the legislature. Borcherding, et al (1977) argue that public employees effectively coalesce through their organizations and "capture" civil service commissions over time, altering rules in such a way that effective suppliers of competing labour to public firms become less wage elastic than a free market buyer would otherwise face. This public employee market power is enhanced, they claim, by the fact that public service employees contribute to the election of the ultimate "bosses", definitely not an option for a private sector union. In some sense then, public employees can alter the position of the derived demand schedule for their services by (a) "nudging" the final demand schedule for public services to the right and (b) specifying rules that lower both the elasticity of substitution between themselves and rival factors and the elasticity of supply of these close substitutes. Both (a) and (b) will tend to raise wages, but they may raise employment too, since, in effect, the budget and tie-in effects may offset the usual substitution effects one might derive out of the neoclassical models of labour demand in the presence of a simple monopoly. De Alessi (1974), in another paper, argues that given the relative loose monitoring of public enterprises by the political review authorities, a rational position for the latter given the gain-sharing results of assiduous monitoring, managers will indulge their taste for security rather more than in private firms. He finds evidence consistent with the risk-

---

5 Compare Schneider and Frey (1988), Bartel and Schneider (1991) and Pardo and Schneider (1996) and Schneider (2002).

6 For example for Austria, Upper Austria and Styria compare Schneider (2002) and Bartel and Schneider (1991).

avoiding hypothesis. Public managers' tenures are more secure, of a longer duration, and their fluctuations in real wages are lower than their private counterparts.

In conclusion, according to the public choice scholars, governmental agencies and firms have distinct biases leading to higher production costs, just as the property rights literature suggests, but also excessive outputs. The latter obtains because the staff of the bureaucracy can affect demand more readily under monopoly public ownership by the strength of its members' votes and/or lobbying efforts. The absence of a civil service and the constraint on strong unions under more competitive types of supply, public or private, are thought to reduce the ability of members of such bureaucracies to offer their services to the legislature on disadvantageous terms compared to potential competitors. On the other hand, the bureaucracy is not likely to have sole "capture" rights over the bureaus, but to share the ownership claims with other interests.

To sum up this part, the public choice approach not only recognizes the differences in behaviour between publicly owned and managed firms and private ones, owing to the limited transferability of ownership. It also considers the likely oversupply of public services owing to the lack of competition in their provision and production. This oversupply is then quite often used for the selfish re-election goals of politicians and can result in higher employment and higher wages in certain regions for a certain time.[7]

2.3 Summary of main findings

Summarising the two approaches, one clearly comes to the result that, as already noted in the introduction, there are various reasons to privatize public utilities or enterprises in order to stop the misuse of such policies. In the next section I investigate to what extent privatization has occurred in the European Union and in Austria.

3. The Amount of Privatization in Austria

3.1 General results

Privatization and proceeds from privatization have been substantial all over the world. Since the beginning of the 1980s, numerous instances of privatization in market orientated industrial countries, but also in transition and developing countries, have been taken place.

A detailed picture of the privatization proceeds of single countries is given in table 10.1.

Comparing Germany with Great Britain, it is evident that the largest privatization proceeds were achieved at the beginning of the 1990s, with US$12.9 and US$21.8 billion in the years 1990 and 1991 in Great Britain. In the following

[7] The Austrian type of Keynesian policy used the public enterprises and state-owned firms for such purposes quite successfully over the period 1971-1986. Compare section 3.2 and Schneider (2002).

years, in Great Britain the privatization proceeds were decreasing but still sizeable. By contrast, in Germany, it is evident that the privatization proceeds were greatest in 1996, with US$13.228 billions. This means that in this year 30 per cent of all privatization proceeds of the 15 European Union countries came from Germany. Apart from this year, the privatization proceeds are much smaller, compared with other larger European countries.

If one considers the small open economies the results are presented in table 10.2.

Table 10.2 shows that, in the beginning of the 1990s, the amount of privatization was quite moderate with the exception of Belgium. The Belgium government privatized extensively in the year 1993 and received proceeds of US$956 million, which are roughly 30 per cent of all privatization proceeds of the small open economies in Table 10.2. The second highest privatization proceeds in this year were received by the Netherlands with US$780 million. This was followed by Portugal, which had a quite ambitious privatization program over the years 1993-1998, with privatization proceeds over US$12 billions over those years. Many well known public utilities in Portugal were privatized, such as the power plant EDP, the highway system BRISA and cement factories ZINPOR. In Austria, the privatization proceeds have also been quite large. In the year 1997 in Austria the government privatized firms with proceeds of US$2.02 billion. In Austria the selling of 25 per cent share of the public telecommunications firm was the biggest sale, where proceeds of US$2.33 billion have been achieved.

3.2. Further Remarks about the Privatization Efforts in Austria

(1) General Privatization Efforts and Proceeds

The Austro-Keynesian era of stabilization policy lasted from the mid 1970s to the mid 1980s can be viewed as an attempt of "direct employment policy" in the public utilities and the public industrial sector, mainly in the heavy, machinery and chemical industry. The primary goal of this type of short-term policy in private goods markets was to stabilize employment and real income in the nationalized industry and, by way of interindustrial relations and the multiplier process, in the private sector as well.

Table 10.1 Privatization proceeds of single countries[8]

Country	Privatization Proceeds in million USD of the year								
	1990	1991	1992	1993	1994	1995	1996	1997	1998
Australia	19	1.042	1.893	2.057	1.841	8.089	9.052	16.815	7.146
Austria	32	48	49	142	700	1.035	1.251	2.020	2.935
Belgium	-	-	-	956	549	2.681	1.222	1.562	1.467
Canada (5)	1.504	808	1.249	755	490	3.998	1.770	-	11
Denmark	644			122	229	10	366	45	4.502
Finland	-	-	-	229	1.166	363	911	835	1.999
France	-	-	-	12.160	5.479	4.136	5.099	8.189	13.467
Germany (2)	-	325		435	240	-	13.228	1.125	364
Great Britain (3)	12.906	21.825	604	8.523	1.341	6.691	7.610	4.544	-
Greece	-	-	-	35	73	44	558	1.395	3.892
Hungary	38	470	720	1.842	1.017	3.813	1.157	1.966	353
Ireland	-	515	70	274		157	293	-	-
Iceland	-		21	10	2	6	-	4	129
Italy (4)	-	-	-	1.943	6.493	7.434	6.265	27.719	13.619
Japan	-	-	-	15.919	13.773	-	6.379	4.009	6.641
Korea	-	-	-	817	2.435	480	1.866	539	600
Luxem-burg	-	-	-	-	-	-	-	-	-
Mexico	3.122	10.757	6.859	2.503	766	167	73	2.690	995
Nether-lands	716	179		780	3.766	3.993	1.239	831	335
New zealand	3.895	17	967	630	29	264	1.839		441
Norway	73	-	-	-	118	521	660	35	28
Poland	23	23	238	245	385	714	749	2.179	2.020
Portugal	1.192	1.198	2.326	500	1.132	2.425	3.011	4.968	4.271
Spain	172	-	820	3.223	1.458	2.941	2.679	12.522	11.618
Sweden	-	-	378	252	2.313	852	785	1.055	172
Switzer-land	-	-	-	-	-	-	-	-	4.426
Czecho-slovakia (6)	-	-	-	-	1.077	1.205	994	442	469
Turkey	486	244	423	546	412	515	292	466	1.009
USA	-	-	-	-	-	-	-	-	3.100

Table 10.1. (continued)[8]

Total OECD	**24.822**	**37.451**	**16.617**	**54.895**	**47.284**	**52.537**	**69.348**	**95.955**	**86.009**
Davon: EU 15	15.662	24.090	4247	29.573	24.940	32.765	44.518	66.812	58.641
Other countries (7)	5.078	10.413	19.845	23.976	18.111	21.115	27.911	57.827	28.533
World-wide total	**29.900**	**47.864**	**36.462**	**78.871**	**65.395**	**73.652**	**97.259**	**153.782**	**114.542**

- = Zero or insignificant

To achieve this political target, various steps were taken by the public management:

- the maintenance of the greatest possible level of production in the face of diminishing prices and demand;
- the greatest possible hoarding of employees even in situations when rationalization measures (dismissals) were required (resulting in unemployment on the job);an over-dimensioned propensity to invest (primarily with regard to the income effect of investment);
- an expansionist wage and fringe benefits policy with respect to buying electric power (causing high labour costs); and the (tacit) financing of the firms' deficits out of the federal budget.

---

[8] (1) Gross receipt from privatizations.
(2) Up to 1997 no information about privatization proceeds were available.
(3) Debt sales in Great Britain were between 1990 and 1997 (fiscal year) GBP 5.347 million, GBP 7.924 million,GBP 8.189 million, GBP 5.453 million, GBP 6.429 million, GBP 2.439 million and GBP 4.500 million respective.
(4) Inclusive convergeable bonds, INA, which could be transferred and shared among these utilities with the amount of US$2.055 million. in the year 1996 and indirect privatization proceeds of US$2.658 million. in the year 1996 and US$2.620 million. in the year 1997.
(5) In the year 1997 there have been no privatizations on the federal level.
(6) The cumulated amount for the years 1991-1993 is US$2.240 million.
(7) *Source* for the years 1990-1996 is the Worldbank and SBC Warburg; for the year 1997 the source is IFR Securities.
All other sources: National statistics, and OECD Financial Market Trends, No 72, (1999), Paris.

Table 10.2 Privatization proceeds in small open economies in the years 1993, 1995, 1997 and 1998

	1993			*1995*		
Country	*US$ million*	*in % of total*	*rank*	*US$ million*	*in % of Total*	*rank*
Austria	142	4%	7	1.035	9%	4
Belgium	956	29%	1	2.681	22%	2
Denmark	122	4%	8	10	0%	9
Finland	229	7%	6	363	3%	7
Ireland	274	8%	4	157	1%	8
Iceland	10	0%	9	6	0%	10
Netherlands	780	24%	2	3.993	33%	1
Norway	-	-	-	521	4%	6
Portugal	500	15%	3	2.425	20%	3
Sweden	252	8%	5	852	7%	5
Switzerland	-	-	-	-	-	-
Total	3.265	100%		12.043	100%	

	1997			*1998*		
Country	*US$ million*	*in % of total*	*rank*	*US$ million*	*in % of Total*	*rank*
Austria	2.020	18%	2	2.935	14%	4
Belgium	1.562	14%	3	1.467	7%	6
Denmark	45	0%	7	4.502	22%	1
Finland	835	7%	5	1.999	10%	5
Ireland	-	-	-	-	-	-
Iceland	4	0%	9	129	1%	9
Netherlands	831	7%	6	335	2%	7
Norway	35	0%	8	28	0%	10
Portugal	4.968	44%	1	4.271	21%	3
Sweden	1.055	9%	4	172	1%	8
Switzerland	-	-	-	4.426	22%	2
Total	11.355	100%		20264	100%	

\- = Null or insignificant

Source: Own calculations with the help of table 10.1.

With regard to the social and re-election problems arising from unemployment, the direct employment policy in public industrial firms was intended to smooth the inevitable adjustment process to the rising requirements of global competitiveness in the long run. Naturally, the type of stabilization policy pursued immediately caused substantial effects on the public industrial firms' productivity, thriftiness and profitability, thus reducing international competitiveness and augmenting deficits in the short run (Nowotny, 1982). Nonetheless, production and employment could not be maintained permanently at a high level, because the rationalization measures could not be postponed any longer. Since the mid 1980s, the Austro-Keynesian stabilization policy has been increasingly criticized for its doubtful long-term efficacy. Finally, the troubling rise of the losses of the state-owned firms in the iron and steel, chemical, machinery and vehicle industry caused an about-turn in public opinion and economic policy. The amount of subsidies to public industrial firms covering the deficits and financing investment was limited to a fixed total in the the period until 1989. This change of policy emerged when the government realized that, due to the critique of the opposition, mass media and private entrepreneurs, as well as to the people's fear of tax increases, a majority of voters would not tolerate further subsidies to public industrial firms. Prior to this change of mind, politicians had formed coalitions with the management of the relatively big and locally concentrated public firms in order to secure the subsidies that rendered inefficiencies possible and served the local constituency. Moreover there have been powerful shop stewards who were simultaneously members of the legislating National Council and therefore succeeded in financing the expansionist enterprise policy out of the federal budget.

From the end of the 1980s there was a turnaround in the Austrian policy with respect to the public industrial sector and public utilities. Not only were there many privatizations in the 1990s, but also these enterprises were much less used for re-election purposes. This was partly due to the fact that, after joining the European Union and the deregulation of former monopolies into competitive markets, it was much less attractive to use the public utilities and industries for re-election purposes. In the 1990s, the privatization of Austrian state-owned industrial firms and state-owned utilities has yielded over US$6 billions over the period 1993-1998 (see Table 10.3). However, the privatization potential in Austria in the mid 1990s is still quite large. Taking the federal, the state and community levels and including all public utilities, there is a privatization potential of €45 billion of which the federal government owns 62 per cent, the city or state of Vienna 13 per cent, all other states (e.g. Upper and Lower Austria) 14 per cent and the communes (without Vienna) 11 per cent. The latest privatization proceeds of the federal government over the years 1999 to 2001 are presented in Table 10.3.

In 1999 9.4 per cent of the Austrian tobacco company was privatized, which yielded US$7.82 billion.

In 2000 100 per cent of the postal bank was privatized and the proceeds were US$1.115million. Also 24 per cent of the state owned Telecom utility was privatized with proceeds of US$878 million. In total in 2000, US$2.003 million of privatization proceeds were received. In 2001, a further 41.1 per cent of the

Austrian tobacco state-owned utility was privatized, which brought privatization proceeds of US$670 million.

In total, over the years 1999-2001, US$2.823 billion privatization proceeds were received. This is quite sizeable and helped the Austrian government to reduce the federal debt.

Table 10.3 Privatization proceeds in Austria (Federal government) over 1999-2001[9]

Year		Proceeds (€ million)	Proceeds (US$ million)
1999	Privatization of 9.4% of the		7.82
	Austrian Tabacco AG	6,8	
2000	100% PSK (Postal Bank)	969.5	1114.93
	24.4% Telecom	763.8	878.37
	100% State Printing Office	2.2	2.53
		1742.3	2003.65
2001	17.38% Airport Vienna AG	54.1	62.22
	41.1% Austrian Tobacco AG	582.2	669.53
	100% Dorotheum	55.6	63.94
	100% Strohal Rotary Printing	21.1	24.27
		713.0	819.96
Total 1999-2001	**2,455.3**		**2,823.61**

Source: Ministry of Economic Affairs, Vienna, 2002.

(2) Some specific remarks about the privatization of the Vienna Airport

The first "wave" of privatization of the Vienna Airport spanned the years 1992 to 1995. Before 1992, the federal state owned 50 per cent of the airport and the city of Vienna and the province of Lower Austria each owned 25 per cent. The first wave of privatization transferred 27 per cent of the shares from public to private shareholders. Now the federal state owned "only" 36.5 per cent and the city of Vienna and the province of Lower Austria each owned 18.5 per cent. After the second wave of privatization in 1995 private share holders owned 48.86 per cent and the city of Vienna, the province of Lower Austria and the federal republic each owned 17.38 per cent. The last wave of privatization of Vienna Airport took place in March and April 2001. The 17.38 per cent of the federal republic which was owned by the Austrian Industrial Holding Agency (ÖIAG) was sold to the following institutions/investors:

(1) 5.24 per cent to the province of Lower Austria and the city of Vienna,
(2) 3.22 per cent to a foundation of Vienna Airport workers/employees,
(3) 0.7 per cent to an Austrian Institutional Investor via the Deutsche Bank, and
(4) 8.18 per cent to Austrian and Foreign Institutional Investors in form of a block trade in March 2001.

---

[9] [US$1.15 ~ €1]

In sum, the federal republic achieved net sale proceeds of US$163,882 million (€142,506million) and the average value of the "airport share" was US$45.3 (€39.4 Euro) in 2001.

Currently (1/2003) we have the situation that the Vienna Airport is 50 per cent owned by private shareholders, another 10 per cent by the employees of the airport the city of Vienna and the province of Lower Austria each own 20 per cent. Overall, Vienna Airport is now partly privatized, and the increasing number of airport privatizations that are taking place through the world demonstrate that growing acceptance of this process as a method of tackling some of the challenges many airports face nowadays.

However, airport ownership and control are always likely to be controversial: for many countries transferring airports, which are considered to be nationally important assets, to the private sector remains highly politically sensitive. This is the reason why the public still holds 50 per cent of the shares of Vienna Airport. This is so because the quasi monopolistic position of many airports will continue to be of concern to politicians and airport users. The fear is that priority will be given to private shareholders or investors and that the interests of the users and community might be neglected. This is in contrast to the situation for commercial airlines where competition can be quite intensive. Airports are likely to be a natural monopoly because competition is not so easy to create. In the case of Vienna, the nearest airports are in Bratislava, Prague and Budapest, but they all are some distance away and do not have the same level of facilities as Vienna Airport. For this reason it is an open question whether Vienna Airport will be totally privatized, and whether this step will be a success or not. So far, the three privatizing steps have been quite successful in terms of profitability and growth. Vienna Airport is a very profitable one and total passengers at Vienna Airport raised from roughly 5 million in 1990 to roughly 12 million in 2000. During the period from 1979-1999 revenues have grown by 9.5 per cent p.a. to US$460million (€400million). Since 1991, when new accounting procedures were adopted, profit before interest and tax increased from US$34.5 million (€30 million) in 1991 to US$97,8 million (€85 million) in 1999 - an annual average growth rate of 13.9 per cent.

4. Summary and Conclusions

Privatization has certainly been a key element of structural reform in the European Union countries, including Austria, and proceeds from privatization have been substantial in most of these countries. Gross receipts that can be transferred to the budget are affected by actions prior to sale, the sales process and the post-privatization regime. An evaluation of the potential uses of privatization receipts or proceeds should reflect the implications for government net worth and their macroeconomic impact. In so far as government net worth is concerned, proceeds from privatization do not often themselves indicate then the government is better off. Privatization has longer term implications in terms of revenues forgone and/or expenditures that will not be made in the future and government decisions on the use of proceeds should reflect these long run effects. Government net worth will rise to the extent that private sector ownership leads to an increase in efficiency and the government shares in this gain. In the Vienna Airport case, the governments have been keen to obtain the revenues from partial privatization. They have, however, been wary of fully privatizing the airport given its market power, and the concern that it might use this market power to the detriment of users.

References

Alchian, A.A. (1961) Some Economics of Property Rights, *Rand Corporation*, Santa Monica.

Alchian, A.A. (1965) Some Economic of Property Rights, *Il Politiquo* 30/4, pp. 816-829.

Baron, B. and Myerson, F (1982) Principal Agents Theory, *Econometrica* 50, pp. 911-930.

Bartel Rainer and Friedrich Schneider (1991) The "mess" of public industrial production in Austria: A typical case of public sector inefficiency?, *Public Choice* Vol. 68/1, pp. 17-40.

Boes Dieter and Friedrich Schneider (1996) Private Public Partnership: Gemeinschaftsunternehmen zwischen privaten und der oeffentlichen Hand, *Zeitschrift fuer Unternehmens- und Gesellschaftsrecht*, pp. 519-543.

Borcherding Thomas, Bush W.C. and R.M. Spann (1977) The Effects on Public Spending on the Divisibility of Public Outputs in Consumption, Bureaucratic Power and the Size of the Tax Sharing Group, in: T.E. Borcherding (editor), *Budgets and Bureaucrats: The Sources of Government Growth*, Durham, NC, Duke University Press, pp. 211-228.

Borcherding Thomas, Pommerehne Werner W. and Friedrich Schneider (1982) Comparing the Efficiency of Private and Public Production: The Evidence from 5 Countries, *Zeitschrift fuer Nationaloekonomie/Journal of Economics* 89 (Supplement 2), pp. 127-156.

De Alessi L. (1974) An Economic Analyses of Government Ownership and Regulation: The Theory and the Evidence from Electric Power Industry, *Public Choice* 19/1, pp. 1-42.

Grossman, F. and Hart, B. (1983) Principal Agents Theory: What is New, What is old, *Econometrica* 51, pp. 7-45.

MasColell, G., Winston, B, and Green, H. (1995*) Microeconomic Theory*, New York-Oxford, Oxford University Press.

Megginson, W.R. and Netter, J (2001) From state to market: a survey of empirical studies on privatization, *Journal of Economic Literature*, 39/3, pp. 321-389.

Niskanen W.A. (1971) *Bureaucracy and Representative Government*, Chicago and New York, Chicago University Press.

Niskanen W.A. (1975) Bureaucraths and Politicians, *Journal of Law and Economics* 18/4, pp. 617-643.

Nowotny Ewald (1982), Nationalist Industry as an Instrument of Stabilization Policy, *Annalen der Gemeinwirtschaft* 51/1, pp. 41-57.

Pardo José Casas and Friedrich Schneider (1996) *Current Issues in Public Choice*, Cheltenham, UK, Edward Elgar.

Schneider Friedrich (1997) Deregulierung und Privatisierung als Allheilmittel gegen ineffiziente Produktion von oeffentlichen Unternehmen?, in: *Wieviel Staat, wie viel Privat?,* Sammelband von der Arbeitsgemeinschaft der wissenschaftlichen Wirtschaftspolitik, Vienna, pp. 33-59.

Schneider Friedrich (2002) Privatisierungen und Deregulierungen in Oesterreich in den 90er Jahren: Einige Anmerkungen aus Sicht der neuen politischen Oekonomie, in: Hartmut Berg (editor), *Deregulierung und Privatisierung: Gewolltes – Erreichtes – Versaeumtes?*, Schriften des Vereins fuer Socialpolitik (Neue Folge, Band 287), pp. 89-120.

Schneider Friedrich and Markus F. Hofreither (1990) *Privatisierung und Deregulierung in oeffentlichen Unternehmen in westeuropaeischen Laendern: Erste Erfahrungen und Analysen*, Vienna: Manzsche Verlags- und Universitaetsbuchhandlung.

Schneider Friedrich and Bruno Frey (1988) Political Business Cycles: A Survey, in: Thomas Willet (editor), *Influation and the Political Business Cycles*, Durham, NC, pp. 239-275.

Sigmund Ulrich (1998) Die Treuhand 1990/1991: *Spezialfall, Privatisierungsmonopol und Staatsversagen?,* Universität Kiel: Institut fuer Weltwirtschaft, Kiel.

Chapter 11

Regulation in Times of Crisis: Experiences with a Public-Private Price Cap Contract at Hamburg Airport

Thomas Immelmann

Introduction

No doubt, the current environment is a hard time for the aviation industry, when even airports - such as Cologne or Stuttgart - suffer heavy operating losses and may even come close to bankruptcy. In this situation, talking about airport regulation in terms of a price or fee cap may be cherished by some airlines[1] but few airport shareholders or authorities. It will be shown subsequently that at Hamburg Airport, a sophisticated price cap regulation proves to be crisis resistant. A concise planning of the processes and the ability to have an annual validation, produced price cap regulation that both proves to be stable in bad times and keeps up its originally intended regulatory function for a fair airport-airline fiscal relation.

Hamburg Airport

Founded as an airfield serving more airships than the young airplane industry in those years, Hamburg Airport was founded on a sheep's meadow a couple of miles away from what was the heart of Hamburg city in the year 1911. Since then, it has grown to an airport serving almost 10 million passengers and 70 airlines in 2000, with the traffic structure of a European "classic origin & destination" airport (see Figure 11.1). In 2000, Hamburg accounted for 165,000 flight movements, of which some 152,000 were commercial. In 2001, passenger development fell back to 9.5 million passengers and 159,000 flight movements, followed by 8.85 mio passengers and roughly 150,000 flight movements in 2002. In economic terms in Hamburg this was the worst year in recent civil aviation history. Still, with a net income of €21 million and €190 million in sales revenues Hamburg Airport proves to be one the most profitable airports in Europe, though the economic development has steadily grown worse since 2001.

---

[1] Compare with i.e. Thomas C. Lawton´s remarks upon the airport charges as a structural barrier against low cost airlines in: *Cleared for Take-Off*; Ashgate; Aldershot, 2002, p. 67f.

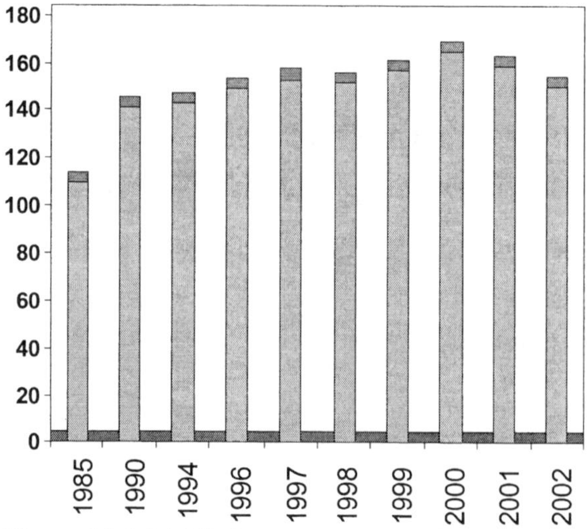

Figure 11.1 (a) Flight movements 1985-2002

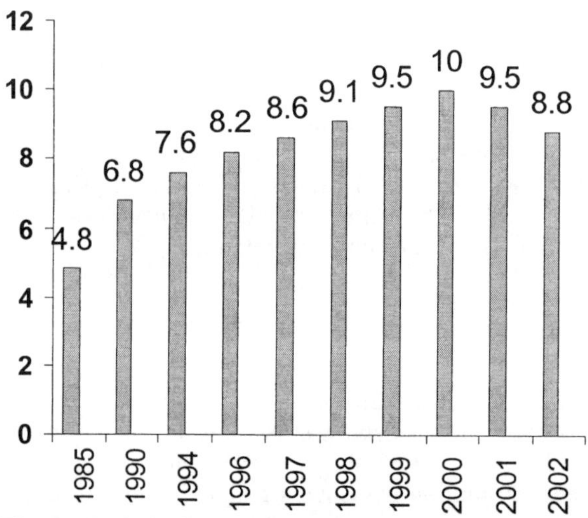

Figure 11.1 (b) Passenger movements 1997-2002

Located now within the city limits of Hamburg, which has grown around the airfield in the past 90 years, Hamburg Airport is not only the oldest international airport still in place at its founding location, but it also has quite complex regulatory requirements due to the fact that more than half a million people live in the direct neighbourhood of the airport. Environmental and noise restriction regulations were initially applied in 1983 and have constantly tightened.[2]

Another feature about Hamburg airport which should be mentioned, since it has implications for airport regulation, is the management of services. A modern business approach was developed well in advance of European airport deregulation. The management of Hamburg Airport saw quite early the challenges to be faced with the deregulation of airport business, especially in the business field of ground handling. The airport has been trying to cope with these challenges, creating a number of subsidiaries to the former Airport Authority, Flughafen Hamburg GmbH. A number of strong companies specialised in certain ground handling business fields have been founded and have successfully established themselves in the market. This strategy took some pressure from the regulatory issues to be clarified before privatization, while some of the former monopolist ground-handling services have been made ready for competition.

Table 11.1 Organization of Hamburg Airport and subsidiaries 2002

40 %	AHS Hamburg - Aviation Handling Services GmbH
100 %	AIRSYS Airport Business Information Systems
100 %	ANG - Airport Networks GmbH
100 %	CATS - Cleaning and Aircraft Technical Services GmbH
100 %	CSP - Commercial Services Partner GmbH
100 %	GAC - German Airport Consulting GmbH
100 %	GroundSTARS - Groundstars GmbH & Co. KG
100 %	SecuServe - Aviation Security and Services GmbH
60 %	SAEMS - Special Airport Equipment & Maintenance Services mbH
51 %	STARS - Special Transport and Ramp Services GmbH & Co. KG

Regulation: Privatization Background

Another background feature of the regulatory framework at Hamburg Airport definitely has to be mentioned: the political will to privatize or at least partially privatize public infrastrucuture. Apparently, the public shareholders of Hamburg Airport - the Free and Hanseatic City of Hamburg (64 per cent), the Federal State of Schleswig-Holstein (10 per cent) and the Federal republic of Germany (26 per cent) were quite aware of the danger of a misuse of the airport's monopoly role by

[2] See the contributions of Hans-Martin Nieme ier and Axel Schmidt in T. Immelmann et al. (Eds), *Aviation versus Environment?* Papers of the 2nd Hamburg Aviation Conference. Peter Lang, Frankfurt/M. 2000

a new private owner.[3] As one of the principles of the public-private partnership before the privatization process, the public shareholders and the Ministry for Economy of Hamburg, being the executive authority for all aviation issues in the federal state of Hamburg, made the decision to establish a form of price cap regulation for all airport fees regulated by German federal law (§ 43 LuftZVO).[4] This included passenger handling, parking, landing and noise emission fees, but neither ground handling service fees, security/safety charges or charges for central infrastucture issues such as baggage handling etc, nor other airport revenues from other business fields (i.e. non-aviation related rents and revenues) were to be included.

The goal was, however, to prevent a private shareholder from simply cashing in on windfall profits. The price cap contract was finally signed in 2000 with a duration of five years from 2000 to the end of 2004.[5] Thus, the price cap contract would be one of the "sine-qua-non" conditions to a future public-private shareholder partnership that had been established in 2000 by the acquisition of 40 percent of Hamburg Airport by the appointed private consortium Hamburg Airport Partners (HAP), owned by Hochtief Airport, an affiliate of the largest German construction company, and Aer Rianta, the worldwide successful Irish airport company.

The Price Cap Regulation

Prior to privatization, in the negotiations between representatives of executive authorities, public shareholders, airlines and other important customers and users of Hamburg Airport, the Government of the Free and Hanseatic City of Hamburg and the Federal Republic of Germany, the conditions of the public private contract and the price cap regulation were brought into one formula. This formula set the reference quotient as a benchmark and a method of regulation to define the future level of fees per passenger:[6]

$$RQ_{2001} = RQ_{2000} * (1 + CPI_{2000} - Z\%) \{-scs\}$$

[3] In fact, Hamburg Airport and the Ministry for Economy of Hamburg supported several scientific surveys on this issue before the airport privatization was underway; see W. Pfähler, H.-M. Niemeier et al, *Airports and Air Traffic Regulation, Privatization and Competition,* Peter Lang, Frankfurt/M. 1999.

[4] Luftfahrtzulassungsverordnung der Bundesrepublik Deutschland

[5] „Öffentlich-rechtlicher Vertrag über die Festsetzung und Anpassung regulierter Flughafenentgelte. Abgeschlossen zwischen der Freien und Hansestadt Hamburg und der Flughafen Hamburg GmbH." Hamburg, April 2000. The following is referred to as "Price cap contract". The author was the responsible spokesman for the airport in the negotiations on the price cap contract; quotes are made from the author's final draft, which was identical to the signed contract paper.

[6] Price cap contract p. 4.

where RQ is an abbreviation for reference quotient, which represents the sum of all regulated fees per passenger charged by Hamburg Airport in 1999. To define the maximum limit of regulated fees per pax and fiscal year for the following year, the price cap formula is applied. CPI stands for the consumer price index, clearing the regulation from nominal monetary effects. Z represents the minimum decrease rate on airport fees that the airport company has to accomplish – a rate of minus 2 per cent. {-scs} means - not exactly arithmetically correct - that the increase of productivity at Hamburg Airport - also the avoidance of windfall profits by sheer scale effects of rapid passenger development - had to be shared between airlines and the airport company defined by a "sliding scale model".

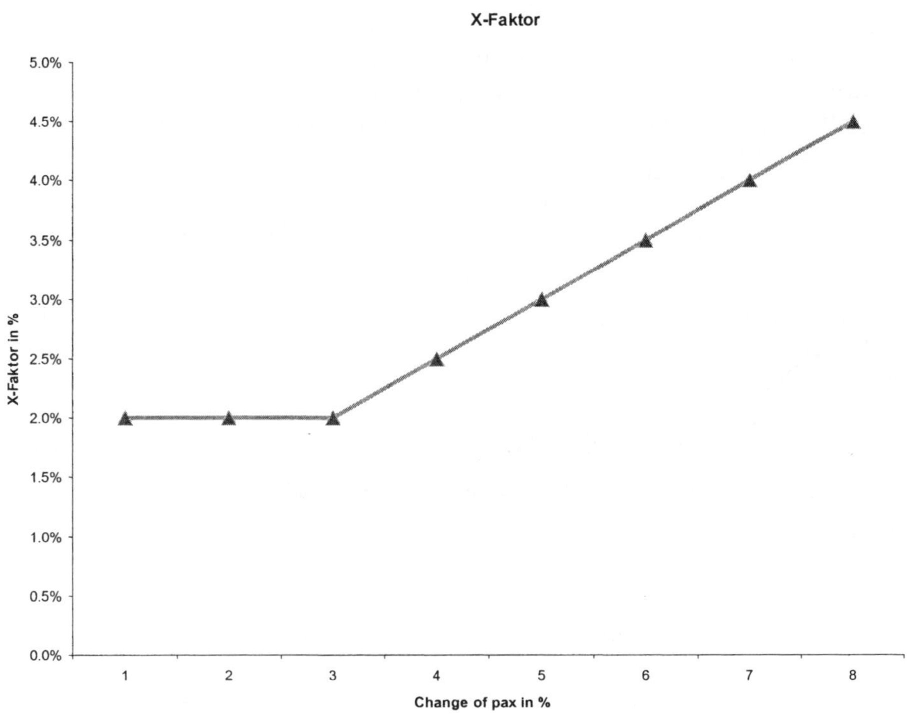

Figure 11.2 Sliding scale model

For each percentage of annual passenger growth above 3 percent - the average growth at Hamburg Airport in the 15 years before the introduction of the price cap contract - in a current year, the reference quotient of the following year has to be decreased by an additional 0.5 percent[7]. Fig. 11.3 gives an example of how the price cap reference quotient would be determined:

[7] Price cap contract p. 5f.

given pax growth: 6%
given Consumer Price Index: 1%

$RQ_{2001} = RQ_{2000} * (1 + 1\% - 2\% - (3 \times 0.5\%))$
$RQ_{2001} = RQ_{2000} - 2.5\ \%$

Figure 11.3 The cap reference quotient

This decrease may seem negligible at first look, but the effect of this "productivity sharing" on the market proved to be positive and underlines the marketing character of the price cap regulation - especially at an origin-destination-airport like Hamburg, where comparably small changes in the regulation framework may have huge effects on market structure.[8]

As shown in Figure 11.4, the effect on the development on the price cap reference quotient was relatively small, due to the fact that the second year of the price cap application at Hamburg Airport was 2001, which had a date in September to be long remembered.

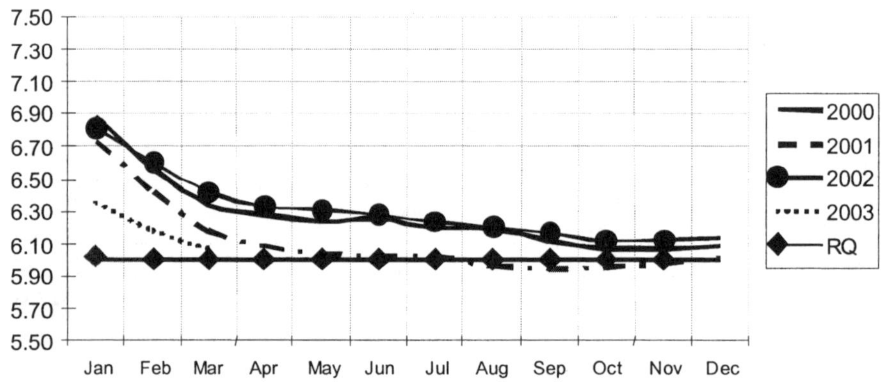

Figure 11.4 Reference quotient 1999-2003 (cum.)

To understand the question why the price cap regulation had a quite limited negative impact on Hamburg Airport's economic performance, a change of paradigm has to be seen. The radical, if not revolutionary change in this price cap model of airport charges and fees for the airport company was the "head count principle", measuring all formerly regulated revenues by numbers of passengers instead of maximum-take-off-weight-tons, landing fee per aircraft type, duration of aircraft parking or other traditional ways. This was the very moment when the airport management and shareholders had to find an answers to a - at first glance -

[8] Compare with David W. Gillen et al, *The Impact of Liberalizing International Aviation Bilaterals,* Ashgate, Aldershot 2001, where the effects of liberalization of international traffic rights on a relatively small Hamburg, respectively north German market are shown.

simple question: what happens if passenger growth rates decline? What happens in times of crisis in aviation industry?

Crisis and Price Cap: Management Tools for an Acid Test

First, price cap protection tools in the case of a - sudden or slow - decline in the aviation market is the communication between producer and market, airport and airline, infrastructure unit and environment. None of the rules set up in the public private price cap contract are static. As described in the two annexes of the contract,[9] a number of boards and control units had to be established by the airport company - not only for crisis management reasons, of course, but also for normal conditions for the surveillance of the airport's service level performance. Further, annual passenger service reports produced under demographic standards have to show the observance of high quality standards in infrastructure and service levels for passengers as well as for airlines or other business-to-business-customers. A landside customer board - a group of retailers, car rental managers and other landside concessionaires - an airside customer board - manned by airline operation representatives such as station and cargo managers - and a neighbourhood community board - have at least one session a year, with the opportunity to discuss all potential claims and critical items directly with the airport's management. In case the claims could not be answered satisfactory, the according board representatives have the right and the ability to pass on their claims to the executive regulatory authority of the Free and Hanseatic City of Hamburg - a procedure that - quite remarkably - has not happened yet. In Hamburg, this communication structure gave airlines as well as the airport the opportunity to react closely and jointly and - not least - very cost-effectively on the change of security paradigms after September 11.

The most important control and steering unit is the Price Cap Review Board with executive level representatives of airlines and airline associations such as BARIG and ADL. This board meets at least once annually and is in the position to change virtually any of the price cap regulation contract paragraphs. The most important change in the price cap regulation since its inauguration in 2000 was the abandonment of the sliding scale clause immediately after September 2001, which proved to be an emergency exit - and an important one - out of the dangers of a totally passenger-figure-driven price cap at Hamburg Airport and which was decided in total accordance with the airport company. The advantage for the airport is the chance to recover faster from the sudden decrease in passenger demand in all aviation-related business fields, the advantage for airlines is the preservation of a long-term and safe scheme of airport fee decrease.

Another dimension of the immunity of the price cap contract against the general economic crisis is the real valuation/inflation index of the reference quotient. In the Hamburg case, this valuation is tied to the general consumer price index in the Federal Republic of Germany. As it seems to be one of the natural laws in the world's economy, a general economic downturn comes hand in hand with

[9] Price cap contract p. 7-9 and annex 3, A, B, C.

high inflation, so the real value of regulated fees safeguards the airport's infrastructure prices against rapid devaluation.

Conclusion

When establishing price cap regulation in an aviation infrastructure unit such as an airport, no "plan for the unplanned" may really survive its first encounter with reality. But it seems to be possible to build in emergency exits that allow partners to leave the once-defined path of regulation and comply with an abrupt change of the economic situation. To cope with the price cap's substantial decrease of airport fees by increasing productivity and cost reduction is definitely a demanding task for the airport company, but the history of regulatory performance at Hamburg Airport in the past three years has comprehensively shown that an everlasting growth in passenger figures is neither a necessity nor an absolute living condition for a price cap. And very definitely, an economic downturn or even the chance of a sudden evolving economic crisis are no argument against a price cap in principle. On the contrary, on an aggregate level, a price cap has a thorough character of providing a marketing incentive that survives in bad times and may serve as a preparation for fitness in times of declining yields and a growing uncertainty in the entire aviation industry (which has been a general trend since the late 1990s[10]). Or to put it more practically: an airport among the first to reasonably value its services and infrastructure in good times is the last to be visited by airline managers that desperately and dramatically seek to reduce costs in bad times - and finally reduce traffic by cutting frequencies or cancelling destinations, leaving the airport and its expensive infrastructure in even worse economic conditions.

[10] Compare with Rigas Doganis, *The Airline Business in the 21st Century,* Routledge, London 2001, p. 9f.

Chapter 12

Capacity Utilization, Investment and Regulatory Reform of German Airports

Hans-Martin Niemeier

1. Introduction

The two issues of capacity utilization and expansion, and price regulation, and the links between them, are explored in this paper. In Germany, there is a perceived problem of the adequacy of airport capacity to meet demand. Excess demand can be met by building more capacity, but capacity can also be rationed more efficiently than it is at present, by price and other means. The system of price regulation that is implemented will influence the price structure, and hence how urgent are investments in extra capacity.

Since September 11th 2001 passenger volumes decreased significantly by 11.6 per cent, freight by 9.0 per cent, and commercial movements by 8.2 per cent at German Airports (ADV). Given that the current crisis in aviation, which started with the worldwide slump at the end of 2000, will probably last longer than the Gulf crisis and might even lead to structural changes (Costa et al, 2002), capacity extension of airports seem to be an odd theme. However, even the most pessimistic scenarios assume that after a period of three or four years of gloom, growth rates of the aviation industry will be back at the high levels of the last decades. Thus, the topic of expanding capacity or the inadequacy of airport infrastructure, as the aviation industry has called it, will soon be back on top of economic and political management of the industry.

In the meantime it might be useful to step back and ask how serious the capacity problem is, whether there is really a "capacity crisis", how capacity problems have been so far dealt with, and whether or not there are options for improved solutions. In this chapter I shall first try to assess the capacity problem at German airports by looking at the situation before 9/11 and the forecast situation for the year 2010. It will become clear that the airport system as a whole is in a situation of persistent overcapacity, but at the same time, there exist partial capacity shortages because the price mechanism does not work effectively. Thereafter, the shortcomings of the price mechanism and the politics of airport extension will be analysed in sections 3 and 4. I shall argue that the current practice lacks economic rationality and leads to an inefficient allocation of resources (section 5). Therefore, in section 6, it seems necessary to look critically at the rules of the game, namely the current cost based regulation of airports. I shall argue that this type of regulation is not appropriate for overcoming the current misallocation of resources and should be reformed. Several options are discussed briefly in section 7 and price cap regulation is favoured (section 8). While price cap regulation has the advantages of leading towards an cost efficient infrastructure and to a better utilization of existing capacity in the short run, the regulation is said to have certain dynamic drawbacks in the long run, namely poor incentives for investment. This charge will be analysed in section 9. Finally, before summing up I shall argue that price cap regulation should be part of a larger reform of setting incentives for an efficient static and dynamic allocation of airport resources.

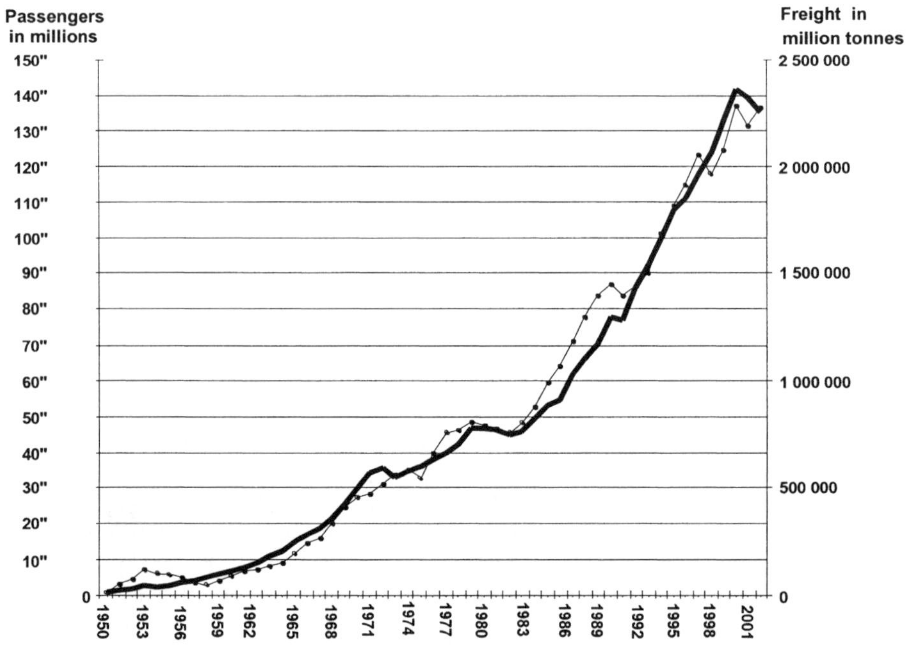

Figure 12.1 Passenger and freight movements at German airports
Source: Arbeitsgemeinschaft Deutscher Verkehrsflughäfen

2. Capacity Constraints at German Airports

Germany has 18 international airports and over 20 regional airports with scheduled or charter traffic. In 1990, the international airports served 80 million passengers and in 2000 143 million (+79.7 per cent). Freight volumes rose from 1.5 million tonnes to 2.3 million tonnes (+53.8 per cent). Commercial movements increased by 54 per cent from 1.2 million to 1.85 million in this period.

Instead of giving an overall picture of capacity problems I shall look at four representative examples. I shall start with Frankfurt airport and then look at the airports of Stuttgart, Hannover and Hamburg.

Frankfurt airport, Lufthansa's original hub, is the largest airport of Germany with 48 million passenger movements, 1.476.374 tonnes of freight and 448.499 commercial movements. It serves twice as many passengers as Lufthansa's secondary hub at Munich and has a market share of 35 per cent of passengers and 67 per cent of air freight in the German airport market. At a first glance, Figure 12.2 shows that the slots for arrival and departures are fully utilized (crosses) for almost all hours of the day.

	arr							dep							ttl						
	1	2	3	4	5	6	7	1	2	3	4	5	6	7	1	2	3	4	5	6	7
0000 - 0059	-	-	-	-	-	-	-														
0100 - 0159	-	-	-	-	-	-	-														
0200 - 0259	-	-	-	-	-	-	-														
0300 - 0359																					
0400 - 0459			c	x														c			
0500 - 0559	x	x	x	x	x	x	x								x	x	x	x	x	x	x
0600 - 0659	x	x	x	x	x	x	x	c	c	c			c	c	x	x	x	x	x	x	x
0700 - 0759	x	c	x	x	x	c		x	x	x	x	x	x	x	x	x	x	x	x	x	x
0800 - 0859	x	x	x	x	x	x	x	x	x	x	x	x	x	x	x	x	x	x	x	x	x
0900 - 0959	x	x	x	x	x	x	x				c				x	x	x	x	x	x	x
1000 - 1059	x	x	x	x	x	x	c	x	x	x	x	x	x	x	x	x	x	x	x	x	x
1100 - 1159								x	x	x	x	x	x	x	x	x	x	x	x	x	x
1200 - 1259	x	x	x	x	x	x	x	x	x	x	x	x	x	x	x	x	x	x	x	x	x
1300 - 1359	x	x	x	x	x	x	x		c						c	x	x	x	x	x	x
1400 - 1459	x	x	x	x	x	x	x	x	x	x	x	x	x	x	x	x	x	x	x	x	x
1500 - 1559								x	x	x	x	x	x	x	x	x	x	x	x	x	x
1600 - 1659	x	x	x	x	x	x	x	x	x	x	x	x		x	x	x	x	x	x		x
1700 - 1759	x	x	x	x	x	x	x								c	x	x	x	x	c	x
1800 - 1859	x	x	x	x	x	x	x	c	c	c	x	c		c	x	x	x	x	x	x	x
1900 - 1959			c					x	x	x	x	x	x	x	x	x	x	x	x	x	x
2000 - 2059								x	x	x	x	x	x	x					c		
2100 - 2159																					
2200 - 2259	-	-	-	-	-	-	-														
2300 - 2359	-	-	-	-	-	-	-														

UTC HOURS which are:

curfewed:	--
full:	x
close to full:	c
none of above:	

Figure 12.2 Slot coordination at Frankfurt Airport (summer 2001)
Source: Deutsche Flug Sicherung

At Frankfurt Airport the demand for slots is greater than the supply. It is obviously a congested airport. Taking a closer look, however we see that certain hours are only close to full (c) and even that still some slots are still available at certain less attractive times. The picture of a capacity crisis does change dramatically by looking at other German airports. At Stuttgart airport, with 7.6 million passengers the sixth largest German airport, no crosses appear (see Figure 12.3). However, the airport obviously has a peak problem in the morning and evening times of weekdays. In these hours the capacity is close to full and the hidden demand is probably greater than the capacity.

Such peak problems also occurred at Hamburg airport in the 1990s. A new apron has increased capacity by 25 per cent, now allowing 51 movements per hour instead of 42 so that, at Hamburg airport, the peak problem has almost vanished. At Hannover airport the situation looks even better. Only from 8 to 9 a.m. are the slots for arrival nearly fully utilized so that even at peak times the demand for slots does not reach the capacity limit. This situation is typical for all German airports with the exception of the heavily congested Düsseldorf airport, which is not allowed to use its second runway for environmental reasons. None of the other 13 airports has yet reached its capacity limit and this is even more the case for the small regional airports.

	arr							dep							ttl						
	1	2	3	4	5	6	7	1	2	3	4	5	6	7	1	2	3	4	5	6	7
0000 - 0059	-	-	-	-	-	-	-	-	-	-	-	-	-	-							
0100 - 0159	-	-	-	-	-	-	-	-	-	-	-	-	-	-							
0200 - 0259	-	-	-	-	-	-	-	-	-	-	-	-	-	-							
0300 - 0359	-	-	-	-	-	-	-	-	-	-	-	-	-	-							
0400 - 0459																					
0500 - 0559								c	c		c	c									
0600 - 0659																c	c		c		
0700 - 0759																c	c		c		
0800 - 0859			c	c	c										c	c	c	c	c		
0900 - 0959			c	c	c										c	c	c	c	c		
1000 - 1059																					
1100 - 1159																					
1200 - 1259																					
1300 - 1359																					
1400 - 1459																					
1500 - 1559																					
1600 - 1659																					
1700 - 1759																			c		
1800 - 1859	c	c	c	c	c														c		
1900 - 1959	c	c	c	c	c														c		
2000 - 2059																					
2100 - 2159								-	-	-	-	-	-	-							
2200 - 2259	-	-	-	-	-	-	-	-	-	-	-	-	-	-							
2300 - 2359	-	-	-	-	-	-	-	-	-	-	-	-	-	-							

UTC HOURS which are:

curfewed:	--
full:	x
close to full:	c
none of above:	

Figure 12.3 Slot coordination at Stuttgart airport (summer 2001)
Source: Deutsche Flug Sicherung

The situation in 2001, just before 9/11, can be summarized as follows. The main hub of German airports, Frankfurt, suffers from excess demand, but out of secondary hubs (with the exception of the environmental constrained Düsseldorf) only a few airports such as Stuttgart and Hamburg are facing peak problems, while all the other airports have idle capacity.

Will this situation change in the future? According to the latest forecast of the DLR, capacity problems will become more severe (Urbatzka et al, 1999).[1] The DLR has developed three scenarios. The first scenario assumes that no capacity constraints hinder the development of aviation. Passenger movements at German airports should rise from 113 million passengers in 1996 to 181 million passengers in 2010. The airlines are forecast to use relatively small aircraft so that the supply

[1] Given the current overcapacity one might argue that the forecast is out of date. I think that this is an open question. On the one hand the forecast is a point forecast of the year 2010 assuming normal conditions. By the year 2010, the crisis might be over and might have not changed the underlying structure of the aviation industry. On the other hand, the rise of low cost carriers and the response of a full service carrier might lead to a market segmentation radically changing the structure of the industry.

of seats per flight stays at the level of 1996. The rise of passenger demand will lead to an increase of total movements from 1,980,000 to 2,952,000 with commercial movements up from 1,519,000 to 2,383,000. Capacity problems will become acute at certain airports. Frankfurt and Düsseldorf will be heavily congested. At peak times, demand increases of up to 165 per cent of capacity at Frankfurt airport, and 195 per cent of capacity at Düsseldorf airport are forecast. For Berlin, Stuttgart, Munich and Hamburg peak problems are also forecast.

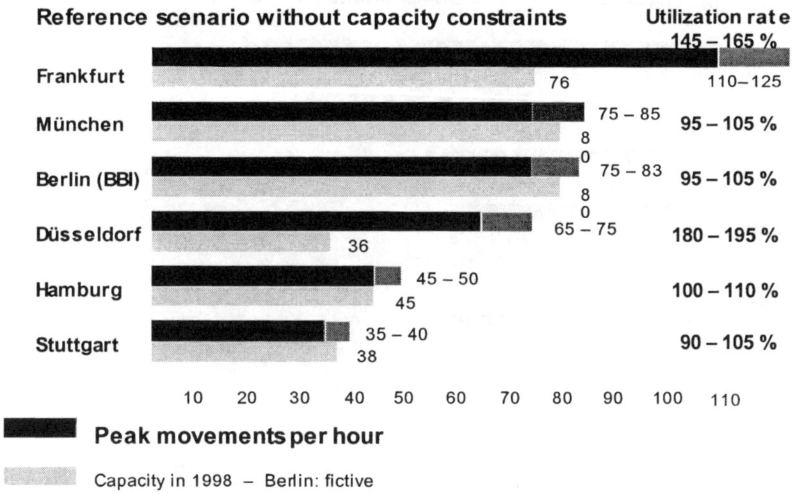

Figure 12.4 Peak demand and supply in the unconstrained scenario for the year 2010
Source: DLR

In order to balance this excess demand the DLR develops two further scenarios. The first one is supply driven and projects increases in aircraft size and load factors without altering the airport choice of the traveller. This leads to a significant reduction of total movements to 2,759,000. The margin of excess demand decreases by 35 per cent at Frankfurt airport and by 45 per cent at Düsseldorf airport. However, this reduction still does not balance demand and supply. Therefore, the DLR develops a third so called "market based scenario" assuming an increased capacity at the six airports with capacity problems in a range between 5 and 20 percent,[2] a partial shift of leisure traffic from Frankfurt and Düsseldorf to smaller airports, and a shift in the modal split due to new high-speed trains and a closer cooperation of Lufthansa and German railways. Total commercial movements stay at the level of the second scenario, but movements at

[2] Düsseldorf with an increase from 36 to 75 movements is an exception as the use of the second runway is assumed, which cannot be used currently due to environmental restrictions.

Frankfurt and Düsseldorf are again slightly reduced thereby balancing supply and demand. Munich, Berlin, Hamburg and Stuttgart are all forecast to have peak problems in 2010 (Figure 12.5).

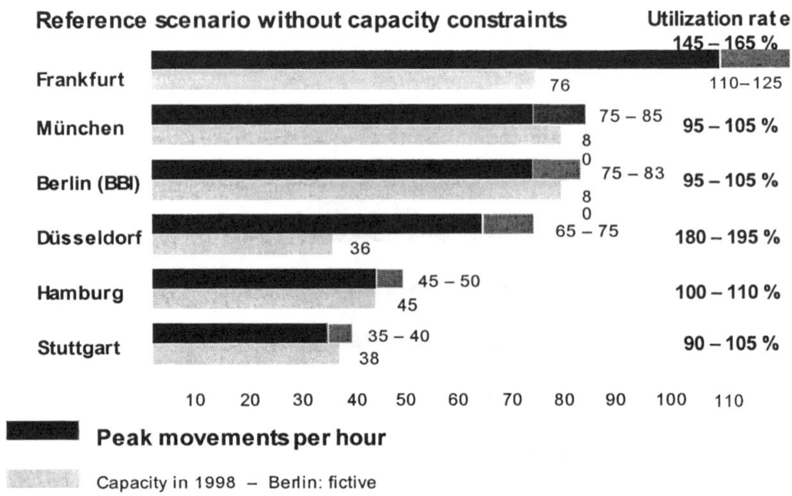

Figure 12.5 Peak demand and supply in market based scenario for the year *2010*

Source: DLR

According to this forecast, German airports face capacity problems, but speaking of an overall capacity crisis seems to be misleading. There are likely to be three groups of airports. The first group of airports are small international airports such as Bremen, Hannover or Saarbrücken and regional airports such as Kiel, Lübeck and Hahn. These airports are by far the majority. They provide enough idle capacity with slots still having the character of a public good such that there is no rivalry for landing and departures. The second group consists of airports with high utilization rates and excess demand at peak times such as Hamburg and Stuttgart. Slots cease to be a public good and become an ordinary private good. Thirdly, we have the group of airports facing excess demand for much of the day. Only at Frankfurt and Düsseldorf are slots permanently scarce.

3. Pricing at Airports

Comparing the market for airport investment and pricing with a well functioning market, it becomes obvious that something must be fundamentally wrong with the industry. It seems that idle capacity and excess demand prevail at the same time for relatively long periods with inefficient rationing and slow reactions of prices and new capacity. The short and long term reaction of an industry to a rising demand was first worked out by Marshall (1890), refined by Viner (1931), and then made its way into standard micro economics and transportation economics. According to Button and Stough (2000, p. 191) the "generally accepted position" assumes[3] that the airport industry has a modified L-shaped average cost curve with initially decreasing cost and economies of scale and density flattening out after a certain level (compare Figure 12.6).

The market clears initially at price of p1 with output at x1 thereby inducing the airport to increase supply along the short run marginal cost curve to the level of x2. Markets clear at a price of p2. Again the price at level p2 induces airports to expand capacity and to increase supply along the short run marginal cost curve leading to another round of price and output expansion. Step by step the airport industry adds capacity until the long-term equilibrium is reached, where supply and demand balances without inducing an expansion. In this point welfare is maximized as the output is produced with minimal average costs.

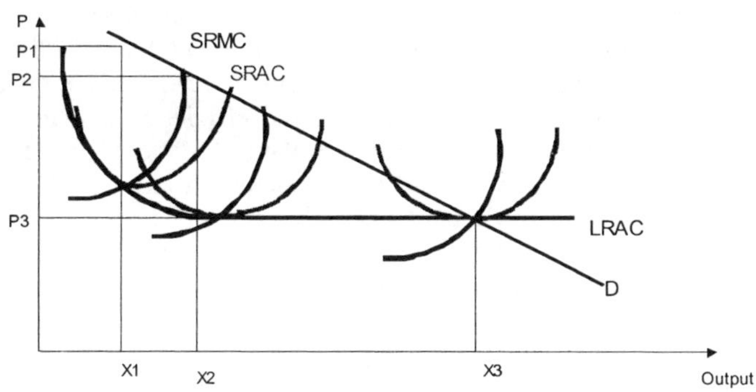

Figure 12.6 Expansion of the airport industry
Source: Button and Stough (2000)

Why is the airport industry not operating in such an ideal way? I would argue initially that the price mechanism is not working very efficiently and later that the regulatory framework sets incentives such that this inefficiency is encouraged (section 6). In the airport industry, two mechanisms are used to allocate resources, namely airport charges and slot allocation by the IATA procedure guide. Airport charges for landing and take off are weight based, the passenger charge is related to the number of passengers, parking charges are weight and sometimes time

[3] From my point of view this well-behaved function should be interpreted very carefully. Its purpose is more to show how an industry with a functioning price mechanism could work than how it realistically will work. As the function does not take account of the lumpiness character of airport expansions a very important aspect of the airport industry is neglected. With lumpy investment the pattern of prices would fluctuate more (cf. Vickrey, 1971). On the level of the industry the lumpiness of adding capacity at a single airport might be smoothened by the aggregation process if substitutes are available, but this is rather unlikely.

based. These charges were quite successful in financing infrastructure in a regulated environment. However, they are not suited for a liberalized aviation market as they are not efficient, in an economic sense. Various studies have shown that the current charges have the following disadvantages. At an uncongested airport, charges have only a relatively weak relation to costs and do not set incentives to airlines for a cost minimizing use of the take off and landing system. They are not strictly based on first best marginal pricing or second best pricing such as Ramsey pricing (Morrison, 1982; Doganis, 1992).[4] This means that at most German airports with idle capacity an inefficient pricing regime is practised. However, these inefficiencies become more important at those German airports with peak problems and with congestion. At these airports, airport charges based on some average cost concept do not incorporate the external effects of congestion or reflect the scarcity of slots. No effective peak pricing and no congestion pricing has been practised at German airports with scarce capacities in the past decade (Niemeier, 2002a).

The IATA rules of slot allocation stem from the period of a regulated aviation market. They give commercial traffic priority over general air traffic and give grandfather rights to slot owners. In a regulated environment these rules make some sense as they give planning security to scheduled traffic and reduce the congestion. However, they are not appropriate for the efficiency demands of a liberalized market, as economists have pointed out in the last 30 years (e.g. Levine, 1969; Fridström et al., 2002). The conclusion of economists is almost unanimous; the current slot procedures result in an inefficient allocation of resources as slots are not allocated to those who value them the most. The IATA rules distort competition among airlines by erecting barriers to entry and the rents from slots do not flow to the airports that could expand capacity and eliminate the slot scarcity. These inefficiencies lead to the situation at congested airports that charges are set at some measure of average cost so that the airports can live quite well and the airlines receive all the scarcity rent as the airline eliminates the excess demand by changing their passengers market clearing prices into/out of the constrained airport (Figure 12.7).

This situation seems to be quite stable.[5] At least for the last couple of decades the coalition of rent seeking airlines and rent providing airports has worked smoothly. German airports have shown no or relatively little initiative in installing a workably efficient price mechanism. They have not used the degrees of freedom the legal system offers in utilizing differential charges. Only the partial privatized

---

[4] Weight-based landing charges are sometimes interpreted as quasi-Ramsey prices because heavier aircraft are able to pay a higher charge than small aircraft (Productivity Commission, 2002) . This interpretation is correct, although the system has its shortcomings and can probably never be designed in a perfect way, as the Australian Competition and Consumer Commission (ACCC, 2001) points out. The important thing is that, as Morrison (1982) shows, the approximation can be improved easily.

[5] Figure 12.8 shows an efficient allocation of slot capacity. However, the current slot distribution rules have the danger of reducing welfare (Starkie, 1998). If the historically determined initial distribution of slots prevails because of institutional obstacles, the demand might be suppressed by inefficient carriers.

Düsseldorf airport has commissioned a study (Ewers et al, 2001) to reform the price mechanism, but it has so far not implemented an efficient pricing strategy.

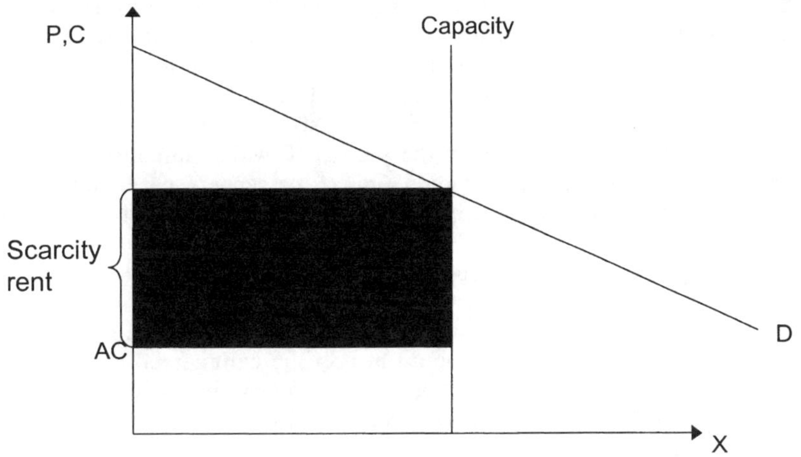

Figure 12.7 Slot scarcity

4. Irrational Policies of Airport Expansion

While German airports have not adopted an efficient pricing strategy they have focused their strategy on the expansion of capacity, which involves almost natural politics because of the negative environmental impact. German airports have developed a strategy based on a predict and provide philosophy and on a logic of jobs versus the environment. A complete analysis of the politics of airport expansion lays outside the scope of this paper. I shall confine myself to two representative examples. The first is the expansion of the apron at Hamburg airport. The second example is the mediation process of Frankfurt airport for a new take-off and landing system. It shows the logic of jobs versus the environment.

In the 1990s the state-owned Hamburg airport still had enough runway and terminal capacity, but growth was seen to be restricted by limited space for aircraft parking positions. In addition, the airport was forced by a court ruling to seek permission for any expansion through a process of public inquiry. Hamburg airport based its application for its development plan in 1996 on a forecast of passenger demand and movements (Flughafen Hamburg GmbH, 1996). At about the same time the Ministry of Economic Affairs of Hamburg had also commissioned a forecast by MKmetric (Mandel, 1997). Comparing each forecast with the other and with the actual development up to the year before the current crisis provides an interesting evaluation, as it shows the intentions of the airport management. Both forecasts expect similarly strong growth of passenger demand in a range between 13 (MKmetric) to 13.85 million passengers (Hamburg airport) in 2010. The forecasts largely diverge in the prognosis of commercial movements. Hamburg airport forecasts 195,000 commercial movements in 2010 while MKmetric forecasts 155,000 and 172,000 at maximum (see Figure 12.8). These differences can be largely explained by the fact that Hamburg airport extrapolates a trend of commercial movements independently from the passenger forecasts while MKmetric derives the number of commercial movements from passenger demand. Given the supply of aircraft orders and the tendency towards rising load factors at the point of forecasting in 1995/6, MKmetric forecasts a relationship of 77 to 86 passengers per commercial movement in the year 2010 while Hamburg airport's method resulted in a marginal rise from 68 to 71 passengers per commercial movement. The latter could only happen if the airlines reverse their former decisions and order smaller aircraft and/or reverse their policy of increasing load factors. Neither explanation seem to be very realistic in a liberalized aviation market with a strong growth of leisure traffic.[6] The high numbers of movements seem to reflect an inconsistency between the number of movements and the passengers. To be more precise, at Hamburg airport the commercial movements follow the forecasts of MKmetric and are, in 2000, about five to ten thousand commercial movements below the forecast of the airport with a widening gap up to 40,000 commercial movements in 2010.

The airport management insisted on the validity of its forecast and based the airport expansion on this over-optimistic forecast. It seemed to follow the logic of predicting and demanding as much growth as possible with the hope that politics will follow the expertise of the airport and provide permission for the expansion.

This strategy involves major risks. Firstly, it leads to a tendency that too much capacity is provided too fast. It leads to relatively capital intensive production with relatively high fixed costs and low marginal costs. Yet, since airports must break even, the financing charge leads to a high average charge per aircraft and passengers. Secondly, the expansion of peak capacity is generally paid by all users, resulting in too low charges for the peak times served by the incumbent national carrier with grandfather rights and too high charges for off-peak times generally used by charter and new entrants. This tendency might result in a high yield market with lower passenger volumes and less attractive connections.

Finally, the strategy increases the risk of losing the acceptance of the airport in the adjacent neighbourhoods as the negative environmental impact is inversely related to movements. In the case of inner city airport Hamburg, the noise emissions, based on the movement forecast, were rising dramatically up to a level which would be sufficient for 20 to 23 million passenger movements. The policy in Hamburg reacted by accepting the forecast of MKmetric and implementing a noise budget, capping the noise levels at the level of 1997 (Niemeier, 2000). At other German airports such a rational outcome might not be reached and the expansion of airports might be blockaded.

In the past, the expansion of Frankfurt airport produced severe opposition leading to "one of the biggest and longest lasting political controversies of the

[6] Compared with network airlines, charter airlines use larger aircraft with narrow seating and high load factors. The rise of low-cost airlines was not foreseen in 1995.

Federal Republic of Germany" (Hujer and Kokot, 2001). The airport's plan to build a new runway will therefore not to be easy to achieve. Before going through the official public planning process, a mediation process should decide on the question of whether or not Frankfurt airport should be extended.

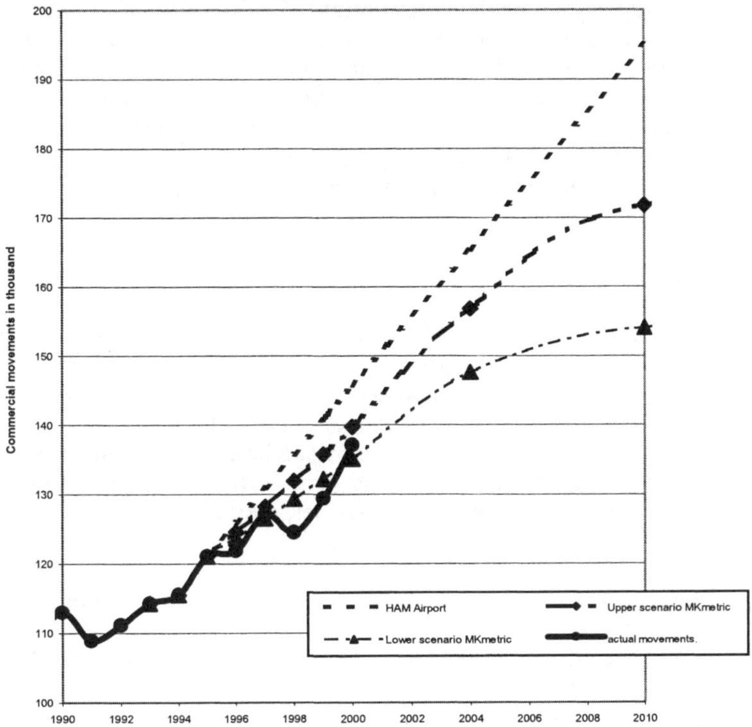

Figure 12.8 Comparison of forecasts for Hamburg airport

Mediation started in summer 1998 and the report was issued at the beginning of 2000. Several studies about the economic, ecological and social consequences were conducted on behalf of the three mediators and the supporting mediation group. All studies were thoroughly discussed in working groups and the scientific advice was cross-checked by other scientists. Five scenarios were defined, ranging from a reduction of movement over the current status to a full-scale expansion. Crucial for the decision was the result of the Input-Output study by Hujer and Kokot (Bulwien et al, 1999). The study came to the conclusion that while currently 142,000 jobs are directly or indirectly dependentd on the airport in the federal state of Hessen, the full-scale expansion would create an additional 57,000 jobs.

The concept of a mediation process is, in principle, a useful instrument. The transparency, rationality and the democratic legitimization of such a major infrastructure project can be increased compared with the ordinary planning process because, at a very early stage, all parties can participate. This presupposes a certain trust in the independence and rationality of the whole process. However, not all parties have such trust as most of the citizens refused to participate. No doubt, excellent studies with new insights were conducted. However, the logic of the mediation process is totally misleading. The mediation report discussed in detail the option not to extend the airport, but "*after valuing all aspects*" (Mediationsgruppe Flughafen Frankfurt, 2000, p. 178, my translation) recommended the full scale expansion. The mediation group valued the economic impact for Hessen and the Federal Republic of Germany to be of such a magnitude that the expansion became a necessity. However, this is not a rational economic decision because nothing is said as to how all the "benefits" of thousands of new jobs[7] are valued against the internal and external cost of the project; in effect a comprehensive social benefit-cost assessment was not carried out. There might be other investment projects with a higher return. Investment decisions are principally a question of the benefits and costs and not a question of direct or indirectly created jobs. Not even the internal costs are mentioned in the mediation report. Given the environmental externalities the political question of whether or not to undertake the expansion of Frankfurt airport should be better rationally decided by an appropriate benefit-cost analysis. The strategy of Frankfurt airport is typical for German and even for European airports, as the Airports Council International recommends the use of such economic impact studies. Investment decisions become then a question of how many jobs can be created by more or less precise input-output analysis so that the public accepts that the people must suffer the negative effects on the environment (Niemeier, 2001).

5. Preliminary Conclusions on Airport Capacity and Expansion

To avoid any misunderstandings, the argument is not so much about the expansion or otherwise of Frankfurt, Hamburg or any other airport. Expansion may indeed be warranted on economic grounds - however this has not yet been established.

The analysis of the previous three sections leads to the following four conclusions.

(a) In the next decade it is expected that only one of the two German hubs and one of the secondary hubs will be congested, some secondary hubs will have peak problems while the majority of German airports have excess capacity.
(b) The scarcity of airport infrastructure is not currently correctly evaluated by a functioning price mechanism as airports do not charge efficiently and slot trading is prevented by law. Relative prices have lost the function to give guidance to the question at what time and to what extent which of the German airports should be extended. When excess demand exists, it is not rationed away efficiently, but rather, expensive additional capacity is provided.
(c) The question of airport expansion becomes more and more a political question. In this political process the airports have developed a "predict and provide" strategy based on a logic of "jobs versus the environment". Airports hope that

[7] The mediation process also overlooks that the results have a bias towards full expansion and that the induced effects which amount to at least a fifth of the total effects are independent of the decision to expand capacity at Frankfurt Airport (Niemeier, 2001).

high growth promises based on optimistic forecasts and employment effects generated by input-output models will lead to an acceptance of the negative effects of growth, namely noise and pollution in the neighbourhood.

(d) The strategy is logically flawed, especially because the expansion is a question of the social net return on investment, which cannot be answered by an input output analysis, but only by a benefit-cost analysis. Therefore the strategy of airports is very risky as not only the economics of airport expansion but also the politics of airport expansion become economically irrational. It is doubtful whether a political consensus on airport expansion might be reached.

6. The Effects and Defects of Cost-based Regulation

The German system of airports shows all the signs of an inefficient allocation of resources and it is just these phenomena which regulatory economics expects from a system of low-powered cost-based regulation. The loosely defined German system seems to be a rate-of-return regulation as it allows charges to be raised with increasing costs allowing for an normal rate-of-return on capital (Niemeier, 2002).

(a) Inefficient choice of inputs (Sherman, 1989). If the allowed rate of return on capital is above the cost of capital the airport has an incentive to expand the capital base to increase profits (Averch Johnson effect). Furthermore, there are high incentives for cost-padding leading to productive inefficiency. In short, the German type of regulation sets incentives for costly airport infrastructure with excess capacity and gold plated terminals.

(b) Inefficient price structure (Sherman, 1989). Under cost-based regulation, the airport has no incentives to adopt peak pricing, but "rather lower the price of capital intensive peak demand in order to justify more capital assets, and charge a monopoly price at off-peak times to realize profit that greater capital will justify" (Sherman, 1989, p. 241). From this perspective, average pricing without time-related price differentiation is the expected outcome at German airports.

(c) Regulation of price structure according to book-keeping principles. Cost-based regulation fixes the price of different services in relation to the costs facing the problem how to allocate common costs. The whole procedure involves a very detailed procedure, which very often as in the case of German airports, is not done. The rather loose practice leads to a relatively uniform price structure with some not very effective price differentiation. Akin to such a concept are the notions of "willingness to pay" or "opportunity costs", which become relevant under conditions of congestion.

Of course, there might be also other factors such as public ownership[8] which contribute to the misallocation of resources, but as the regulatory framework sets

[8] Public ownership has obviously also a major impact on the performance as very often airports are seen as a tool of regional policy. Airports should increase local employment. Terminals are seen as highlighting the dynamism of a city. No doubt even for commercially run airports these factors are important as long as the owners remain the local government.

the incentives and defines the rules of the game, the cost-based type of regulation plays at least a major role. The more airports tend to become profit-seeking companies the more important these factors will become.

The economic regulation of German airports stems from the times of a regulated aviation market. Unlike the UK, Germany did not change the airport regulations with the liberalization of the aviation market, and even with the beginning of the process of privatization of airports the old system of cost-related regulation of airport charges remained unchanged, with the two exceptions of Hamburg and Frankfurt (see section 8). Germany did not even separate the functions of ownership and regulation so that very often they are done within the same ministry of a federal state.

7. Options to Improve the Situation

Regulatory economics has developed several methods to increase the efficiency of a system (for an overview cf. Kunz, 2000). I shall confine myself to three concepts that are currently debated by airport regulators and analyse whether these concepts are appropriate for the present situation of the German airport system with its specific institution. In other words, I do not intend to argue in general that the two other options are inferior. The first option is to give up ex-ante regulation and rely on general competition law. It is an option recommended by David Gillen for Canada (Gillen et al, 2001) and David Starkie for the UK (Starkie, 2001). Monitoring, the second option, is the new regulatory system for Australian airports, which supersedes the former price cap regulation (Productivity Commission, 2002). Thirdly, I will discuss the merits of the price cap regulation (see section 8), which I find appropriate for German airports.

Gillen and Starkie argue in short that the airport industry has lost the character of a natural monopoly. The abuse of monopoly power is limited by competition among airports and from other transport modes. Furthermore, the complementarity of revenue from competitive non-aviation and monopolistic aviation business provides an incentive for airports not to charge monopoly prices. The profit-seeking motive will lead even the monopolist to differentiate prices, introducing peak and congestion pricing. As all types of regulation are far from perfect and might result in distortions, the balance shifts towards liberalization and giving up ex-ante regulation. In case airports abuse monopoly power position, the competition regulator can step in.

In the past, airports were depicted as almost natural examples of natural monopoly.[9] It is one of the merits of Starkie to have questioned this belief as early as the mid 1980s (Starkie and Thompson, 1985). The empirical support is not conclusive because only a few studies have been carried out. However, research seems to indicate that average costs decline up to a level of 150,000 movements and 12.5 million passengers, stay constant and finally increase as hubs experience

[9] Ex-ante regulation is commonly justified by a combination of economies scale and scope and sunk costs relative to demand. A different reasoning is that even if scale economies have been exhausted, it may not be possible to build additional airports for environmental reasons. Thus, airports have a locational monopoly.

diseconomies of scale, due to congestion and environmental constraints (Pels, 2000, Productivity Commission, 2002). There is an agreement about the sunk cost character of airports.

However, the crucial question of up to what level the range of economies of scale and scope prevails relative to demand for a particular airport is hard to answer as the slope of the average cost curve and the borders of the local market are not known. As a first rough guess it seems that Frankfurt and Munich are definitely beyond that range. Düsseldorf might have no cost advantage over Cologne. All secondary hubs such as Hamburg, Stuttgart, Berlin and small airports like Bremen, Dresden, Hannover and Leipzig seem to have a natural monopoly in their origin destination traffic.[10] This strong market position is enhanced by legal barriers to entry so that even the hubs face no strong competition in the origin-destination market and only some competition in the transfer market. Perhaps with the exception of the Rhine area around Cologne and Düsseldorf the competitive pressures will be rather low. This at least the case in the North German market, where Hamburg faces an inelastic demand, and doubling the level of airport charges would decrease passenger demand by only 10 per cent Mandel (1997).

Given the mild pressures of competition it is doubtful if airports will be prevented from abusing their monopoly power in Germany. However, the complementarity of the different airport services might be an effective counter force. The complementary nature of non-aviation and aviation services is evident. The question is how strong this relation is.[11] I believe that it might be rather less powerful, as a first reaction of an airport management facing the complementarity would be to differentiate airport charges in order to increase traffic and thereby non-aviation revenue. This has not happened at German airports. Giving up ex-ante regulation for Germany might not change much. It may just stabilize a system with monopolistic slack and an inefficient price structure unsuited to deal efficiently with the capacity problems. Also, this inefficient system would have no reason to fear the power of German ex-post regulation. The ruling of the court in the case between Düsseldorf Airport and the airline Hapag-Lloyd is in this respect very instructive. Hapag-Lloyd, as with other airlines, refused to pay an 7.5 per cent increase in charges in April 2000. The court compared the charges of Düsseldorf with other German airports. As the charges were about the same level the court ruled that Düsseldorf was not abusing its monopoly power. The lower charges of price capped Hamburg airport were explicitly treated as an exception (Landgericht Düsseldorf, 2001). The German competition law, at least as practised by the courts, is quite ineffective in setting incentives for efficiency or even preventing the abuse of monopoly power.

---

[10] Of course, this is just a rough estimation. What is necessary is an industry analysis taking into account also the competition of other transport modes. The multi modal approach by Mandel (1997) for Northern Germany could be extended for German airports including the competition from other European airports.

[11] While the Productivity Commission finds "an incentive for airports to temper prices for aeronautical services" (2002, p. 188) the Network Economics Consulting Group on behalf of the Australian Competition and Consumer Commission concludes that the price elasticity for aeronautical services is rather too low to temper prices (ACCC, 2001).

Price monitoring is another option. On 13 May 2002, the Australian transport minister decided to abolish price cap regulation and to adopt a more light-handed regulation, namely price monitoring of the main airports for a period of five years with an independent review and the right to reverse powers of price control in case of abusive pricing. The decision is based on a study of the Productivity Commission, which analysed the two options of an improved price cap regulation and a monitoring system. The Commission recommended the latter one (Productivity Commission, 2002) and the minister agreed because monitoring should give "greater scope for airports to price, invest and operate efficiently (Commonwealth Treasurer, 2002, p. 3). In respect to capacity problems, the monitoring system explicitly encourages efficient price systems with price discrimination, peak and congestion pricing.

Monitoring differs from abolishing ex-ante regulation insofar as the behaviour of airports is closely followed. It claims to be more light handed and to avoid regulatory mistakes, but from my point of view these claims are doubtful. Price cap regulation gives the airport a price ceiling under which the airport can set freely the relative prices, thereby giving incentives to adopt efficient price structures. The Australian price monitoring system simply sets a range of price ceiling by the qualitative aim of preventing the abuse of market power. Furthermore, it encourages price differentiation by defining it as a review principle. Thus, the differences might be not as great as they appear at first sight.[12]

To be effective, monitoring needs a credible threat (Kunz, 1999). This has not been the case in New Zealand, as the Productivity Commission points out. Given the expertise gained in five years' experience of price capping and the strong institutional backing of the Productivity Commission, the threat against monopoly abuse and the incentives for efficient pricing may be sufficient in Australia. However, this institutional setting is not present in Germany, which even lacks the institution of an independent regulator. Therefore, monitoring might create a situation similar to New Zealand, where agreements between the airport and its users have led to long lasting litigation, and in the case of Auckland Airport, excessively high prices, such that the Commerce Commission of New Zealand recommended ex-ante regulation (New Zealand Commerce Commission, 2002). Such litigation is a sign that the transaction costs due to opportunist behavior are substantial and a severe problem of the relationship between airports and airlines. The court case between Düsseldorf airports and Hapag Lloyd might be just the beginning of long lasting court actions. Ex-ante regulation by price cap has the advantage of reducing transactions costs as it brings all parties involved together in an orderly described discourse.

[12] For a more critical assessment compare Forsyth (2002). So far, monitoring is a rather loosely defined concept. Therefore, a possible outcome might be a system similar to cost plus regulation as Forsyth argues.

8. Price Cap Regulation

The most serious problem[13] of German airports is the inefficient distribution of traffic due to a malfunctioning price system leading to the inability of rational investment decision making and to irrational planning processes of airport expansions. In addition, the lack of an independent regulator increases the potential for increasing transaction costs, as the Düsseldorf court case shows.

I would argue that in this specific situation price cap regulation copying the Hamburg model is the best way to improve the current situation of German airports (Niemeier, 2002). This process is gaining momentum as Frankfurt airport has also adopted a kind of fee cap. The price cap regulation of Hamburg airport has been effective from May 2001. It is intended to regulate only the bottleneck facilities. Thus, the price cap is based on a dual till principle, leaving the non-aviation business unregulated. The X is to be determined by the projected growth of productivity without rate of return considerations. Quality of services is being monitored taking into consideration the different quality levels airlines demand. Users are informed through improved consultations. Although the implementation has some shortcomings, for example, not covering the fee for central infrastructure for ground handling, or the asymmetry of the sliding scale factor in case of a downturn in traffic, the model (see below) could easily be developed to be an effective model for regulation of German airports. Essential for such a reform is the establishment of an independent regulator for the industry on the federal level (Niemeier, 2002; Wolf, 1997). The pro and cons of such an approach are as follows.

(a) Price cap defines a ceiling of the average price level so that the airport is free to differentiate the particular charges. The airport has an incentive to increase traffic by lowering charges for price elastic traffic and by increasing charges for price inelastic traffic. Therefore, price cap regulation might lead to an efficient price structure over a relatively short period of time as airport managers are undergoing a learning process from running an airport as a public utility to a profit seeking company. They have not yet acquired the knowledge about demand elasticities for Ramsey pricing, peak pricing or congestion pricing, which is largely new territory. However, once the rules are set in a way that such price regimes do pay off the learning process will accelerate.

(b) Acceptance by airlines. Price differentiation increase uncertainty as there are always some airlines better off and some airlines worse off. It was very instructive that the airlines accepted a new system of noise charges at Hamburg airport effective from 2002. The new system has its winners and losers, but because average charges had to be decreased according to the price cap formulae, the group of airlines accepted it. Price cap regulation combines the effects of an efficient price structure, which led to winners and losers with the promise to pass productivity gains to all airlines. Therefore it decreases the transactions cost of a reallocation of resources.

---

[13] On the problem of productive inefficiency see Niemeier (2002).

(c) Transparency and openness of consultation. These two principles seem to be self-evident. However, very often self-evident principles of good regulation are not practised, as in the current German system. The airlines appreciated that, because of their demands, a price cap review board was established providing more information, and that the *X* with a value of 2 was changed to a sliding scale with an *X* of 2 for passenger growth rates and a higher *X* for higher growth rates. All parties agreed, showing that transparency and openness of consultation processes are essential to the reduction of transactions costs. Trust in the impartial outcome of a consultation process is essential as trust reduces transactions costs (Williamson, 1985).

The cons of such a reform are mainly related to the question of how in practice price cap regulation works. Price cap regulation was intended by Littlechild as a pragmatic approach for a workable regulation of a monopolistic bottleneck without the negative incentives of cost based regulation. In the following discussions, price cap regulation lost some of his theoretical elegance and merits (Bös, 1991). In the static setting, incentives for cost reduction are lessened if the regulator bases his decisions on *X* on the cost of the regulated firm or on its rate of return. The Australian Productivity Commission has taken up this well known fact and argued that price caps "converge towards cost-based regulation … with associated high levels of regulatory involvement and risks of regulatory error..." (Productivity Commission, 2002, p. 308). However, from my point of view this argument is not conclusive as the regulator tries to estimate future productivity gains by avoiding gold plating. This intention is limited by the fact that the regulator does not want to set the *X* below the cost of the firm thereby risking bankruptcy, and also the limited knowledge of the regulator on the cost and demand function of the airport. However, the lag or price cap sets incentives to reveal not all, but at least some of the potential productivity gains.[14] Furthermore, benchmarking although far from perfect might be useful to prevent the regulator from underestimating the cost potential in a large degree. "The worse he is informed about costs or demand, the lower the X he must choose", writes Bös (2001, p. 18). However, the opposite can also be true.

One should not expect more from the pragmatic price cap method than it promises, namely fairly good regulation. Bös concludes his theoretical analysis on different regulatory methods that price cap regulation "implies a satisfactory compromise between information requirements for the regulator and negative incentives for the public" (Bös, 2001, p. 6). How well or badly price cap regulation performs in the airport sector has so far been not studied, but the results from other industries at least indicate that incentive regulation reduces prices and costs and performs better than traditional cost-based regulation (Ai and Sappington, 2001, Giulietti and Waddams Price, 2000).

The cons of price cap regulation must be taken seriously: however, they focus on the question how much of a possible productivity gain can be passed to the

[14] In the dynamic setting strategic behavior might induce the regulated firm to have relative high costs at the end of the review period so that the potential of the increase of productivity is hidden from the regulator (Bös, 1991).

airlines and the final consumer by price cap regulation. They do not directly[15] effect the first necessary object of reform, namely to establish an efficient price structure without high transaction costs in order to use the given capacity more effectively and to have the right price signals for investment. In other words, price cap regulation might not create such good incentives for productive efficiency as some have hoped, but it creates good incentives for Ramsey prices (Bradley and Price, 1988) and peak pricing (Brunekraft, 1998). Therefore, I think it is worthwhile to risk price cap regulation in Germany.

9. Price Cap and Underinvestment

It would be naive to expect that excess demand will vanish forever once prices are established, reflecting the relative scarcity of airport infrastructure. Sooner or later investment in airport infrastructure will be necessary. This raises the question of whether price cap regulation provides sufficient incentives for investment.

Investment in new terminals or in a new runway are long term projects with sunk costs while price caps have a shorter period, usually of five years. In the first stage the regulator sets the price cap, then the airport makes its investment decision and in the final stage the regulator reviews the previous price cap. Obviously, the airport might be subject to opportunistic behaviour of the regulator as it might reduce prices below long run average costs so that the return on investment becomes too low. The regulation might cause underinvestment and the investment decision depends on the credibility of regulation to allow for a fair return on investment (Vickers and Yarrow, 1988).

Helm and Thompson (1991) found that "there are some grounds for believing that privatized utility regulation - as practised in the UK - may result in underinvestment on the part of firms with high sunk cost infrastructure" (Helm and Thompson 1991, p. 238). They named BAA as an example for possible underinvestment. They acknowledged that the empirical question is open and I may add that it still is - both in general for public utilities[16] and, in particular, for the UK airports.

The CAA faces the particular problem of regulating Heathrow airport along with Manchester and the other BAA London airports. Heathrow airport faces heavy excess demand. The building of Terminal 5 has been discussed for years. The CAA is confined by law to the economic regulation in the narrow sense, leaving the external benefits and costs of such an investment to be decided in a public planning process. The statutory objectives of the CAA are among others "to promote the efficient, economic and profitable operation of such airports … and to

---

[15] Of course, an efficient price structure on a too high level due to productive inefficiency is still an inefficient outcome in the strict sense of Pareto. However, we are here aiming at something very pragmatic, namely some price differentiation and some decrease in the price level.

[16] Lieb-Doczy and Shuttleworth (2002) name three examples for a hold up problem between regulator and private firm, but Ai and Sappington (2001) found that aggregate investment of US telecommunications does not vary systematically under incentive regulation relativel to rate-of return regulation.

encourage investment in new facilities to satisfy anticipated demands" (CAA, 2001, p. ix). The investment is characterized by large sunk costs for fixed 'lumpy' capital with relatively low operating costs. The historic accounting values are below the opportunity costs given the land valuations of such an attractive site in west London. In order to address this problem, the CAA has evaluated several options for setting the price cap (CAA, 2001).

Firstly, the CAA finds the current standard model with average accounting costs on a single till basis inappropriate as it would lead to the greatest divergence of prices from the market clearing level. Furthermore, it argues that regulation should focus on monopolistic bottlenecks, but not extend to services, where market works work more or less effectively and high profits reflect the scarcity of specific sites. The single till might distort commercial business in the non-aviation sector.[17] Secondly, it proposes a revised regulatory cost base (RRCB) on dual till basis with revaluation of existing assets and returns allowable on future capital reflecting alternative use value. This focuses regulation on a monopolistic bottleneck with prices above single till prices, but below market clearing levels and below forward looking incremental (long run average) costs, thereby increasing incentives to invest. The CAA proposes to set the price cap for current outputs (up to 70 million passengers) on this basis. Thirdly, it proposes a price cap based on the incremental cost of new capacity at Heathrow for a price path beyond 2008 with existing output based on RRCB plus a premium for additional aircraft movements delivered by existing runways. The premium should reflect the difference between the cost of additional output for the airport and the value of additional output for users. Furthermore, contracting between airport and users is recommended, a service quality term should be introduced and enhanced information on capital investment planning should be provided to the airlines (see Andrew and Hendricks, 2002).

This package addresses the central problem of a credible commitment very well. Of course, the current regulator cannot bind the future regulator, but establishing a clear framework clearly signals to the airports that the regulator will leave the airport a fair return on investment for cost effective investments. The whole process is transparent to all parties, strikes a good balance between various interests, and should lead to relatively low transaction costs. It avoids the risk of a fully liberalized system, in which an unregulated monopoly might increase capacity too slowly to reap scarcity rents. It is superior to the German cost-related regulation of investment, where the airlines miss even the basic rights of information on investment programmes given to UK-airport users for years. Adopting such a regulation for German airports would enhance the economic rationality of investment decisions in narrow sense and could be a basis for a rational decision addressing the environmental problem.

[17] For an extensive discussions of the pro and cons of the single till principle see "The Single Till Approach to the Price Regulation of Airports" by Starkie and Yarrow (2000) Surprisingly the Competition Commission finds the "arguments and current evidence for moving to the dual till ... not persuasive" (CAA, Press Release, 13 August 2002).

10. Price Cap Plus Enhancing Competition

Price cap regulation is not a "panacea" (Armstrong et al, 1994, p. 193), but only an imperfect substitute for workable competition. Therefore, it needs to be supplemented by a strategy to promote competition and to decide rationally public policy issues.

- Slot trading. Price cap regulation is an appropriate tool to set incentives for productive efficiency and for peak pricing. However, as the case of Heathrow clearly proves, price cap regulation has its limits, if an airport is heavily congested and an expansion of capacity is blocked for political reasons. Regulated airport charges did not clear the market at Heathrow in the past decade. Slot trading could clear the market and could make the regulation less complicated (CAA, 2001 and Forsyth, 1997).
- Open skies. Restrictive air service agreements limit the competition among airports as airlines are restricted to certain airports and secondary airports cannot develop a niche market. Open skies would lead to a change in market shares among German airports and its European competitors in the long haul market (Gillen et al, 2000).
- Privatization. While, with the exception of the US, a strong trend towards privatization is observable worldwide (Graham, 2001), in Germany the overwhelming majority of airports are owned and sometimes even directly managed by the state or by state agencies. So far only a few private-public partnerships with majority rights for the state have emerged in Germany. Privatization gives the opportunity to increase efficiency by changing the principal-agent structure and by an influx of know-how leading to a more market based pricing policy (Soltwedel and Wolf, 1996).
- Cross ownership control. Horizontal alliances or mergers between airports that are in competition have the potential to effect competition negatively. This is important if more and more airports lose the position of a natural monopoly due to a strong rise in demand. As most airport services have anoverwhelming local content, economies of scale and scope are limited and the welfare loss through strict cross ownership restrictions as in Australia might be worthwhile for Germany (Niemeier and Wolf, 2002).
- Rational decisions on environmental aspects of airport expansion.[18] Once the narrow economics of airport expansion are treated rationally by a more balanced traffic distribution and better use of existing capacity, a more realistic amount of demand for new capacity with less negative environmental impact will emerge. Once the horror scenarios boil down the airports might change their strategy and engage in a rational discourse.

[18] Economic and environmental regulation are analytically two separate issues. Having said that, it is important to address both problems as even the best incentives to invest by good economic regulation cannot overcome blockades of investment projects due to environmental restrictions.

There are two options[19] to address the problem of investment and externalities. Major projects of airport expansions can be assessed in a public planning process on the basis of benefit-cost analysis. The alternative should be chosen which maximizes social welfare. The second option is to set environmental standards like noise or pollution by politics, which must be met by the airport (cf. Baumol and Oates, 1988). The privatized airport bears the risk of investment. Hamburg's Aviation policy has been increasingly guided by the second option in setting a noise budget (Niemeier, 2000) thereby outperforming other German airports such as Düsseldorf airport in the rational management of environmental issues.

11. Conclusions

The assessment of the current and future capacity problems of German airports shows that only one of the two German hubs and one of the secondary hubs has excess demand with a rising tendency. Some secondary hubs will have peak problems, but even in the long term the majority of German airports have idle capacity reserves. These unbalances occur under a system in which prices (charges and slot prices) have lost their function to guide traffic to their best uses and to signal when, where and to what extent capacity should be provided. In this environment the airports have adopted a predict and provide strategy to increase capacity whenever future demand might reach capacity limits at peak times. In order to overcome environmental problems they have adopted a strategy of "jobs versus the environment" relying on regional impact studies showing that that airport expansion creates thousands of new jobs. Both strategies are increasingly risky. Increasing capacity well ahead of time is very costly and furthermore, overestimates the negative impact on the environment making the political process more complicated. Investment decisions cannot be based on impact studies[20], but only by a benefit-cost analysis. Given these risks a political consensus on airport expansion might not be reached.

The economic and political problems are mainly rooted in the inefficient incentive structure of the regulatory framework. Cost plus regulation sets incentives to an inefficient choice of inputs, which leads to costly airport infrastructure with excess capacity and gold plated terminals, and to an inefficient price structure, which leads to average charges with too low prices for peak demand in order to justify capacity expansion.

As an alternative to cost plus regulation, there are currently three regulatory systems discussed, namely liberalization without ex ante regulation, monitoring and price cap regulation. These systems are evaluated as to whether they might be appropriated to increase the efficiency of the German airport system. Relying only

---

[19] There is also the option of voluntary agreements between the airport and it's neighbours along the lines developed by the Coase and Buchanan school. However, because of the public good character of externalities, the greater the numbers affected by airport pollution the lower the probability to reach efficient solutions (cf. Frank, 1983 p. 288).

[20] Impact studies tend to exaggerate the effects on economic activity and do not provide measures of benefits.

on ex-post regulation will probably lead to a system with monopolistic slack and inefficient price structure as German airports are mostly regional natural monopolies and/or sheltered from competition by law. They face no effective competition and German competition law cannot act a substitute for competition. Monitoring presupposes a creditable threat to regulate the industry if monopoly abuse occurs. While it may be argued that, in Australia, the institutions have gained the necessary experience and knowledge of the industry through price cap regulation, German regulators lack these. The threat to regulate cannot be called credible in Germany. Therefore monitoring might lead to a system as in New Zealand with long lasting litigation and high transaction costs.

The pros and cons of price cap regulation are discussed. As price cap regulation is practised at Hamburg airport it may be easily extended to other airports A truly independent regulator should be implemented who will take care of the technical shortcomings of the Hamburg model, like the asymmetry of the sliding scale. Price cap regulation has the advantage of giving the airports more freedom in their pricing policy than cost plus regulation. Incentives are set for a new price structure and a better use of the existing capacity. As a new price structure with peak pricing creates winners and losers among the airlines, it is very important that price cap regulation passes the productivity gains to airlines and to consumers through a lower level. The combination of an efficient price structure and a lower level of charges might even overcome the resistance of those airlines choosing to fly at peak times. Price cap regulation has the advantage of establishing an efficient price structure with low transactions costs. In the short run, price cap regulation could reduce excess demand and install a price system that signals where and when to expand capacity.

Price cap regulation is supposed to lead to underinvestment, if the regulator cannot credibly promise the airport a fair return on investment. The clear, transparent, and robust approach of investment regulation of the CAA shows that a credible promise can be given.[21] Compared to Germany the process is superior as it provides the airlines and the public with more information.

Price cap, far from being a perfect substitute for effective competition, can and should be combined with a variety of measures to promote competition. Slot trading, open skies, privatization with cross ownership controls should be part of a comprehensive reform of the basic rules of the airport industry. Such a reform could lead to a rational management of airport infrastructure with less excess demand and a realistic demand for new capacity. The negative environmental impact would be less than currently forecast, giving the airports an opportunity to engage in a rational discourse on the social cost and benefits of airports' extensions.

In a nutshell, the answer to the question of wheter the German airport industry needs new rules to use and extend capacity efficiently can only be positive. The industry needs less, but effective, regulation with incentives for more competition and for a rational discourse on environmental problems.

[21] Of course, the creditability depends also on future regulators.

Acknowledgements

The author is grateful to Achim Czerny, Heinz Decker, Ingo Fehrs, Peter Forsyth, David Gillen, Cathal Guiomard, Kai Hüschelrath, Benedikt Mandel, Jürgen Müller, Till Neuscheler, Wilhelm Pfähler and Hartmut Wolf for extensive comments on earlier drafts of the paper. The responsibility for any remaining shortcomings remains the author's.

References:

Ai, C. and Sappington, D.E. (2001) *The Impact of State Incentive Regulation on the U.S. Telecommunications Industry*, http://bear.cba.ufl.edu/sappington/papers/itxt4.pdf.

Andrew, D. and Hendriks, N. (2002) *Price cap regulation of airports in the UK*, Paper presented at the German Aviation Research Seminar, "The Economic Regulation of Airports: Recent Developments in Australia, North America and Europe, November 8-9, Bremen.

Armstrong, M., Cowan, S. and Vickers J. (1994) *Regulatory Reform: Economic Analysis and British Experience*, Cambridge Mass, MIT Press.

Australian Competition and Consumer Commission (2001) *Price Regulation of Airport Services,* Submission to the Productivity Commission's draft Report October 2001, www. pc.gov.au.

Baumol, W.J. and Oates, W.E. (1988) *The Theory of Environmental Policy*, 2nd edition, Cambridge University Press.

Bös, D. (1991) Privatization, *A Theoretical Treatment*, Oxford, Oxford University Press.

Bös, D. (2001) *Regulation: Theory and Concepts*, Bonn http://www.wiwi.uni-bonn.de/users/fiwi/www/papers/pps/ppslist.htm.

Bradley, I. and Price, C. (1988) The economic regulation of private industries by price constraints, *Journal of Industrial Economics*, Vol. 37, pp. 99-106.

Brunekreeft, G. (1998) *Price capping and peak-load pricing in network industries*, Discussion Paper No. 73, University of Freiburg.

Bulwien, H., Hujer, R. Kokot, S., Mehlinger, C., Rürup, B., Voßkamp, T. (1999) *Einkommens- und Beschäftigungseffekte des Flughafens Frankfurt/Main*, Frankfurt.

Button, K.and Stough, R. (2000) *Air Transport Networks*, Edward Elger Cheltenham.

CAA (2002) *Competition Commission Current Thinking on Dual Till - CAA statement on process Press Release*, 13 August 2002, London, www.caa.co.uk.

CAA (2001) *Heathrow, Gatwick, Stansted and Manchester Airports Price Caps - 2003-2008: CAA Preliminary Proposals - Consultation Paper*, London, www.caa.co.uk.

Commonwealth Treasurer (2002) *Productivity Commission Report on Airport Price Regulation*, Joint Press Release Minister for Transport & Regional

Services and Treasurer, www.treasurer.gov.au/tsr/content/pressreleases/2002/024

Costa, P.R., Harned, D.S. And Lundquist, J.T. (2002) *Rethinking the aviation industry*, McKninsey Quarterly, 2002, number 2, www.mckinseyquarterly.com/article.

Doganis, R. (1992) *The Airport Business*, London, Routledge

Ewers, H.-J., Tegner, H., Joerss, I., Eckhardt, C. F., Jacubowski, P., Meyer, C.A., Brenck, A. and Czerny, A. (2001) *Possibilities for the Better Use of Airports Slots in Germany and the EU,* Berlin, TU-Berlin.

Forsyth, P. (1977) Price Regulation of Airports: Principles with Australian Applications, *Transportation Research-E*, Vol. 33, No 4, 297-309.

Forsyth, P. (2001) *Airport Price Regulation: Rationales, Issues and Directions for Reform,* Submission to the Productivity Commission Inquiry: Price Regulation of Airport Services, Department of Economics Discussion Paper 19/02, Monash University Clayton.

Forsyth, P. (2002) *Replacing Regulation: Airport Price Monitoring in Australia,* Paper presented at the German Aviation Research Seminar, "The Economic Regulation of Airports: Recent Developments in Australia, North America and Europe, November 8-9, Bremen.

Flughafen Hamburg GmbH (1996) *Antrag der Flughafen Hamburg GmbH auf Planfeststellungsbeschluss gemäß 8 Abs. 1 LuftVG für die Änderung des Flughafens Hamburg durch Errichtung und Betrieb eines Vorfeldes 2 nebst damit im Zusammenhang stehenden und im Antrag konkretisierten Maßnahmen und durch eine neue Lärmschutzhalle vom 23. Dezember 1996,* Hamburg.

Fridström, L. *et al.* (2002) *Competitive Airlines: Towards a more Competitive Policy in Relation to the Air Travel Market*, Report from the Nordic Competition Authorities, Copenhagen, Helsinki, Oslo, Stockholm, www.konkurransetilsynet.no/archive/internett/publikasjoner/nordisk_rapport/nordic_report_competitive_airlines_01_02.pdf.

Frank, J. (1983) *Markt versus Staat. Zur Kritik einer Chicago-Doktrin*, in Jahrbuch Ökonomie und Gesellschaft, Vol. 1, pp. 257-298, Frankfurt.

Gillen, D., Hinsch, H., Mandel, B., and Wolf, H., (2000), *The Impact of Liberalizing International Aviation Bilaterals on the Northern German Region*, Ashgate.

Gillen, D., Henriksson, L. and Morrison, W. (2001), *Airport Financing, Costing, Pricing and Performance in Canada*, Final Report to the Canadian Transportation Act Review Committee, Waterloo.

Giulietti, M. and Waddams Price, C. (2000) *Incentive Regulation and Efficient Pricing: Empirical Evidence*, Research Paper Series No. 00/2 Centre for Management under Regulation Warwick Business School.

Graham, A. (2001) *Managing Airports, An International Perspective*, Butterworth Heinemann, Oxford.

Helm, D. and Thompson, D. (1991) Privatised Transport Infrastructure and Incentives to Invest, *Journal of Transport Economics and Policy*, 25(3), pp. 231.246.

Hujer, R. and Kokot, S. (2001) Frankfurt Airport's impact on regional and national employment and income, in W. Pfähler (ed.), *Regional Input-Output Analysis, Baden-Baden*, Nomos Verlag.

Kunz, M. (1999) Airport Regulation: The Policy Framework, in: Pfähler, W., Niemeier, H.-M. and Mayer (Eds.), O. *Airports and Air Traffic – Regulation, Privatisation and Competition*, Peter Lang Verlag: Frankfurt New York , pp. 11-55.

Kunz, M. (2000) Regulierungsregime in Theorie und Praxis, in: Knieps, G./Brunekreeft, G. (Eds.) *Zwischen Regulierung und Wettbewerb – Netzsektoren in Deutschland*, Heidelberg, Physica.

Landgericht Düsseldorf (2001) *Urteil in dem Rechtsstreit der Flughafen Düsseldorf GmbH gegen Hapag-Lloyd Fluggesellschaft mbH vom 20.6.01*, 34 0 (Kart) 36/01 Düsseldorf.

Levine, M.E. (1969) Landing fees and the Airport Congestion Problem, *Journal of Law and Economics*, 12, pp.79-109.

Lieb-Doczy E. and Shuttleworth G. (2002) *Grundprinzipien eines wirtschaftlich effizienten regulatorischen Prozesses*, London, www.nera.com.

Mandel, B. (1997) *Luftverkehrsprognose für den Flughafen Hamburg*, Untersuchung von MKmetric im Auftrag der Wirtschaftsbehörde der Freien und Hansestadt Hamburg, Hamburg.

Marshall, A. (1890/1920) *Principles of Economics*, 1st edition 1890, 8th edition 1920, London, Macmillan.

Mediationsgruppe Flughafen Frankfurt (2000) *Bericht Flughafen Frankfurt/Main*, Frankfurt.

Morrison, S.A. (1982) The Structure of Landing Fees at Uncongested Airports, *Journal of Transport Economics and Policy* 16, pp. 151-159.

Niemeier, H.-M. (2000) Towards an efficient market-based environmental policy – a view form the Hamburg Region, in Immelmann, T., Mayer, O. G., Niemeier, H.M., Pfähler, W., (editors), *Aviation versus Environment?*, Frankfurt M., New York, Peter Lang Verlag.

Niemeier, H.-M. (2001) On the use and abuse of Impact Analysis for airports: A critical view from the perspective of regional policy, in W. Pfähler (ed.), *Regional Input-Output Analysis*, Baden-Baden, Nomos Verlag.

Niemeier, H.-M. (2002) Regulation of Airports: The Case of Hamburg Airport – a View from the Perspective of Regional Policy, *Journal of Air Transport Management*, Vol. 8, pp. 37-48.

Niemeier, H.-M. and Wolf, H. (2002) Strategische Allianzen zwischen Flughäfen – notwendiges Gegengewicht zur Blockbildung der Fluggesellschaftten? in Knorr, A., *Europäischer Luftverkehr – wem nutzen die strategischen Allianzen?*, Schriftenreihe der DVWG, B 246 Bergisch-Gladbach.

New Zealand Commerce Commission (2002) *Final Report. Part IV Inquiry into Airfield Services at Auckland, Wellington and Christchurch International Airports,* August.

Pels, E. (2000) *Airport Economics and Policy Efficiency, Competition and Interaction with Airlines*, Tinbergen Research Series 222, Netherlands.

Productivity Commission (2002) *Price Regulation of Airport Services; Report No 19*, AusInfo, Canberra.

Sherman, R. (1989) *The Regulation of Monopoly*, Cambridge UK, Cambridge University Press.

Soltwedel, R. and Wolf, H. (1996), *Privatisierung öffentlicher Unternehmen – Eine ordnungspolitsche Reflexion*, in: DVWG (editor), *Privatisierung deutscher Flughäfen*, Bergisch Gladbach, pp. 4-20.

Starkie, D. (1998) Allocating Airport Slots: A Role for the Market, *Journal of Air Transport Management*, Vol. 4, pp. 111-116.

Starkie, D. (2001) Reforming UK Airport Regulation, *Journal of Transport Economics and Policy*, 35, 119-135.

Starkie, D and Thompson, D. (1985) *Privatising London's Airports*, Institute for Fiscal Studies, Report 16, London.

Starkie, D. and Yarrow (2000), *The Single Till Approach to the Price Regulation of Airports*, London, www.caa.co.uk.

Urbatzka, E., Focke, H., Stader, A. and Wilken, D. (1999) *Szenarien des Luftverkehrs im Jahr 2010 vor dem Hintergrund kapazitätsbeengter Flughafeninfrastruktur,* Forschungsbericht 43, Deutsches Zentrum für Luft- und Raumfahrt, Köln.

Viner, J (1931) Cost curves and supply curves, *Zeitschrift für Nationalökonomie,* Vol. 3, pp. 23-46.

Vickers, J. and Yarrow, G. (1988) *Privatization, An Economics Analysis*, MIT Press, Cambridge, Mass.

Vickrey, W. (1971), Responsive pricing of public utility services, *Bell Journal of Economics*, 2, pp. 337-46.

Williamson, O.E. (1985) *The Economic Institutions of Capitalism*, Free Press, New York.

Wolf, H. (1997) *Grundsatzfragen einer Flughafenprivatisierung in Deutschland*, Kiel.

Part D
Towards Institutional Reforms

Chapter 13

Optimal Economic Regulation: A Short Survey of Developments from the 1970s to the 1990s

Cathal Guiomard

> The historic link between subsidies and restriction of competition is an ancient one. In 1690 Louis XIV officially adopted and began to subsidise the ... *Comédie Française*. He gave it the exclusive right to perform all plays by authors no longer living. Many independent ventures were formed, but as they expanded their offerings, the *Comédie* complained and induced the Crown to impose various restrictions on them: Some could let their characters faint or bleed, but not die. Some could let their performers do only acrobatics or pantomime. Two small establishments ... were forced to hang a gauze curtain between actors and audience. One amateur theatre ... could open only at 7, over an hour after the others. (Kahn, 1989, Vol. 2, p. 4)

Introduction[1]

In this paper, I review briefly the recent evolution of the academic perspective on optimal economic regulation by reference to selected representative publications from the 1970s to the 1990s. Other papers in the present volume (for instance, Forsyth and McKenzie-Williams) indicate the extent to which recent reviews of airport regulatory policy incorporate the evolving academic perspective.

Lying behind, and perhaps partly prompting, academic research into economic regulation is the gradual worldwide liberalisation of such economic sectors as aviation, telecoms, electricity, gas, and postal services. A thorough analysis of the technological and economic reasons for this liberalisation of

[1] I am grateful for helpful discussions with, and comments from, my colleagues at the Commission for Aviation Regulation (CAR) during the preparation of this paper; also from participants at the 6th Air Transport Research Society Conference in Seattle, July 2002, and especially from Professor Hans-Martin Niemeier of the Hamburg Institute of International Economics and Professor Peter Forsyth of the Department of Economics of Monash University in Australia. The views expressed in the paper are personal and do not necessarily reflect the opinions or positions of the Irish Commission for Aviation Regulation.

network industries is offered in Newbery (1999). As part of this liberalisation process, many sectoral economic regulators have been created. The academic research agenda addresses the question of how these agencies should go about their work.[2] Over the past 15 years or so, the focus of the academic analysis of economic regulation has substantially changed direction. Some of the main changes are briefly surveyed below.

Marginal-Cost Pricing

In 1970, Alfred Kahn, in a text that remains a classic in the field, set out an exhaustive description and analysis of the regulation of US public utilities, as it was practised at the time and as he thought it could be improved upon.

He laid the greatest possible stress on marginal cost as the basis of efficient pricing. In the reprint of this book, which appeared some 20 years later, Kahn pointed to a particular instance where the marginal-cost principle is still flouted in the US: the charging for landing 'slots' at congested airports according to the weight of the aircraft, rather than by auctioning or with reference to variable marginal costs (Kahn, 1989, p. xxii).

Kahn considered in detail the case of natural monopoly, defining it as:

> an industry in which the economies of scale - that is, the tendency for average costs to decrease the larger the producing firm - are continuous up to the point that one company supplies the entire demand. [Natural monopoly] is a reason, also, why competition is not supposed to work well in these industries. (Kahn, Vol. 1, p.123 - 4)

Spulber, (1989), offers an equivalent though perhaps clearer definition: under natural monopoly a single firm is able to serve the entire market at less cost than could two or more firms, p. 3).

The existence – or otherwise – of natural monopoly conditions is plainly something to be determined empirically.

This definition is more precise than the rule of thumb sometimes applied, namely, industries with large fixed costs. Properly defined, 'fixed costs' are a short-run concept; they are the costs of an input in fixed supply. However, in the longer term, all inputs are variable. Therefore, an industry may be characterised in the short run by fixed costs, but when all inputs are variable, returns to scale may nonetheless be constant or decreasing. For example, agriculture is an industry with very high fixed costs in the short run, but without such economies of scale as to make agriculture production by a single farm the most efficient way to organise production.

---

[2] These new institutions have become topics of sometimes-heated discussion. Following the first report of the Irish CAR on airport pricing, a columnist with an Irish daily newspaper remarked: "Have you heard about regulators? It rhymes with terminators and they're like a sort of new gunslinger in town." Fergus Finlay, Irish Examiner newspaper, 1st September 2001.

Kahn goes on to draw out the implication of economies of scale for a (socially) optimal economic organisation. Such a company's marginal costs will be lower than average costs and therefore a contradiction arises between two fundamental rules for a social optimum:

1. Buyers should pay (only) marginal costs, and
2. Total revenues should cover total costs.

There are only two ways out of this contradiction: either marginal-cost pricing *for all buyers*, or commercial break-even, has to be sacrificed. If break-even is abandoned, a company can survive only if it receives a subsidy from taxpayers. In practice, this has not been the route policymakers have mostly opted to go.

Alternatively, marginal-cost pricing must be sacrificed. As Kahn argues, the justification for marginal cost pricing lies entirely in the elasticity of demand: consumers buy more, or less, than the optimum according to the price charged. Then why not charge customers (in practice: classes of customers) according to their different willingness to pay? This would allow total revenues to cover total costs while permitting a level of output closer to the optimum through seeking to avoid turning away any class of buyer (up to the optimum output) by charging them no more than they are willing to pay for that output.

Of course, such price discrimination is one area at least where there could be tensions between the approaches of economic regulators and of competition authorities. Price discrimination is open to abuse, particularly where buyers have no choice of supplier. Furthermore, if different prices are charged to customers who are themselves commercial rivals - for example, competing transport modes - competition in *their* industry may be impaired, requiring a trade-off between the importance of different inefficiencies to be evaluated.

When is price discrimination justified? In theory, the answer is when three tests are met:[3]

1. Lower charges are required to bring forward the additional demand.
2. The cost of meeting the extra increment of business is less than the average cost of the total operation before satisfying the extra demand.
3. The elasticity of demand of the new business is large enough to increase total revenues by at least the additional costs incurred.

Did price discrimination in regulated US industries generally meet these conditions? Kahn comments on the case of US aviation (before 1970) as follows.

> Consider for example promotional airfares ... As long as reduced fares are for standby service or travel on off-peak days or seasons they are not discriminatory; they merely reflect (perhaps even inadequately) the lower marginal costs of travel that makes no marginal demand on capacity. To the extent that they are offered to select groups - young people under 21, wives and children accompanying husbands - they are discriminatory but the discrimination may be justified because

[3] An alternative to price discrimination would be two- (or multi-) part tariffs.

> (1) of the presence of short-run decreasing costs at times when capacity is in excess and (2) the demand by these classes of travellers may well be more elastic than by single unaccompanied adults, many of them travelling on business. But to the extent that the purpose of such fares, or of the subsidies paid to the airlines that serve smaller towns or the discriminatory low rates on short-hop trips, is merely to 'promote air travel' or the habit of using airplanes, without reference to whether the travel promoted is on-peak or off-peak, it seems to lack economic justification, in view of the apparent absence of economies of scale in the air transport business in the relevant range. (Kahn, 1989, Vol 1, p.149-150).

Even in the relatively narrow set of circumstances in which he considers economic regulation to be justified, Kahn does not underestimate the practical difficulties in applying the principle of marginal-cost pricing. At least the following set of issues falls to be considered by an economic regulator:

1. Quality of Service
2. Operating Expenditures (Opex)
3. Capital Expenditures (Capex)
4. The Rate Base (or regulatory asset base, the RAB, in UK parlance)
5. The Allowed Rate of Return
6. The Rate Structure

There is an evident challenge in seeking to carry out this large set of difficult tasks. But, in addition, Kahn is concerned about the possible organisational culture of regulators' offices. He argues that, at least historically, the 'regulatory mentality' has suffered from an anti-competitive bias. The result is that regulation has often *not* supplemented (inadequate) competition but in fact has supplanted it.[4] This leads to a general regulatory dilemma.

Imperfect Knowledge

An important shortcoming of the approach to economic regulation just discussed is that it makes formidable data and computational demands on regulators. But, far from having perfect information, economic regulators may know relatively little about

1. The demand relationships for the regulated firm's products;
2. The firm's total costs and how these vary with output; and
3. How new investments will raise or lower costs.

In the 1980s, the alternative concept of regulation by 'price caps' was devised and implemented in the UK. This approach arose out of the prospect of substantial deregulation of utility businesses in the UK, the corresponding requirement to set

---

4 As illustrated by the quote on the cover page.

up a regulatory regime, and the known informational asymmetry between the regulator and the regulated entity.

The logic of price-cap regulation has recently been assessed for the UK Civil Aviation Authority by Professor David Sibley (Sibley, 2000).

Sibley notes that, in the simplest version of price caps, the regulator does nothing except impose a cap on the regulated firm's prices and enforce adherence to that cap. The cap typically declines from one year to the next at a given percentage rate *X*. The theory assumes that the firm has superior information about demand and costs, as compared to the regulator. Using this superior information, the firm simply acts to maximize profits, discounted into the future, subject to the price cap.

Price-cap regulation mimics a competitive market in which the producer cannot influence the price and can increase profits only by reducing costs. *As long as the cap is set at the economically correct level*, this creates powerful incentives for the firm to behave efficiently. In any given time period, the firm gains by trimming its costs and reducing waste. Furthermore, because the market value of the firm is the present value of the future stream of its profits, the firm also gains from efficient investment behaviour over time. Price caps also allow the firm to price discriminate so that economic efficiency may rise as well, as the firm offers prices that are determined by consumer tastes.

However, Sibley stresses that for these attractive properties of price cap regulation to hold, there is one key requirement: the regulator must be able credibly to pre-commit to refrain from opportunistic behavior towards the firm. Suppose that the firm has been operating under a system other than price caps and is put under a price cap scheme. The regulator may have formed some understanding of the firm's costs and marketing abilities under the old system, which will be shown to be false under the new one.

If the firm does indeed respond to the incentives offered by the price cap plan by reducing costs or pricing more efficiently than before price caps, the regulator, observing the new, lower costs and more efficient prices, may wish to respond by requiring the firm to return some or all of the resulting extra profit. In a price cap system, a common way to accomplish this is to increase the *X* factor, even after the regulator has committed to a particular level of *X*. Unless a regulator credibly commits to refrain from such behaviour, the firm's incentive to pursue efficiencies is considerably reduced.

An example, discussed in Forsyth in this volume, was the 2002 decision of the Australian authorities to lift airport price-cap regulation (and replace it with price monitoring), only five years after its introduction, because, Forsyth argues, price-cap regulation against a difficult economic background led to serious profit volatility and the risk of firm failures.

There exists a large academic literature on optimal regulatory incentive schemes in the presence of informational issues such as adverse selection and moral hazard.[5] Although the schemes described in this literature are generally too complex to implement directly, they all have one element in common: optimal

---

[5] Some of this literature is surveyed in Laffont and Tirole (1994).

regulation with informational asymmetries involves some degree of earnings sharing. Thus, appending at least a small amount of earnings sharing to a price cap scheme increases economic efficiency.

As the discussion of commitment above makes clear, despite good intentions, in practice regulators often do not honor initial commitments to a regulatory scheme. There will always arise political pressures to increase X if the firm is making large profits, even if those profits are due to no more than responding to incentives put in place by the regulator. Similarly, if the firm's earnings are unexpectedly low for too long, there will be pressures to modify the scheme so as to increase earnings.

Sibley proposes a potential response to this problem: periodic adjustment of the *X* factor according to a formula that is known in advance to the firm, and is not opportunistic.

Balancing Market and Regulatory Failures

From today's perspective, one of the striking features of the original approach to the analysis of economic regulation is that the regulatory process itself generally lies outside the analysis. Economic regulators arrive from out of the blue to correct the imperfections of the market without themselves being analysed as entities pursuing their own institutional or other objectives within the same world that the other actors also form part of. This is part of the reason for Kahn's comment that:

> The ... major limitation of any mere exposition of the normative rules of economic behaviour and performance [is] that they tell us absolutely nothing about how to achieve these results ... by what kinds of institutional arrangements can we obtain the maximum assurance ... that the goals will in fact be achieved?

That shortcoming is being made good. Spulber (1989) offers a thorough (graduate-level) survey. He argues that a full analysis of regulation needs to take account of the following drawbacks to regulation.

> Regulation may entail high administrative costs. The formulation and implementation of regulation may entail policies that not only are redistributive in nature but that interfere with allocative efficiency. Regulation of markets is subject to all of the problems that attend economic planning. The regulator operates with imperfect information. Regulatory policies may be second best, reflecting rules of thumb, administrative procedures, and institutional constraints. Even well-intentioned public policies can create incentives for inefficient private behaviour. (Spulber, 1989, p.65)

In the Spulber approach, a three-part 'market failure test' is used to evaluate the need for economic regulation (or, equally, competition policy). First, the market in question must be shown to depart from the first-best equilibrium. Second, it must be shown that regulation - facing the same institutional, technological and informational constraints (that likely are the cause of the market failure) - can alleviate or correct the market failure. Third, the potential benefits of a regulatory remedy must justify market intervention, taking account of the costs and any distortions of economic regulation.

Spulber presents his analysis using the contestable markets framework. His argument for doing so is that this amounts to the framework of perfect competition but without the need to assume that there are a large number of firms that can compete only by varying output (but not price). In particular, contestabilty allows for natural monopoly. Spulber argues that this is the best basis for the study of significant scale economies because, if contestable markets perform well under scale economies, then natural monopoly cannot justify regulation. But if natural monopoly and departures from contestability - such as sunk costs or other barriers to entry - lead to market failure, regulatory policy may be desirable. However, it must then focus on both the natural monopoly and the non-contestability features of the market failure.

For example, Spulber concludes that under natural monopoly conditions, if public policy seeks 'zero-profit subsidy-free' prices,[6] then contestability without regulation is sufficient to produce these prices, since only by setting zero-profit subsidy-free prices can the incumbent make the natural monopoly sustainable.

However, subsidy-free prices may not be welfare maximising. For example, Ramsey prices may involve cross-subsidies so are not sustainable. This leads to a trade-off between the welfare gains of Ramsey pricing (plus regulatory costs) and the welfare attainable under subsidy-free prices (without regulatory costs).

Spulber analyses a series of different (increasingly information-intensive) price-setting policies that regulators might set - including cost-based prices, break-even prices, price discrimination, and perfect price discrimination - but concludes that *for the contestable market case*, the most economically efficient approach is an auction for the right to supply the market in question. Where there are barriers to entry (and hence non-contestability) the franchise cannot be used repeatedly so traditional forms of economic regulation may be required. A market solution for sunk costs is, of course, the long-term contract. Spulber evaluates economic regulation - itself a form, he maintains, of implicit contract - against privately negotiated and enforced contracts. Regulation may reduce the cost of negotiation (in a market with many agents) and the cost of contract enforcement.

Spulber's analysis is at a very high level of abstraction and is some way from offering a set of practical tools for economic regulation, though these may well be developed. Indeed, one of the book's key conclusions – that franchise contracts be substituted for the apparatus of formal economic regulation – could be challenged by one of the lessons being drawn from the bankruptcy of the UK company Railtrack.

In October 2001, a columnist with the *Financial Times*[7] argued that Railtrack followed 'the 1990s orthodoxy' (of concentrating on its 'core competence' of managing the rail network) and outsourcing much else including track maintenance

---

[6] In a multi-product firm, subsidy-free prices are those such that the revenue generated by any subset of output levels does not exceed the stand-alone cost of producing those output levels.

[7] Peter Martin, "Lessons from Railtrack", *Financial Times*, 9 October 2001, p. 21.

to contractors. The approach, he argued, suffered from three flaws: first, even well-specified contracts cannot replicate the operations of integrated businesses; second, while information technology has lowered the costs of information *exchange* it has left the costs of trust-building and alignment of interests as high as ever; finally, while contracts may work well against a stable economic and political background, after a crisis, such as a rail accident, they may become very unstable.

Conclusion

The logic of sectoral economic regulation is strongest – at least from the viewpoint of economic efficiency[8] - in an industry marked by significant economies of scale. The existence of a natural monopoly can justify a certain level of economic regulation to seek to protect consumer welfare. But how is such a worthwhile aim to be achieved?

Marginal-cost pricing remains sound in principle but difficult to implement with precision because sufficient information may not, in general and in practice, be available. In addition, once the government agency is made endogenous to the analysis of regulation, the theoretical case for economic regulation is weakened and novel contract-based forms of regulation may have theoretical attractions to earlier approaches. However, inter alia, the UK Railtrack collapse of 2001 has suggested that contract-based regulation, at the present stage of knowledge, may also be difficult to put into practice.

At a less technical level, it is helpful to recall that the objective set for the UK Office of Fair Trading is "to make markets work well for consumers". Carefuly attention to developments in the theory of optimal economic regulation can help regulatory agencies to pursue the interests of consumers successfully.

References

Kahn, Alfred E (1989) *The Economics of Regulation* (reprint), MIT Press, Cambridge MA, published in two volumes in 1970 and 1971, by Wiley.

Laffont, Jean-Jacques and Jean Tirole (1994) *A Theory of Incentives in Procurement and Regulation*, MIT Press, Cambridge MA.

Newbery, David M (1999), *Privatization, Restructuring and Regulation of Network Utilities*, MIT Press, Cambridge MA.

Sibley, David (2000) "Economic Analysis of the CAA's Initial Incentive Regulation Proposal for the National Air Traffic Services", available at www.caaerg.co.uk/erg/.

Spulber, Daniel F. (1989) *Regulation and Markets*, MIT Press, Cambridge MA.

---

[8] For example, the Aviation Regulation Act 2001 charges the Irish CAR with the task of setting maximum airport charges in such a way as to seek to promote "the operation and development of cost-effective airports that meet the requirements of users".

Chapter 14

Airport Privatisation and Regulation: Getting the Institutions Right

Hartmut Wolf

1. Introduction

Airport privatisation has been - and still is - on the agenda of national air transport policies of many countries throughout the world. Privatisation may take many different avenues, ranging from only a minor divestiture of airport companies by public shareholders (for example in Germany) to a complete sell-off of (former) public airports to private investors (for example in Australia). Privatisation can be restricted to the operation of public infrastructure facilities by a private firm (for example in Bolivia), or it can also involve privatising the airport's infrastructure (for example in the UK). As infrastructure facilities of airports are usually regarded to be non-contestable monopolies, privatisation is typically accompanied by some form of price regulation.[1]

The regulation may take a variety of forms, ranging from strict rate-of-return to price-cap regulation (with various sliding scale mechanisms in between).[2] It may be restricted to the airside activities of airports (for example Hamburg Airport), or it may also cover non-airside activities (for example in the UK). Not least, airports can be privatised while all markets for airport services are fully deregulated (as in New Zealand). Against this variety of institutional settings that govern the airport sector, policy makers might ask what form of privatisation, and what design of the institutional setting within which privatised airports will have to operate, will prove to be most adequate to ensure efficient operation of privatised airports.

This chapter analyses the determinants of the appropriate design of ownership structures in the airport sector and of the institutional setting for airport service

---

[1] A noticeable exemption is New Zealand, which privatised its major airports without any accompanying price regulation.

[2] The new airport at Athens may serve as an example for the application of rate-of-return regulation, the BAA airports in the UK may serve as examples for airports that are regulated by a price-cap regime, and the airside charges of Vienna Airport are subject to a sliding scale mechanism.

markets. The analysis is based on The New Institutional Economics.[3] This paradigm focuses on asymmetric information and incomplete contracts and the institutions that govern these contracts. Contracting parties are aware of the dangers of opportunism that might emerge because of informational asymmetries and the incompleteness of contracts, and they design governance structures to protect their own quasi-rents against opportunism by their respective partners. A governance structure is efficient if it minimises transaction costs, the latter comprising the operating costs as well as the incentive costs that are generated by that structure. The efficient design depends on the specific characteristics of the transaction in question. The main dimensions are the asset specificity of supporting investments and the frequency of transaction. Asset specificity refers to the dedication of investments to specific uses and/or transaction partners (for example complex baggage systems for hub and spoke carriers represent highly specific assets while land - although it is immobile - generally does not). Thus, a high degree of asset specificity makes the economic value of that investment highly dependent on the transaction in question and hence locks the investor into that transaction.

The chapter is organized as follows. Section 2 describes the choice of airport ownership structures and the design of airport regulation as a contract problem. Section 3 evaluates alternative governance structures and identifies complementarities between the distribution of ownership rights and the design of the institutional setting within which privatised airports operate. Within section 4, some general guidelines on how to appropriately design airport privatisation policy will be derived from the results achieved so far. Finally, the overall results of this chapter will be summarised in section 5.

2. Airport Privatisation Policy as a Contract Problem

Following Goldberg (1976), the distribution of ownership rights to airports and the design of price regulation can be analysed as a contract problem. As he argued, regulation may generally be viewed as a transaction cost saving device for controlling the behaviour of natural monopolies in cases where transaction-specific investments lead to non-contestability of monopoly markets while at the same time locking the seller's investments into that transaction.[4] Hence, it is not only the buyer of the natural monopolist's services that needs to be protected against opportunism by the seller (i.e. monopoly pricing), but also the seller needs security of expectations, otherwise she would not invest specifically in that transaction. Regulation as a governance structure has to protect both parties' reasonable interests, otherwise inefficient outcomes will occur.

As regards the airport sector, aprons, runways, and - to lesser degree - also terminals represent immobile investments dedicated for specific uses and with long

---

[3] For an overview see Richter and Furubotn (1996).

[4] See also Williamson (1976).

working lives. Once these investments have been made, the future economic fate of a regulated airport is bound to future decisions by the regulator. On the other hand, the social welfare effects of airport regulation depend on the willingness of airport authorities to invest in such facilities. Because airport infrastructure is often a regional non contestable monopoly, the regulator (as an agent for the airports' users and regions) is typically tied within bilateral relationships with the airport authorities. Hence, both sides (i.e. airport authorities and the regulator) need protection against opportunism by the respective partner either by self-insuring or self-action or by a third party.

If all transaction-specific investments were dividable into fairly small steps the regulatory risk of an airport authority would be minimal. She could employ a trigger strategy realising her planned investment step by step, making her particular next step depend on the regulator's past decisions. As long as the regulator is interested in ongoing investment the airport authority may exercise a threat of not realizing the next step of investment if the regulator behaves opportunistically by exploiting the airport's quasi-rents. Also, the regulator could retaliate for opportunistic behaviour by the airport by lowering the level of airport charges below long run marginal costs. Both threats would make the regulatory contract self-enforcable without collateral institutional safeguards (Salant and Woroch 1991). However, in reality expanding major infrastructure facilities has to be done in large discrete steps, which seriously restricts the ability of airport authorities to retaliate to an opportunistic regulatory policy once these investments have been realized. Because indivisibilities in airport infrastructure investments prevent self-enforcement of regulatory contracts without institutional safeguards against opportunism, appropriate governance structures have to be implemented.

Airport regulation means that the task of controlling the behaviour of the airport company is not performed by the users of that airport, but by a regulator, who simultaneously acts as a principal for the regulated airport and as an agent for the airport users. Asymmetric information and bounded rationality prevent perfect (i.e. in the sense of neoclassical economics: first best welfare maximising) regulatory outcomes. Instead, dangers of opportunism might exist. In this respect, opportunism may come in three ways. First, informational disadvantages of the regulator about the real conditions of production for the airport might lead to opportunistic behaviour by the airport company, which would result in allocative and/or productive inefficiency.[5] Second, transaction-specific investments create a lock-in effect for the airport company which might give the regulator ex post-opportunities to expropriate the firm's quasi-rents. And third, as the results of price regulation usually affect all airport's users regardless of their individual efforts to

[5] Productive inefficiency is likely to occur if the airport company cannot fully transform rents into profits for her shareholders because the regulator would tax that profit away. Then she may have incentives to transform potential profits into rents for the insiders within the firm (X-inefficiency) as it is much more difficult for the regulator to detect and expropriate insider-rents than profits.

control the regulator, their control efforts might be socially suboptimal,[6] which provides the regulator with opportunities to behave opportunistically against the users' interests.[7] To achieve efficient outcomes of airport privatisation, the governance structure that defines the relationship between airport company, regulator, and airport users has to be designed carefully to protect the reasonable interests of airport companies and airport users. In this sense, the design of airport privatisation policy does not only mean a change in the ownership structures in the airport industry, but to design an institutional setting for the airport sector that guarantees the maximum of social welfare gains that can be realised by privatisation.

3. Governance Structures in the Airport Sector

Williamson (1986: 112 pp.) generally identifies four prototypes of governance structures, namely (1) market governance, (2) trilateral governance (neoclassical contracting), (3) transaction-specific governance (relational contracting), and (4) unified governance (internal organisation). *Market governance* is the main governance structure for non-specific transactions of both occasional and recurrent contracting. Such transactions do not need institutional safeguards against opportunism, as all transacting parties have outside options for their investments and hence have the opportunity to end the transaction without incurring sunk costs. Buyers can easily turn to alternative sources, and suppliers can sell output intended for one order to other buyers without difficulty. Ground handling fits into that kind of transaction, as buses and cargo loaders can easily be transferred between different airports and customers. These costless exit options prevent opportunism. A *trilateral governance structure* means that the contracting partners choose an independent institution as an arbitrator for conflict resolution, for example the legal system and its courts may act as an arbitrator. However, a precondition for an effective trilateral governance structure, i.e. a governance structure that effectively protects the contractors' quasi-rents, is a regulatory contract that is either almost complete or entails unambigous conflict resolution mechanisms, so that the arbitrator is able clearly to detect contract breeching and to identify clearly the party that has breached the contract. *Transaction-specific governance* means that the contractors do not rely on conflict resolution by an independent arbitrator, but instead agree on self-enforcing contracts that protect each other's quasi-rents. A contract is self-enforcing if the partners supply hostages to each other in order to commit to ongoing contractual relationships (Williamson 1983). Finally, a *unified governance structure* means vertical integration between the contractors. Vertical

---

[6] Any Airport user is affected by the results of regulation regardless of the individual efforts to control the regulator.

[7] Regulatory capture (i.e. the regulator identifies herself with, and pursues the aims of the regulated firm against the airport's users' interests) fits into this type of opportunistic behaviour.

integration eliminates the danger of losing quasi-rents as a result of opportunistic behaviour by the partner. However, agency problems within the unified governance structure might occur, as vertical integration eliminates the disciplinary exit option of market governance.

In the airport sector, and with respect to privatisation, leaving transactions solely to the *market* would mean total privatisation without any regulation. This would avoid dangers of opportunistic behaviour by a regulator and related under-investment by the airports. Markets for ground handling are highly contestable, hence markets are appropriate institutions for governing transactions in handling services. Infrastructure facilities, however, may be non-contestable monopolies in their location. If so, the regions that are served by these facilities depend on the behaviour of the monopoly supplier of infrastructure services. It might be expected that unregulated airports with strong market power would raise the level of infrastructure charges well above long run marginal costs in order to reap monopoly profits. It has been argued in the literature, however, that this should cause no concern with regard to efficiency considerations, as airports could engage in almost perfect price discrimination. Perfect price discrimination would lead to the production of the maximum of output of infrastructure services that cover its costs. Hence, reaping monopoly rents by unregulated airports would only generate a fairly small welfare loss in terms of allocative efficiency while the airports would have all incentives to produce efficiently. In particular, regulation-induced over-capitalisation (or under-investment), X-inefficiency and costly rent seeking behaviour by the airports in a regulatory process would be avoided. That would probably overcompensate for the small loss of allocative efficiency that has to be expected (Forsyth 2002: 21).

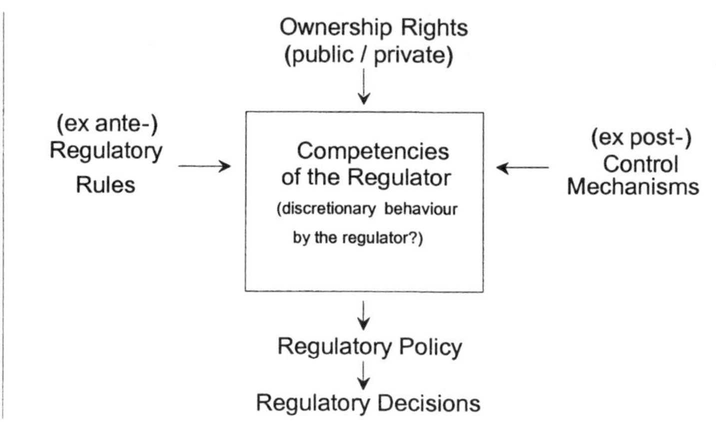

Figure 14.1 Elements of a regulatory system
Source: Wolf (2003)

Note, however, that full deregulation of the markets for infrastructure services does not automatically mean that the economic behaviour of airports is not subject to control by state authorities. Instead, even the services of a fully privatised airport are typically supervised by a national competition authority on the grounds of common competition law. Further, recall the lumpy character of the airport's investments in major infrastructure facilities, which means that differentiation of airport charges according to the price elasticities of different markets lies at the heart of the problem of ensuring efficient usage of the infrastructure facilities. In contrast, common competition law is often not suited to encourage efficient price differentiation. For this reason, competition authorities might refuse efficient differentiation of airport charges.[8] Hence, it might be doubtful if almost perfect price discrimination would occur after the markets for airport infrastructure services had been fully deregulated. Therefore, political reliance on the functioning of fully deregulated markets for infrastructure services may generate high social costs. If common competition law in the country under consideration is not suited to allow for perfect price discrimination, it might be wise to install another governance structure, i.e. either an internal, a trilateral, or a transaction-specific one.

Accordingly, airport regulation may come in three ways (Figure 14.1). First, regulation may be performed by means of internal regulation, which means that the state as owner of an airport company exercises ownership rights to control the behaviour of the company by internal command. With respect to airport privatisation, a precondition for internal regulation is only partial divestiture of airport companies by public owners. Internal regulation eliminates the regulatory risk to the airport company (because expropriation of the airports' quasi-rents by an opportunistic regulatory policy that sets the level of charges below long run marginal costs would harm the regulator herself) and hence avoids related problems of under-investment in specific airport facilities. In effect, such a structure provides a set of incentives that leads the airport to superior if not optimal investment decisions. However, public ownership probably leads to inefficient outcomes for political-economic reasons: the regulatory process is likely to be influenced by pressure groups and self-interested politicians and hence by political considerations that might not be in the interests of the airport's users. Without going into political-economic details here why - and if always - public ownership is likely to generate

---

8 In some countries (for example in Germany) decisions by the national competition authorities against anti-competitive behaviour may be challenged by the offenders before courts, which could overrule the competition authorities' orders. The effect on the efficiency of market outcomes might be twofold: on the one side such a governance structure might protect the suppliers' quasi-rents against opportunistic orders by the competition authorities. On the other side, it might lead to a tendency by competition authorities to base their orders against monopolistic misbehaviour on considerations with regard to the suppliers' costs or on a comparison with a particular supplier's prices in different markets on which the supplier operates (which can be clearly seen for example from the historic track record of the German competition authority). In this way, the competition authorities might try to base their decisions on objective and clear criteria in order to avoid overruling of their orders by the courts, which could, however, reduce the firms' incentives to enhance productive efficiency.

considerable inefficiencies[9] it might be noticeable that airport privatisation is often justified as a means to improve the efficiency of airport services by altering incentives for the airport's management. Obviously, as incentive structures of an airport's management are shaped by the objectives of owners, expectations about improved efficiencies of privatised airports must rest on the assumption that privatisation leads to a depoliticisation of the regulatory process. That is only credible if state authorities cannot influence the airport's management decisions by internal regulation, i.e. if full privatisation (or at least a major divestiture of public airports) takes place.

Alternatively, and second, regulation can be strictly bound to ex ante-specified rules which are enforceable before courts, thus leaving the regulator no discretion. Such rules would effectively protect the airport company's quasi-rents and thus would facilitate complete airport privatisation without inducing problems of under-investment. However, while eliminating the dangers of opportunism by the regulator, such governance structure might give airports the opportunity to behave opportunistically, as such rules are unavoidable inflexible. For example the well known rate of return-regulatory mechanism, that guarantees the airport company a fair and reasonable rate-of-return on employed capital whatever its costs, represents such a rule, which eliminates the (otherwise existing) hold-up problem of the airport operator, but also gives the company incentives for over-capitalisation (Averch and Johnson 1962). Furthermore, ex ante-rules make regulation heavy handed because the rules must be tailored to control for all action parameters of the airports, otherwise price regulation could be easily undermined by non-pricing strategies of the airport operators. For example a fixed price-cap gives the airport incentives to lower the quality of its services in order to circumvent regulatory restrictions unless rules are implemented that explicitly control for service quality. A rate-of-return mechanism gives the airport incentives to set an inefficient structure of charges in order to create additional demand at peak times (which can be used to justify the building of additional airport capacity) unless the structure of charges becomes subject to regulatory control (Bailey and White 1974). All in all it is very doubtful if regulating a private airport by strictly defined ex ante rules leads to better results in terms of social welfare than internal regulation by means of public ownership. Indeed, as Vickers and Yarrow (1988: 40) conclude after examining the results of empirical studies about the relative performance of private and public companies, private companies that are heavily regulated tend not to perform better than public ones.

Inflexible and heavy handed regulation may be avoided by allowing for discretion by the regulator, especially by giving her the opportunity to sanction opportunistic behaviour by the airport by lowering charges ex post, thus making

---

9 There exists a considerable body of literature on this subject that suggests that public ownership is not in itself going to generate inefficiencies but incentives and broader public mandates can explain some of the inefficiencies. Thus, giving the same incentives to public managers should lead to the same results as in the private sector. For an overview see for example Vickers and Yarrow (1988: 11) and Brenck (1993: 56).

regulation a repeated game between the airport and the regulator. This might probably reduce incentives of the airport to exploit informational advantages from the beginning, which in turn reduces the need for continously ex ante control of all action parameters of the company. For example regulatory discretion would enable the regulator to lower price-caps if she detects quality dumping by the airport, thus weakening the airport's incentives to lower the quality of her services, and, hence, making ex ante specification of quality standards by inflexible rules avoidable. However, a precondition for efficient outcomes of a discretionary policy is again the existence of institutional safeguards that protect the airport's quasi rents. Otherwise, regulation may fail to achieve efficient infrastructure investments by the airport.

These considerations lead to the third prototype of regulatory governance, namely ex post control of regulatory outcomes. Implementing a governance structure that relies heavily on ex post control mechanisms means giving the regulator freedom to skim monopoly rents from the airport ex post by lowering charges below long run marginal costs for a while. At the same time, they can protect the airport's quasi-rents by exerting a threat of sanctions on the regulator if regulatory outcomes prove to be inefficient. The idea is to make regulation more light handed by designing a relational regulatory contract that is self-enforceable.

The self-enforcement of relational contracts, as we have stated, needs collateral that each of the contractors provide to their counterparts. The investments by the airport in major infrastructure facilities represents such collateral, as such investments bind its economic fate to the future decisions of the regulator. For the part of the regulator, her competencies to regulate may represent an effective hostage that might protect the airport's quasi-rents. Hence, protection can be provided by the threat of the regulator losing her capability. To make this threat credible, regulatory outcomes have to be controlled by an independent institution that is allowed to stop regulation, but even this control institution might behave opportunistically. Therefore, guidelines are needed as to what constitutes inefficient outcomes of regulation. In order to preserve flexibility in the system, these guidelines necessarily have to be somewhat vague. A further safeguard could be a division of competencies between different institutions (a) of assessing the efficiency of regulatory outcomes and (b) of deciding about the future of regulation. If so, those institutions that are commissioned to detect inefficient regulatory outcomes would not profit from the abolition of regulation. This would probably reduce the incentives to cheat. To sum up, a precondition for improving the efficiency of regulation is the implementation of a system of checks and balances with various institutions involved.

However, such an institutional setting remains to represent an incomplete contract with only vague guidelines on what constitutes inefficient regulatory outcomes. Hence, it would be wise to install additional elements into the system that may serve as safeguards to protect the airport against unduly regulatory decisions. Appropriate safeguards may be (a) the abolition of the single till principle, which would mean that the airport's revenue from non-airside activities is shielded from misbehaviour by the regulator, and (b) delegating the task of regulating designated airports to an institution that is responsible for regulation of all airports that are subject to regulation (or even also of other regulated industries like electricity, gas, and telecommunications). If so, the regulator has to take into account the effects of her decisions regarding one particular airport on the whole airport system (respectively on the system of all regulated industries). Note, that different airports will realise their investments at different times. Therefore, exploitation of one airport's past investments in immobile assets by the regulator would harm this airport, but would also probably lead to the unwillingness of other airports to further invest in major infrastructure facilities. Hence, the responsibility for the whole airport system would defuse the problem of indivisibilities of infrastructure investments, which lies at the heart of the credibility problem.

Although the introduction of a regulatory system that heavily relies on ex post control mechanisms may improve the efficiency of regulatory outcomes, the building and operation of the needed institutions comes not without costs. These costs may probably be higher than maintaining public ownership or designing a set of strict ex ante rules. They must be weighted against the expected improvements in efficiency through regulation by ex post controls. It may be expected that these costs will become smaller compared to the benefits of such a system the more airports will become subject to ex post control under a unified legal framework, as the operation of the needed institutions is likely to be characterised by economies of density. In contrast, it can be expected that the smaller the number of airports that will become subject to privatisation, the less attractive is the introduction of effective ex post-control mechanisms. Thus, the building and operation of an institutional setting that heavily relies on ex post controls is more attractive, the more airports that operate under that setting.

The discussion so far leads us to the following results with regard to the appropriate design of privatisation policy for the airport sector. First, complementarities exist between the optimal choice of the form of privatisation and the design of the legal framework within which privatised airports will operate. Full privatisation is only feasible if the institutional framework guarantees effective protection of the airports' quasi-rents (Figure 14.2). Otherwise airport privatisation has to be restricted to a minor divestiture of public airport companies or to the operation of public infrastructure facilities by a private contractor. The latter would mean that the state would be responsible for infrastructure investments.

Second, if the governance structure ensures effective ex-post control of regulatory policy, inflexible ex ante-regulatory rules can be avoided, and regulatory policy could be more light handed than if it is based on such rules. Hence, light handed regulation needs strong institutions that interact within a system of checks and balances.

Finally, the building of ex post control-mechanisms will be especially suitable in countries that had privatised (or plan to privatise) not only a single but a greater number of airports.

<table>
<tr><th>Need for specific infrastructure investments \ Ex post Control of Regulatory Policy</th><th>effective</th><th>not effective</th></tr>
<tr><td>small</td><td rowspan="2">Freedom for discretionary regulatory policy
<u>and</u>
full privatisation</td><td></td></tr>
<tr><td>big</td><td>Regulation by ex ante rules
<u>or</u>
public ownership of airports</td></tr>
</table>

Figure 14.2 Governance structures in the airport industry: Complementarities

Source: Wolf (2003).

4. Some General Guidelines for the Design of Airport Privatisation Policy

The following guidelines for the appropriate design of an airport privatisation policy that aims at enhancing the efficiency of the airport sector may be derived from the results achieved so far.

- Full privatisation is a necessary (although not sufficient) condition for enhancing the efficiency of the airport sector by privatisation. Hence, airport privatisation policy should be directed to total divestiture of airport companies by public shareholders.
- In order to facilitate full privatisation, policy makers should ensure protection of the airports' quasi rents against opportunistic (or simply wrong) decisions by regulatory authorities, either by abolishing regulation or by restricting regulation to infrastructure services and implementing institutional safeguards into the regulatory system that shield the airports' investments against expropriation by the regulator.
- In order to facilitate light handed regulation, policy makers should (a) shift the responsibility for regulation to a central layer of government (i.e. to a regulator who is responsible for regulating all airports or even all regulated network industries), (b) design an institutional setting of checks and balances within the regulatory system, and (c) abolish the single till principle for the regulation of airport charges.

5. Conclusions

The discussion in the preceding sections has shown that complementarities exist between the legal framework for the airport sector and the privatisation strategy of public owners. Designing privatisation policy means deciding simultaneously on the airports' ownership structures as well as on the legal framework that cover the airport sector. Privatisation will only lead to improved efficiency of airport services if it is accompanied by full deregulation of the airport sector or - if full deregulation is not feasible - by implementing a governance structure that allows for light handed regulation. However, light handed regulation needs strong institutions that may act discretionally, and discretion needs to be supervised, otherwise inefficient outcomes will occur.

References

Averch, H. and L.L. Johnson (1962) Behaviour of the Firm under Regulatory Constraint. *American Economic Review* 52 (5): 1052–1069.

Bailey, E.E. and L.J. White (1974). Reversals in Peak- and Off-Peak Prices. *Bell Journal of Economics* 5 (1): 75–92.

Brenck, A. (1993) Privatisierungsmodelle für die Deutsche Bundesbahn. In W. Allemeyer, A. Brenck, P. Wittenbrinck and F. v. Stackelberg (Eds.), *Privatisierung des Schienenverkehrs*. Vandenhoek & Ruprecht, Göttingen.

Forsyth, P. (2002) Privatisation and Regulation of Australian and New Zealand Airports. *Journal of Air Transport Management* 8 (1): 19-28.

Goldberg, V.P. (1976). Regulation and Administered Contracts. *Bell Journal of Economics* 7 (2): 426–452.

Richter, R., und E. Furubotn (1996) *Neue Institutionenökonomik. Eine Einführung und kritische Würdigung*. Mohr, Tübingen.

Salant, D.J. and G.A. Woroch (1991) Crossing Dupuit's Bridge Again: A Trigger Policy for Efficient Investment in Infrastructure. *Contemporary Policy Issues* 9 (2): 101-114.

Vickers, J. und G. Yarrow (1988) *Privatisation: An Economic Analysis*. MIT-Press, Cambridge, Mass.

Williamson, O.E. (1976) Franchise Bidding for Natural Monopoly in General and with Respect to CATV. *The Bell Journal of Economics* 7 (1): 73–104.

Williamson, O.E. (1983) Credible Commitments: Using Hostages to Support Exchange. *American Economic Review* 73 (4): 519–540.

Williamson, O.E. (1986) *Economic Organization. Firms, Markets and Policy Control*. Wheatsheaf, Brighton, Sussex.

Wolf, H. (2003) *Privatisierungspolitik im Flughafensektor. Eine ordnungspolitische Analyse*, Springer, Heildelberg.

Chapter 15

On the Institutional Setting of Ex-Post Regulation in Regulated Industries

Bernhard Duijm

1. Introduction

In several countries there has been a trend to transform highly regulated markets into competitive markets. Most economists agree that in many cases the introduction of competition in markets previously dominated by state monopolies or vertically integrated firms cannot be achieved simply by abolishing the old anti-competitive regulations. Often, pure market forces would not lead to the development of competition even if the anti-trust laws were strictly applied. Therefore, the process of liberalisation of these sectors should be accompanied by a new kind of regulation policy, not aiming at preventing competition, but at making competition possible and fostering it.

This competition-orientated economic regulation[1] may include obligations for the incumbent firm to give access to certain facilities to new entrants in the market at prices (or more general: conditions) fixed or at least permitted by a regulator. While competition-orientated regulation policy and competition policy share the same objective, namely fostering competition, the methods of both fields of policy differ considerably. The usual goal of competition policy is to prevent anti-competitive behaviour and concentration processes which are expected to reduce competition. With the exception of merger control, the instruments of competition policy are applied ex post. They are used in a manner to *forbid* certain economic activities (including doing mergers and acquisitions that would lead to a dominant position or strengthen an already existing dominant position).

On the other hand, the instruments of regulation policy are applied ex ante. Usually, they *prescribe* the regulated firms to act in a specified manner, or in other words, they fix some of the variables or the way of setting the variables indicating market performance, such as prices and quantities for example, the prices that a privatized airport charges may be set in advance by the regulator.

Of course, competition policy is also a kind of regulatory policy and is sometimes called ex-post regulation policy. For the sake of clarity, in this paper the term "regulation" is used in the sense of ex-ante regulation only.

---

[1] Aspects of technical regulations will not be discussed in this paper.

In a market economy, market performance is usually the outcome of market forces. In such a system, the replacement of the market forces by the settings of a regulator[2] can be justified only in certain circumstances and where other policy instruments would be ineffective, e.g. in addressing particular market failures or in achieving specified policy objectives. In order to prevent any misuse of regulation policy, there is general agreement that regulators should be politically independent. This requirement is fulfilled when there are independent regulatory agencies separate from the government. Autonomous ministerial agencies linked to a ministry may be able to act with a substantial degree of independence (OECD/IEA, 2001, p. 4). However, a minister acting directly or indirectly as a regulator may use his regulatory power to achieve non-competition goals, e.g. reducing regulated postage rates during an election campaign.

In respect of the regulator's sectoral scope of authority there are three main approaches (Estache and de Rus, 2000, p. 45):

- An *industry-specific* approach leads to separate regulators for all regulated industries, e.g. one for electricity, one for gas, one for water, one for rail, one for inland waterways, one for airports, and so on.
- In a *sector-specific* approach, a regulatory agency deals with a group of related industries, e.g. an energy regulator for electricity and gas and a transportation regulator for railroads, inland waterways and airports.
- In a *multi-sectoral* approach there is a single regulatory agency for all or most regulated sectors.

These institutional designs differ with regard to the sectoral breadth of authority; which of them is optimal depends on various determinants. Industry- or sector-specific regulators might be superior when regulations in different sectors or industries differ considerably. Main advantages of a single regulatory agency are seen in savings from "economies of scope" and in the avoidance of regulatory inconsistencies across industries (Hewitt, 1999, pp. 196 ff.).

However, in the view of most economists, even well designed regulation is inferior to a functioning market. Not least because of regulatory failure, regulation should be limited to specific situations and activities, as when natural monopolies or other structural factors impede the development of a functioning competitive market. Therefore, even in regulated industries, not all economic activities should be subject to ex-ante regulation, for example most of the non-aeronautical activities of airports. The rules of the competition law(s) are, of course, applicable to those activities, and - depending on the legal system - even to activities permitted by the regulatory agency.

Thus, some industries are subject to regulation rules as well as to general competition law and perhaps to sectoral competition law. Then the question arises which authority should be in charge of competition law enforcement in regulated industries. As there is interaction between competition and regulation policy (or in other words: ex-post and ex-ante regulation) the conduct of competition policy in a

[2] Regulator, regulatory authority, and regulatory agency are used as synonyms. For the institutional design of regulatory agencies see OECD/IEA (2001, p. 23).

certain industry may influence the conduct and even the need for (ex-ante) regulations in this industry and vice versa. The assignment of authority in the field of competition policy is therefore a very important political decision.

2. Assignment of Authorities in the Field of Competition Policy

For the sake of simplicity, let us first assume that there are one or several regulatory agencies separate from the general competition authority. The second assumption is that there is only a general competition law; sector-specific competition laws do not exist. There are at least five main ways of assigning the power to apply the competition law.

(1) Regulatory and competition policy competencies[3] are combined within the regulatory agency giving this agency the exclusive right to apply independently the general competition law to the firms in industries regulated by the agency.
(2) As in (1) only the regulatory agency can apply competition law, but there are rules concerning the co-operation with the competition authority. Different degrees of co-ordination exist: the influence of the competition agency is relatively low, when it has only the right to be informed before the regulatory agency takes action based on competition law. The highest degree of influence is the right of the competition agency to veto decisions of the regulatory agency. But even then, only the regulatory agency can initiate actions based on competition law.
(3) There is a concurrent authority to apply the competition law. Thus, both the regulatory agency and the competition agency can act independently.
(4) In contrast to (2) the competency of applying competition law lies with the competition agency, but in the case of regulated industries co-operation with the appropriate regulatory agency is compulsory. Here, competencies in regulation and competition policies are institutionally separated while a certain degree of formal co-ordination exists.
(5) The strictest form of separating regulatory and competition authorities is to give the competition agency the exclusive right to apply competition law absolutely independently to all industries including the regulated ones.

In practice, the situation might be more complex. The kind of assignment may not only differ from industry to industry. It might be different also within one industry depending on the kind of anti-competitive activity concerned. Generally,

---

[3] In this paper competency in competition policy and regulation policy means the power to apply the competition law or the laws concerning economic regulations (regulation law). Usually, both types of law give considerable discretionary powers to the agency applying the law. Competency in the sense of making laws is not discussed, although the agencies in charge of conducting policies might play an important role in designing the legal framework. See OECD (1997, pp. 19 ff.) for the role of competition agencies as advocates of deregulation. Of course, courts also have important competencies concerning competition policy, but they are omitted in this paper.

regulatory agencies are more involved in mergers and acquisitions than in the application of rules concerning anti-competitive behaviour of firms.[4] The official institutional design may lie between some of the five "pure" ways of assignment described above. And the institutional design practised in reality may be different from the one laid down in laws. This might be especially true in the field of co-operation between the regulatory and the competition agency.

There is a more general aspect one has to deal with when the assignment of competencies is discussed: can general competition law be applied to issues laid down in a (specific) regulation law or not? Or in other words: does the application of a (specific) regulation law exclude the application of the general competition law or are both laws equally applicable?[5] If the latter is the case then all regulatory decisions can be supervised by the agency in charge of competition law enforcement.

3. Combining Regulation and Competition Policy Enforcement - Pros and Cons

3.1 Pros

One possible advantage of combining regulation and competition policy enforcement within one agency may be the avoidance of inconsistent decisions. As both fields of policy deal with promoting and protecting competition - although those sub-goals have different weights in both policies - a decision taken on the base of the appropriate regulation law might counteract decisions based on competition law and vice versa. These inconsistent decisions can be avoided in cases where a single agency is in charge of applying the relevant regulation laws and general competition law.

Inconsistencies of regulation and competition law enforced by two different agencies may cause severe problems for the regulated firms. The same or similar activities which are permitted by the regulator under regulation law may be forbidden by the competition agency under competition law. But even the simple fact that regulators and the competition agency have concurrent competencies for the same activities may lead to higher costs for the firms.

It can be assumed that every regulator is reluctant to leave a case to the competition agency when he is empowered to deal with that case under the relevant regulation law. If he has the authority to apply the competition law equally, he will probably choose the most appropriate regime (regulation law or competition law) to solve the problem (Hewitt, 1999, p. 185). If he does not have these concurrent powers he must use regulation law, even in cases where the application of competition law would be sufficient. The result is that detailed rules

---

[4] Especially in the US, some regulatory agencies have the power to approve mergers and acquisitions; see Victor (1998, p. 520) and Calvani and Robb (1998, pp. 515 ff.). However, there are important deviations from this rule.

[5] In Germany, this question is discussed especially with regard to the telecommunications sector; see Möschel (2001).

(based on regulation law) have to be observed by the regulated firms with negative consequences for competition.[6] Regulatory interventions may also affect investment and hence economic growth in the long run, especially when many indivisibilities in investment exist, e.g. in increasing the capacity of airports by constructing a new runway.[7]

This argument of over-regulation is based on a static point of view. It can be modified slightly for a dynamic point of view. Many regulations are presumed to be temporary. They are expected to be applied only until a functioning competition has developed. This process might be speeded up by technical progress, international integration of markets[8] and so on, but also by the conduct of regulation policy. In order to ensure that regulations remain only temporary, many laws contain obligations for regular assessments concerning the need for continued regulation and in some cases the need for the regulatory agency itself (Haffner, 2000, p. 212). Such a regulation policy cannot be evaluated continuously, but in intervals of for example three to four years. Making regulation superfluous as soon as possible is not in the interest of the regulator when the abolition of regulation is connected with the abolition of the regulatory agency. Therefore, the regulator might be inclined to retain more regulations than necessary in order to demonstrate the need of regulations and the need for the regulatory agency.

Empowering the regulatory agency with competition law enforcement in the relevant industry may act as an incentive to reduce regulations sooner and faster, for under this institutional design the agency does not lose "responsibilities", as long as there are reasons for maintaining the agency. Only the instruments adopted have to be changed.

Another advantage of combined competencies is the possibility of synergies. Within an agency, information gathered for regulatory decisions are available for competition decisions, while the exchange of information between different agencies might be hindered. There might only be a few people with in-depth knowledge of a certain industry. Then, scarce human resources can be used in a more efficient manner when regulation and competition law enforcement is combined. Other possibilities of saving costs may also exist.

3.2 Cons

Combining regulatory and competition law competencies can have some serious drawbacks.

The conduct of regulation policy might influence the conduct of competition policy concerning the non-regulated activities of the regulated companies as well. For example, a regulator being used to set prices according to a certain rule when applying the relevant regulation law might ask for detailed commitments before

---

[6] See Boyfield (2000, p. 38) for examples of over-detailed regulations.

[7] See Nicoletti (2001, pp. 22 ff.) for network industries.

[8] For example, international liberalization of the airline industry might increase the number of potential origin airports within a certain region (especially within border zones), thus intensifying competition between airports and reducing the number of airports that can be regarded as a natural monopoly.

giving his consent to a merger of two firms.[9] This can lead to a permanent supervision of the behaviour of the merged firms which is not intended by competition law. The differences in the conduct of regulation and competition policy then diminish by implicitly expanding regulations to the non-regulated areas of economic activities. But here, the de facto ex-ante regulation (instead of a pure ex post regulation) might lead to a reduction in competition.

This "bias" towards regulatory measures may be reinforced by a least two factors:

(1) Regulatory agencies do not exclusively pursue the goal of "protecting and fostering competition", but are assigned a wider set of policy objectives. Being in charge of competition law enforcement in the relevant industry, the agency is enabled to use the instruments of competition policy for achieving all of their objectives. This might reduce competition, e.g. when the regulator grants an exemption to the general prohibition of cartels in order to achieve his objectives.

(2) Due to the wider range of objectives - compared with the competition agency - including those with considerable distributional importance, that regulatory agencies have to pursue, they are often less politically independent than the competition agency. Even if the political independence is guaranteed by law, it may be difficult for newly set-up agencies to make use of it. A lack of de-facto political independence allows politicians to achieve their goals even through competition law rules applied by the regulatory agency because a potential counteracting agency enforcing the competition law is then missing.

Compared with the competition agency, a regulatory agency may show a less strict or even lax attitude towards actual or potential violations of anti-trust law. This can be explained by the fact that the regulatory agency might resort to the instruments of regulation law in cases where the anti-competitive behaviour leads to unwanted market performance. The result of the inappropriate application of competition law is more regulation than necessary. By doing so, the regulation agency can demonstrate the supposedly still existing need for regulation and for its existence.

Therefore, there are reasons for applying sunset legislation with respect to temporary regulation. But combining regulation and competition policy enforcement might make it more difficult to put through sunset legislation as competition law enforcement is a permanent task to be pursued also after all regulations of an industry have been abolished. It is hardly acceptable that a separate "regulatory" agency should exist any longer in order to apply general competition rules to an industry when no specific ex-ante regulations are applicable any more. As one can assume the employees of the regulatory agency are reluctant to give up their jobs, especially when some of their tasks, namely applying the competition law, still exist, they will continue to regulate ex ante as long as possible. An agency which has only explicitly temporary regulatory tasks can be dissolved with less resistance. In this way of looking at the assignment,

---

[9] For other examples see Hewitt (1999, p. 184).

combining regulation policy and competition policy within the regulatory agency will lead to a rather long life of the latter.

4. Separating Regulation and Competition Law Enforcement

A division of tasks between the regulatory agencies and the competition agency giving the latter the exclusive power to enforce competition law might be advantageous for several reasons (Duijm, 2000, pp. 16 ff.).

(1) The centralised design of competition policy conduct will ensure that competition law rules are equally adopted throughout the whole economy, in regulated and in non-regulated industries. This is not guaranteed when regulatory agencies can apply competition law independently. If there are sector- or industry-specific agencies, the application of competition law rules can even differ from sector to sector, from industry to industry, causing distortions in competition. Such distortions can be avoided by entitling a single agency to enforce competition law.
(2) The competition policy is likely to be less interventionist when it is conducted by the general competition agency rather than by regulatory agencies. Instead of monitoring firms continuously, like regulators do, the competition agency usually begins an investigation after having received a complaint or other information indicating a possible violation of the competition law. It aims at deterring firms from restricting competition rather than setting the outcome of the market process more or less directly.
(3) A third advantage can be seen in the role of the competition agency as a counteracting institution. There might be situations where the competition agency - applying competition law - can reduce anti-competitive effects caused by regulatory decisions.

5. Co-operation and co-ordination between the competition agency and the regulatory agencies

If the enforcement of competition law and the enforcement of regulation laws are separated, co-operation and co-ordination of the agencies involved is absolutely necessary in order to avoid inconsistencies. Proper co-operation makes it easier for all agencies responsible for an industry or a sector to fulfil their tasks. But even if a regulator has combined competencies for a regulated industry or sector, co-operation with the competition agency is necessary to avoid inter-industry or inter-sector distortions of competition resulting from considerable differences in applying competition law.

Co-operation and co-ordination may include the exchange of information and the common definition of subjects relevant for conducting competition policy, like the definition of markets and of market power. A far-reaching kind of co-operation is realised when the regulatory agencies are required to consult with the competition agency before they can apply competition law, and vice versa the competition agency must request a (non-binding) opinion from the appropriate regulatory agency before taking action against firms in a regulated industry or sector.

6. The Industry Coverage of Regulators

Whether and to what extent the above-mentioned arguments and other arguments in favour or against combining or separating regulation law and competition law enforcement are valid depends on many factors, which cannot be analysed here, except for one. One important factor is the institutional design of regulatory agencies concerning their sector responsibilities, whether there are (many) industry-specific regulators or (a few) sector-specific regulators or one general regulator. Generally, the narrower the industry coverage of a regulatory agency the higher the probability that the regulator is captured by the regulated firms. So, an industry-specific regulator is more likely to be captured by the firms than a sector-specific one, for in the latter case there are probably different interests among the regulated industries, which cannot be taken into account by one regulator conducting a unique regulation policy in all industries he is responsible for. Another reason for industry-specific regulators to be more prone to be captured is the fact that persons preparing and taking regulatory decisions will be well acquainted with the regulated firms after some time because, within the agency, there is no possibility for job rotation. Job rotation would effect a regular change of the industry an employee of a regulator deals with. When the captured regulator is in charge of the enforcement of regulation *and* competition law he will probably conduct both, regulation and competition policy, more in the interest of some or all regulated firms than in the interest of the public. Multi-sectoral or general regulators are expected to be the least capture-prone agencies for they are confronted with a wide range of divergent interests. From this point of view, giving the general regulator the competency of competition law enforcement seems to be the least harmful alternative with regard to a "proper" competition policy.

One has to ask whether this institutional design is really ideal for preserving a proper competition policy.

First of all: does it make sense to create one single regulatory agency in order to enforce different regulation laws? Should not the - in most cases - already existing competition agency[10] be assigned with conducting competition *and*

[10] Möschel (2002), pp. 684 f. argues that in many countries, competition agencies other than ministries are relatively new bodies while some industry-specific supervisory or regulatory agencies have been existing for a long time. This is true for industries where private firms are active - sometimes alongside public enterprises (banking, assurance etc). However, it is questionable whether these regulators are pro-competition. In the case where all enterprises are (still) public-owned (in many countries: airports) generally some kind of an "internal regulation" is applied by the (local) government which acts as the owner and - more or less directly - as the regulator. In the process of privatisation and liberalisation explicit regulation might be necessary. In order to protect the conduct of regulatory policy against particular interests of the public owner (e.g. revenues from privatisation) a *new* institutional design for regulation is desirable.

regulation policy? Such an approach is followed for example in Australia where the Australian Competition and Consumer Commission (ACCC) is the competition authority and a multi-sector regulator in charge of inter alia electricity, gas, telecommunication and airports on the *national* level[11] (OECD/IEA, 2001, pp. 40 ff.).

Here, the question of assignment of competition policy competencies, the question of combining them with, or separating them from, regulatory competencies, is easily answered for there are no alternative agencies. This kind of approach had been favoured by the German Monopolies Commission until recently. It opposed the creation of a Regulatory Authority for Telecommunications and Posts and wanted the regulatory competencies in these industries to be assigned to the Federal Cartel Office. According to the last biennial report - published some months ago (July 2002) - the Monopolies Commission has changed its opinion. Due to the fact that regulatory measures - taken to create and promote competition - seem to be necessary for a longer time than originally expected, the Commission argues for a separation of regulation and competition policies. The Monopolies Commission fears that the conduct of competition policy will be negatively affected if the Federal Cartel Office should gain regulatory competencies, e.g. in the field of the gas market (Monopolkommission, 2002, p. 50*). To avoid a fragmentation of regulation policy it proposes the creation of a general regulation agency for all network infrastructure industries which should be in charge of the economic regulation, whereas technical regulations should be assigned to industry- or sector-specific agencies.

This accepted, the question of assignment of competition policy competencies still remains: should the general competition agency (in Germany: Federal Cartel Office) retain competencies in applying competition Law (in Germany: Act Against Restraints of Competition) to all industries or only to the non-regulated industries while the single regulation agency is in charge of applying it to the regulated industries?

There is no reason to expect different approaches to competition law enforcements across the regulated industries when a single regulatory agency is empowered to apply this law. This is in contrast to a set of sector- or industry-specific regulators where even closely related industries might be treated unequally. But one problem remains even if there is only one regulator - he might apply competition law towards regulated industries in a different way than the competition agency does towards non-regulated industries. If the regulator applies competition law in a regulatory manner, his competency in competition policy has more and farther-reaching effects on competition compared to - small - industry-specific regulators doing so. As even a politically independent central bank cannot ignore fiscal policy in designing the monetary policy, the general competition agency cannot ignore the competition law enforcement in the regulated industries. Otherwise, serious distortions of the level playing field throughout the economy may arise. Assuming he same number of regulated industries, the balance of powers in applying competition law is more affected to the disadvantage of the competition agency when there is only one general regulator than when there are

---

[11] However, there are state-based industry- and sector-specific regulators.

many - smaller - regulators with competition policy competencies. This change in the balance of powers will remain for a long time, although the general regulator will probably be less reluctant to end regulation (and at the same time his competition policy competencies) in certain industries.

Another argument put forward in favour of combining regulation and competition law enforcement is less valid in the case of a general regulator - specific knowledge of a certain industry. This special knowledge can be found in industry-specific agencies, especially when they are also in charge of technical regulations. However, it is doubtful whether there are industries with exceptional production processes or other peculiarities justifying a special approach to competition policy (Behrends, 2001, p. 84 f.). Even when one ignores this objection, there are still some disadvantages in empowering industry-specific regulators with competencies in competition policy:

(1) The narrower the industry coverage of an agency, the more non-competition goals are assigned to this agency, which it will seek to achieve not only by regulatory measures but also by competition law enforcement.
(2) There is empirical evidence that industry-specific agencies especially are captured by the interests of the regulated firms when acting or co-acting as a competition authority. Until the 80s, the German Federal Cartel Office (FCO) had to seek consent with the Federal Banking Supervisory Office before taking action against anti-competitive behaviour of banks. More than once, consent was not found and the FCO could not act (Duijm, 2000, p. 7). In the US, the Surface Transportation Board approved a merger of railroad companies despite a protest of the Antitrust Division of the Department of Justice.[12]

It can be expected that industry-specific agencies would be very reluctant to phase out a special regulatory regime because this phasing out would lead to the end of their existence. The reluctance tends to prolong the separated enforcement of competition law in this industry.

Furthermore, the number of decisions based on competition law made by one industry-specific agency is probably relatively small.[13] This small number creates uncertainty for the firms involved in competition law cases. Furthermore, there is high probability that overlapping competencies exist, resulting from economic activities of firms operating in different industries, for example in the electricity and in the gas markets. Firms operating in both markets are in the interest of customers who want "one-stop energy shopping" (Hewitt, 1999, p. 197). Technical progress may lead to other converging markets, e.g. the communication and the broadcasting market. When there are different agencies for both markets

[12] See Hewitt (1999, pp. 190 ff.) for this example and other cases.

[13] This argument is less valid when the regional scope of the agency in charge is large, e.g. in the case of an EC regulator in place of national regulators in the EC member states. But it is not clear whether centralisation of regulation enforcement is in accordance with the principle of subsidiarity. For an efficient regulation the regulator might have to rely on information and complaints from the consumers, which tend to be more easily available in the case of national regulators.

uncertainty concerning the responsibility arises. If two or more agencies have equal competencies, probably a forum-shopping arises.

Thus, in the case of industry-specific regulators with competencies in competition policy, it is not the individual power of the regulatory agencies which might give rise to concern for the general competition agency, but the potential differences and fragmentation in competition law enforcement.

Therefore, in the case of a general regulator as well in the case of industry-specific regulators there are - albeit different - reasons to give the general competition agency some power to control the actions of the regulators concerning competition law enforcement. For example, the regulatory agency could be obliged to request the opinion of the competition agency when it wants to apply competition law. A publication of the opinion forces the regulator to explain his competitive decisions if not in line with the policy of the competition agency.[14]

There is little need for the general competition agency to supervise or control competition law enforcement by regulators when the regulatory agencies are organised on a sectoral level. On the one hand, the individual coverage of industries of a certain agency is small enough not to impede the general competition agency in conducting competition policy as intended and not to distort the economy-wide level playing field seriously. On the other hand, the coverage of industries is large enough to resist attempts of capture from single industries and to facilitate consistent conduct of competition policy across closely related industries of the sector, provided that *all* industries of the relevant sector are under the regulatory and competitive responsibility of the appropriate agency. The last-mentioned condition is a serious drawback of this institutional design - the agency would have to be empowered to apply competition law to certain industries only because other industries, belonging to the same sector, are regulated. Since, in many countries, not all industries of a sector are regulated (e.g. often the oil market in the energy sector is not regulated) this would reduce the competencies of the general competition agency, when a regulatory agency is created for the network-based gas and electricity market and effect a change of the responsible competitive agency for some industries, which might lead to a change in competition policy in these industries. Therefore, this institutional design is a viable solution only for sectors where all or most industries are regulated.

7. Specific Competition Laws and Rules

Up to now, the analysis was made under the assumption that no industry- or sector-specific competition laws or rules exist. However, industry- or sector-specific laws often do not only contain regulatory rules, but also competitive rules.[15] These specific competition rules might be either equally applicable with the general competition law or might overrule the latter. They might be enforced by the general competition agency or by the regulator(s). When the specific competition

---

[14] This kind of co-operation is adopted between the Italian Central Bank as the regulator of the banks and the Italian Anti-trust Authority; see Wise (2001, p. 100).

[15] See Koenig and Kühling (2001) for the German electricity and railroad industries.

rules are enforced by the general competition agency, the results discussed above have not to be altered significantly.

When they are applied independently by the regulatory agency, most of the problems concerning competition law enforcement by regulators are reinforced - an even greater resistance of regulators against phasing out can be expected, as there are special competition policy (permanent) tasks fulfilled exclusively by them; overlapping applicability of several specific competition rules; divergent application of similar rules, causing uncertainties; and so on.

Some of these problems can be overcome by concurrent competencies of the general competition agency - applying general competition law - and the regulators - enforcing specific competition rules. But this will probably lead to forum shopping if it is not ensured that the strictest policy - in the sense of the most pro-competitive policy - is put through. But uncertainties remain: will a permission of one authority be repealed by another authority? Therefore, specific competition rules - enforced by regulators - call for co-operation between them and the general competition agency.

If specific competition rules or laws exclude the applicability of the general competition law, the need for co-operation also exists. The objectives of specific competition rules and the objectives of general competition law are essentially the same. Instruments, definitions and so on should be used in a similar manner to prevent competitive distortions. There is no place for an uncontrolled competition of competition policies within one economy, although some procedural rules might differ according to different market structures, e.g. the existence of market entry barriers.

8. Some Empirical Evidence

Many countries are undertaking regulatory reforms, some of them, like Ireland, in a public consultation process (Department of the Toaiseach, 2002). One of the key problems in all the countries is the relationship between regulation and competition and the relationship between competition and regulatory authorities. According to the OECD, there are an increasing number of combined regulation/competition laws being tried in the OECD member states, most of them assigning sector specific regulators with regulatory and competition policy tasks (Hewitt, 1999, p. 186).

Such developments have been observed in Germany, where in the telecommunications industry certain competencies concerning competition policy were transferred from the Federal Cartel Office to the Regulatory Authority for Telecommunications and Posts. In the UK, the Office of Gas and Electricity Regulation (OFGEM) was established in 1999. Thus, a sector regulator was created in place of the former industry-specific regulatory agencies for gas supply and electricity regulation. OFGEM has concurrent power in applying the competition act in cases concerning anti-competitive behaviour, but not with regard to mergers (OECD/IEA, 2001, pp. 86 ff.). In Germany, the government gave up plans to extend the federal railroad authority with primary technical regulatory functions into an economic regulator with considerable competencies in the area of competition policy. Nevertheless, the authority is now empowered to investigate ex officio in cases of alleged discriminatory access to the railroad networks.

However, other developments can be observed as well. In Italy, up to 1997, the Broadcasting and Publishing Authority was in charge of enforcing general competition law in these industries. This assignment was repealed in 1997 and the general competition authority has assumed responsibility for these industries. A new Communication Regulatory Authority was established, which has no competencies for competition law enforcement; it can express its opinion on competition policy issues (Wise, 2001, p. 101). This can be regarded as a separation of competencies and as a division of labour according to the supposed relative advantages of competition and regulatory agencies.

In the Netherlands, the regulator for the electricity market was created as a chamber of the general competition agency, but for the telecommunication sector an independent regulatory agency was established, which has to co-operate closely with the general competition authority. This can be seen as an institutional design where the regulators are linked to the competition agency (OECD, 1999, pp. 224 and 232).

It is interesting that in the UK the Financial Services Authority has no important competition policy competencies - contrary to the other sectoral regulators (Hewitt, 2000, p. 38). The same is true for Germany.

So, rather divergent developments in assigning powers concerning competition policy can be observed.

9. A Few Implications for Competition Policy Concerning Airports

What do all these considerations suggest when the institutional design of competition policy in the field of airports is concerned?

First of all, airport regulation policy and airport competition policy seem to be highly mutually dependent. With the exception of very large cities being served by two or even more airports, airports are considered as more or less "natural" monopolies. As they have significant potential to exercise market power they are (still) government owned and/or regulated. However, they are not always monopolies. There are passengers travelling from points located between airports who may consider different airports as substitutes. The same is for true for passengers who are not time-sensitive (for example tourists). Although inter-airport competition is often still not intensive, it might become so when infrastructure is improved, for example by connecting airports and cities by a network of high-speed trains.

Actual and potential inter-airport competition is endangered by collusion and cartels among airports within a region. Individual market power is then transformed into collective market power. Regulation in order to avoid misuse of market power will become a permanent task if restrictions of (potential) competition cannot be prevented. The same is true in the case of mergers of privately-owned airports within a region or when an incumbent airport establishes a new one (for example by purchasing a former military airfield).

Regulation of airports (for example the allocation of take-off and landing slots) influence the competition in the *airline* industry, especially the effects of mergers and alliances in this industry. It can act as an important barrier to entry for new domestic or foreign airlines. In order to overcome these barriers to entry, airlines might purchase other airlines to obtain their slots. In addition, mergers and alliances between two or more airlines influence inter-airport competition. As travellers prefer connecting flights of the same airline to those of distinct airlines,[16] a merger of airline X serving the route from airport A to airport B and of airline Y serving the route from airport B to airport C might make airport A a closer substitute for airport D, from which direct flights to airport C exist. But of course airline mergers and alliances can also reduce inter-airport competition.

From the interdependencies between regulation and competition in the field of "airport-policy" it follows that a high degree of co-operation between the authorities in charge of competition law and regulation law enforcement is necessary. Combining regulatory and competition policy competencies concerning airports might be the best institutional design.

But which authority should be in charge of these combined competencies? As we have seen, inter-airport competition has effects on inter-airline competition and vice versa. Effective competition in the market of air transport requires functioning competition in both markets - airline services and airport services (OECD, 2000*b*, p. 228). This high mutual dependence of the two markets makes an "air transportation authority" superior to a narrowly defined (industry-specific) "airport regulatory authority". Although the air transportation market is a specific market in that sense that other forms of transportation are no (close) substitutes, assigning regulatory law and competition law enforcement to the general competition authority might be advantageous. As mergers and especially alliances between airlines are often across the border they may be subjected to several anti-trust jurisdictions and reviewed by different national authorities. While some international co-operation agreements between competition authorities exist, facilitating consistent decision-making, such an international network of agreements between transportation authorities would have to be developed.[17]

However, drawbacks of this institutional design may also exist. In Germany, the state anti-trust authorities are in charge of applying most parts of the GWB (Gesetz gegen Wettbewerbsbeschraenkungen, Act Against Restrictions of Competetion) as long as restrictive business practises do not have inter-state effects. The state anti-trust authorities are not regional branches of the de facto politically independent FCO, but in most *länder* (states) parts of the state ministries of economics and therefore politically not independent. Thus, in many cases, the realisation of this design would lead to a shift of competencies within the *länder* governments from the ministries of transportation (up to now in most *länder* responsible for the de facto regulation of airports) to the ministries of economics. Regardless of which ministry is in charge, its policy might be influenced by the ministry of finance, representing the interests of the state as owner of the airports.

---

[16] See OECD (2000*a*, p.130) for some reasons.

[17] See OECD (2000*a*), p. 136 for the AA/BA alliance; there was no international arrangement involving the US Department of Transportation.

In the run-up to privatisation, fiscal interests of a state can dominate the economic interests of the whole economy. Other authorities, for example the FCO, might pursue these economic interests in a better way.[18]

This example shows that an evaluation of institutional designs requires a very broad assessment of a wide range of inter alia political, constitutional, juridical, and economic aspects.

Some Concluding Remarks

Why do differences in the institutional design of regulatory and competition agencies exist? Why do they exist between countries and within countries?

There are at least two answers. First, not all governments tried to reform regulation in a systematic manner. In Germany, the energy bill did not contain rules concerning the assignment of agencies in order to circumvent the second chamber of parliament, where the government had no majority (Bundesrat, 1998, pp. 124 f.). The Dutch parliament opposed a telecommunication authority being integrated into the competition authority (OECD, 1999, pp. 224, 232). Thus, even if the optimal institutional design had been known, there was - for political reasons - not always the possibility to realise it.

But - and this is the second answer - the ideal institutional design is not yet known. Which of the "models" described above is ideal depends on many factors, varying from country to country and on time. I will mention just a few factors:

(1) Are regulatory and competition agencies equally politically independent? Especially in the EU, the European Commission is more concerned with the independence of regulatory agencies than that of competition agencies.
(2) How is the market structured? Is the state a major owner of firms in the regulated industries?
(3) How are laws concerning liberalisation and de-regulation designed? Is a light-handed regulation approach applied?
(4) What is the role of courts in competition and regulatory policy?
(5) Are there real possibilities to split off vertically integrated firms?
(6) Is there a wide-spread "spirit of competition" throughout the economy, the administration and agencies?

The answers to these and similar questions are different in different countries. In a negative way, some institutional designs can be excluded as obviously inferior to others, e.g. dozens of regulators, whether with or without power to enforce competition law. But a positive selection is impossible. A "good" regulatory and competition policy can be achieved by various designs, which may sometimes combine some of the described models, e.g. a general regulatory agency with no competition policy competencies and very few sectoral regulators with competencies in competition policy.

---

[18] The predominance of fiscal interests (revenues from privatisation) could be observed in the regulation of the German telecommunication and postal industries.

Whichever policy is adopted, an intensive co-operation of the authorities involved and a clear-cut pro-competitive regulation is essential to foster competition throughout the economy.

References

Behrends, Sylke: *Neue Politische Ökonomie*, München 2001.

Boyfield, Keith: *The Politics of Regulation*, London 2000.

Bundesrat: Stellungnahme des Bundesrates, in: GWB - Gesetz gegen Wettbewerbsbeschränkungen, Wirtschaft und Wettbewerb, special issue, Düsseldorf 1998, pp. 120-130.

Calvani, Terry and Kevin Robb: Market Liberalisation and Competition Policy, in: *International Business Lawyer*, Vol. 26 (1998), pp. 514-517.

Department of the Taoiseach: *Towards Better Regulation*, Dublin 2002.

Duijm, Bernhard: Fachbehörden als Wettbewerbshüter?, in: *ifo-Schnelldienst*, Vol. 53 (2000), No. 12, pp. 3-10.

Duijm, Bernhard: Wettbewerbssicherung nach Privatisierung und Deregulierung: Aufgabe allgemeiner Wettbewerbs- oder sektoraler Regulierungsbehörden?, in: Hartmut Berg (ed.), *Deregulierung und Privatisierung: Gewolltes - Erreichtes - Versäumtes*, Berlin 2002, pp. 9-27.

Estache, Antonio and Ginés de Rus: The Regulation of Transport Infrastructure and Services: A Conceptual Overview, in: A. Estache, G. de Rus (eds.), *Privatization and Regulation of Transport Infrastructure*, Washington, D.C. 2000, pp. 5-50.

Haffner, Robert C.G.: Policy Issues in Telecommunications Reform: The Netherlands, in: OECD (ed.), *Privatisation, Competition and Regulation*, Paris 2000, pp. 207-213.

Hewitt, Gary: The Relationship between Competition and Regulatory Authorities - Background Note, in: *OECD Journal of Competition Law and Policy*, Vol. 1 (1999), No. 3, pp. 177-219

Hewitt, Gary: Bank Mergers - Background Note, in: *OECD Journal of Competition Law and Policy*, Vol. 2 (2000), No. 4, pp. 13-66.

Koenig, Christian and Jürgen Kühling: Institutionelle Regulierungsordnung in der Eisenbahn- und Energiewirtschaft - sektorspezifische Regulierungsbehörden oder Bundeskartellamt?, in: *Wirtschaft und Wettbewerb*, Vol. 51 (2001), pp. 810-820.

Möschel, Wernhard: Ist das Verhältnis von TKG und GWB neu zu durchdenken?, in: *Kommunikation und Recht*, Vol. 4 (2001), pp. 619-622.

Möschel, Wernhard: Das Verhältnis von Kartellbehörde und Sonderaufsichtsbehörden, in: *Wirtschaft und Wettbewerb*, Vol. 52 (2002), pp. 683-688.

Monopolkommission (Monopolies Commission): Netzwettbewerb durch Regulierung. 14. Hauptgutachten der Monopolkommission gemäß § 44 Abs. 1 Satz 1 GWB 2000/2001 - Kurzfassung, 2002.

Nicoletti, Giuseppe, Regulation in Services: OECD Patterns and Economic Implications, OECD Economics Department Working Papers No. 287, Paris 2001.

OECD: The Role of the Competition Agency in Regulatory Reform, *OECD Proceedings*, Paris 1997.

OECD: The Relationship between Competition and Regulatory Authorities, in: *OECD Journal of Competition Law and Policy*, Vol. 1 (1999), No. 3, pp. 169-176 and 220-246.

OECD: Airline Mergers and Alliances, in: *OECD Journal of Competition Law and Policy*, Vol. 2 (2000*a*), No. 2, pp. 127-225.

OECD: Competition Policy and International Airport Services, in: *OECD Journal of Competition Law and Policy*, Vol. 2 (2000*b*), No. 2, pp. 227-261.

OECD/IEA: Regulatory Institutions in Liberalised Energy Markets, Paris 2001

Victor, Paul A.: Interaction Between Competition and Regulatory Regime in Deregulation, in: *International Business Lawyer*, Vol. 26 (1998), pp. 518-521.

Wise, Michael: Review of United States Competition Law and Policy, in: *OECD Journal of Competition Law and Policy*, Vol. 1 (1999), No. 1, pp. 9-70.

Wise, Michael: Review of Competition Law and Policy in Italy, in: *OECD Journal of Competition Law and Policy*, Vol. 3 (2001), No. 2, pp. 65-122.